DAYLIGHT F●REVER

A MEMOIR

MAHVASH KHAJAVI-HARVEY

Print ISBN 978-1-54399-648-7

eBook ISBN 978-1-54399-649-4

Disclaimer:

I have recalled events and conversations from memory. As we know, memory is faulty and so I have taken some creative liberties. Dialogue is not meant to represent word-for-word transcripts, rather the essence of what was said, felt, and meant. In certain instances, I have compressed the events for ease of reading. Most importantly, I have changed identifying characteristics and names of people of the Bahá'í Faith to ensure their anonymity in a world where persecution remains a very real threat.

DEDICATION

To all the refugees of the world, for your great courage and perseverance.

CONTENTS

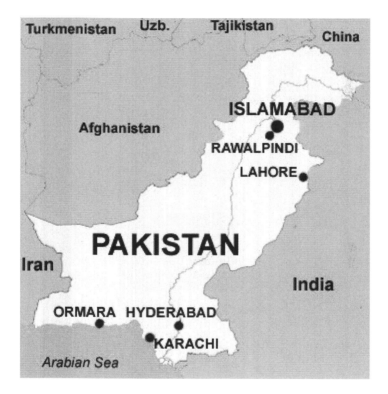

FOREWORD

"[A] new era has begun! Am I not your sister and you my brother? Can you not look upon me as a real friend? . . . how [else] will you be able to give your lives for a great Cause?"

—Tahirih, Iranian poet and first female suffrage martyr

Tahirih was a famous Persian poet who I have long adored. She lived in Iran during the mid-1800s at a time when women were neither seen nor heard. She zealously promoted equality between men and women and spoke out against the oppression of women, inspiring them to reject the diminished status and violence they had been forced to accept for so long. Tahirih was eventually executed for speaking the truth of equality and oneness. Her voice and life cut off by strangulation. Yet her final words were as bold as her life had been: "You can kill me as soon as you like, but you cannot stop the emancipation of women." With her death, Tahirih became a beacon of hope and courage. Her message has endured nearly two centuries and still resonates in the hearts of so many courageous people across the world today. People willing to stand up for the oppressed.

Like Tahirih, there is someone else I fiercely admire for her devotion to the oneness of humankind and the equality of all people—from all walks of life, from all places, and of all orientations. She is my daughter, Parisa. It is for her I write this book.

In 2016, when Parisa was just twelve years old, she felt, for the first time, the pain of prejudice and discrimination. Even in the supposedly safe and progressive sanctuary city of Seattle, the kind of ignorance and fear that leads to hate can be found. It happened in a place of learning—her middle school. A young boy, who felt emboldened and entitled by the rhetoric of the country, which had become increasingly non-welcoming, declared to his peers that there were way too many immigrants in this country, and they should all be deported. Parisa bit her tongue to keep from crying. Her mother was an immigrant. Her uncles, aunt, grandmother and grandfather, family, friends—all immigrants. With great love, my little girl stood up and asked the boy how he could say such a thing when he didn't know every person's story? He did not have any answer. She told him, "My mother is an immigrant. You shouldn't judge immigrants; you don't know their struggles. They work hard to rebuild their lives and they contribute to their community."

When I picked her up at the bus stop that day, her tears flowed long and hard. She was angry because she felt I had been disrespected, but I understood how much deeper that interaction affected her. It is painful and disappointing when the people you call friends, colleagues, fellow citizens, and your community, spew senseless comments that cause pain and hurt. Words have power and words spoken out of ignorance and fear do great and lasting harm. "Write a book, Mom," she told me. "Tell your story. People need to know." I was not sure. My story is not unique, I told her. There are millions of people like me who have escaped war and persecution, becoming refugees in order to build a new life. Millions who have left behind family and loved ones, their homes and their land, and also like me—even their childhood. Millions who cross borders "illegally" in an attempt to leave trauma, fear, and darkness behind. "It's important," Parisa insisted. She said people needed to know what immigrants risk to escape unbearable conditions. People needed to understand their sacrifices, their struggles, and the courage it takes to start over in a foreign place. I weighed her words carefully. I knew the truth in them. If someone has never met or intimately known any refugees, it is nearly impossible to understand what they have suffered. This makes it all the easier to draw conclusions, create stereotypes, and live in fear of them.

My story is a horrendous one to live. I do not wish it on any one, young or old. It is the story of a child who did not get to choose where she was born or raised, and who suffered a lifetime of trauma, enduring an Islamic revolution and religious persecution, a long, bloody war and separation from family at a young age. But like any story, it is also one of hope. Hope for a new life, freedom, and greater opportunities. The hope that we can overcome adversity and that we are more resilient than we realize. If we can hold on to hope, even under the most distressing of circumstances, we hold on to a piece of ourselves. Perhaps it is a piece of our dignity, perhaps our courage, perhaps just a small will to live, but it is enough to keep us going.

As a refugee and now, a proud American citizen, it is my duty to give back to the community that welcomed me with open arms. In doing so, I strive to advocate for the emancipation and acceptance of all immigrants. Parisa's wish for you is that within these pages you will come to understand and appreciate the courage it takes for immigrants to leave behind everything they know and love and to start anew. As well as how immigrants show their gratitude for the opportunity of a better life for themselves and their families by giving back to their communities through contributions and loyalty. My wish for you in reading this book is that my story will help you find greater courage to accept all people and treat them with dignity. The courage to be unafraid to extend a hand and to protect those in need when they are falling.

Mahvash Khajavi-Harvey, June 8th, 2019

(Parisa and Mahvash at the 2019 Women's March)

PREFACE

MAY 1988: ZAHEDAN

"Find something to hold on to," the smuggler says before pinning us under a tarp in the truck bed. Us. Two families with young children, a nineteen-year-old man, and me, fifteen years old and on my own. We sit hunched around gasoline cans and water cans, sealed off from all light. I clutch the tiny gold butterfly pendant around my neck, a gift from my mother, and whisper the prayer my father loves. *Is there any Remover of difficulties save God?*

That old familiar cold sweat runs down my spine and I scream the silent scream that dies in my throat. The engine revs and there is no turning back now. The truck lurches forward. Something to hold on to, he said. I release the butterfly necklace and grab for something, but there is nothing except other bodies bouncing and slamming against hot metal. We ride like this for hours, and in the darkness, I lose all sense of time and nearly my mind. Every bump bruises and I curse my long neck and skinny body. I go over the smuggler's last words before pinning us down: we might never see him again. There might be multiple drivers. The truck might stop suddenly but we must stay put. Stay silent. Eventually someone will return for us. The Pakistan border is just three hundred and seventy miles away, but it could take us a week before we arrive because we have to weave back and forth through Afghanistan multiple times. If we are caught, we will all go to prison, and perhaps worse. I remember the way he looked me up and down slowly and said, "You're very young and very . . . pretty."

A shiver snakes through my body despite the heat. "It is worth it. *It is worth it.*" I tell myself over and over again. I have made my choice. I begged for this moment. This is the moment I have been longing for. To stay in Iran was not a choice but a submission to live at the mercy of sirens and bombs. A surrender to live in fear and darkness.

Nearly every night at dusk for the past eight years, they cut electricity across Tehran so Iraqi jets could not spot us. Every home hung thick, black blankets in the windows. Black to block the light, and thick to block the flying shards of glass. My family, like many others, ate by candlelight inside while the world became eerie and silent outside. We held our breath, waiting for the bombs to fall. Everyone except my father that is. My father would always tell me with a smile, "Mahvash, my love, you can't escape your destiny." As if that would comfort me and ease my terror during the night raids. It did neither.

The truck turns sharply and something hard jabs my ribs. I wish, of all things, for a cushion. When I was younger, I wished on every star for my own spaceship. Lying on my thin mattress on the floor at bedtime, my heart would race, and I would break out in a cold sweat. I could not sleep, and if I did, I would wake up screaming from the nightmares. If I could just get a spaceship, then I would not have to be afraid. Every night I could climb inside and travel to the other side of the world, to the side where the sun was shining bright and warm. And I would not come back until the sun was rising in Iran again. All I wished for then—all I really wish for now—is to live in the daylight forever.

In the dark of the truck, I am as close to a spaceship as I will ever get. This is my chance at freedom, at light. I am leaving my war-torn city and escaping certain death. My father's words resonate in my mind. Does this mean I am outrunning my destiny? Or running right into it?

Only God knows.

PART I: BEFORE

(Pictured left to right: Leila, Baba, and Mahvash in front of the Chevy)

1

COURAGE

MARCH 1977: TEHRAN

The 1956 turquoise Chevy sparkles in the early sun. The shiny white roof makes me squint to look at it. Everything from the antenna to the muffler gleams. My Baba polishes every inch of that car each day after work, from top to bottom, inside and out. "Tell me truly, Mahvash," he asks, "have you ever seen anything so beautiful?" "*Na baba!*" No way, I say, and I mean it. Even at five (and a half) years old, I realize that while we do not live in the poorest neighborhood, we do not live in the wealthiest one either. No one else on our street has a car, and the ones in the city center of Tehran are smaller and less colorful. Our American-made beauty is absolutely the dreamiest thing I have ever seen. The neighborhood men come over to our garage sometimes and watch Baba work. He is always replacing parts, even when it is not necessary, to keep the Chevy in pristine condition. It is always ready for display, like a museum relic. "She is as beautiful as a bride," he boasts, and no one ever disagrees.

Baba spent his entire life savings to purchase the Chevy just a few years back. "I paid a handsome price, a very handsome price, but when you really want something—remember this—you pay more than the asking price for it." I think my life savings right now is about ten rials, which is not even enough to buy a rock candy, but with the New Year celebrations of Nowruz starting soon, I hope to get close to five hundred rials. Everyone always gets money on the new year. But even with five hundred rials, if Mr. Goodarzi at the corner store was to tell me a Kinder Bueno egg cost only one hundred rials, I do not think I would give him two hundred just because I really wanted it. Still, I am happy my Baba bought the Chevy because I like to sit behind the steering wheel, pretending to take treacherous mountain turns without batting an eye, all while Baba polishes the dash and tells me stories from the years he spent as a truck driver.

"In the early days, I couldn't even drive the trucks. I was the sixteen-year-old son of a farmer, with no skills whatsoever. Just my passion. I knew nothing except that I loved cars. So I worked as a helper. I put air in the tires, pumped gas, loaded cargo, and made tea for the drivers. These drivers, they drink a lot of tea, you know," he explains, running a cloth across the hood. "But then you would too if you were up all night, navigating snowy mountain roads. Oh, but I loved it. Just to be around trucks, learning how to work on engines—I was so happy." He smiles and pauses while I double check my mirrors before taking a hairpin left turn. "You know, at night, I would take my mattress to the roof of the cab and sleep under the stars, dreaming about a car of my own." Baba was never prouder than when he was behind the wheel of the Chevy, but if truth be told, riding in it made us all hold our heads a little higher. Even Maamaan, though she pretends not to care. "I swear Aziz, you love that car more than me!" she scolds Baba, coming out of the house with my big brothers, Cyrus and Kia, their arms piled with road trip supplies for Baba to pack on the roof rack: mattresses, blankets, pillows, Nowruz presents for the cousins, and even a sewing machine. A request from a great aunt in Kerman who we are going to visit after picking up our cousins and aunt and uncle in Yazd. "Can we really fit eleven people in our Chevy?" I ask Baba. Kia is quick to answer: "No way! That's why you will have to sit on the top with the mattresses." "Yes," Cyrus says, "It is prime seating, Mahvash. Kia, on the other hand, will have to be tied to the spare tire." Kia takes a punch at Cyrus who dodges the swing. Leila whines, "Where am I going to sit?" "Didn't anyone tell you Leila?" Kia looks over in concern. "You have to stay here and feed the Haft Seen goldfish while we go on the road trip." Even though Leila is four years older than me, she just doesn't like to be teased. Her eyes well up and she runs away to hide. Maamaan scolds the boys. "Go apologize. Now. Or I'll make you stay behind to feed the goldfish."

Maamaan began new year preparations weeks ago. She always starts by going room to room through the house and finding things to deep clean. The Persian rugs get a good beating and washing. During Nowruz, the entire country gets two weeks of holiday from work and school to visit friends and family, so everyone wants to be sure their home is at its best. Today, when Maamaan threw open the windows the scent of new hyacinth blooms filled our home. Hyacinth is the official smell of spring. But there is still some winter to say goodbye to. We will bid farewell tonight during the *Chahar Shanbe Suri*, the fire festival.

"Is everyone packed?" Baba asks. "We'll leave for Naneh's house after the fire ceremony and drive through the night. I don't want to exhaust the Queen by driving her through the heat of the day, and besides, the roads are quieter at night. I like that." Maamaan tells Baba we have been packed forever, it is he who has not yet packed—neither his bag nor the car. Baba just chuckles and continues to stand there, taking in his two-thousand-pound beauty and unconsciously rubbing at the scar on his nose.

The previous year, while Baba was scraping rust from the undercarriage, the Chevy slipped off the car jack and fell on his head. Even though Baba's shoulders are wide and strong and just one of his hands can hold three big pomegranates at once, he was not able to lift that car off his chest. Maamaan ran door to door for help from our neighbors. Several men and several attempts later, the car was finally lifted just high enough for Baba to squeeze out. His big nose was completely flattened like a piece of naan. The good news is that the reconstructive surgery gave him a new nose that looks very much like the old one, save for the deep scar from the sutures— proof, everyone says, of Baba's undying love for the Chevy.

Cyrus and Kia make a game of tossing bags to each other and then up onto the roof. Cyrus will graduate high school next year and Kia the following. They will be the first in all the family to do so; everyone is quite proud. Everyone seems to be forgetting that I am about to be the first one in the family ever to graduate from kindergarten. I feel very proud of this fact. My three siblings did not start school until the first grade. Baba has even promised me a small treat at the end of the school year, if just like my siblings, I keep my grades up. Cyrus received a camera a couple years ago for having such high marks. He is now the official family photographer, always behind the lens, never in the photos. I like the picture from when I am three years old and sitting on Kia's knee on top of the Chevy next to Leila. We munch on apples and our toes dangle on the windshield wipers. There is also one from earlier today, with Leila and I standing on the Chevy's front fender, holding onto Baba from behind and peering around his shoulders. Leila shields the sun from her eyes, and I cling hard to Baba's jacket, worried I might slip and fall. In photos, Baba trades his wide grin for a straight and serious mouth, wrists clasped behind him, brow furrowed. He looks very handsome.

"Can I put on my new Nowruz outfit now?" I beg Maamaan. "Of course not. You know we never wear our Nowruz clothes until Nowruz." I sigh. I know. We bought our new clothes nearly two weeks ago and the wait has been unbearable. Every day I go into Maamaan's closet to stroke the soft, light wool of my new sweater or run my finger along the pleats of my new skirt. Sometimes I find my brothers already in there, eyeing their sharp new suits and starched, white button ups, or Leila, coveting her new plum colored dress.

"Baba, how long is the drive to Great-Grandma Naneh's again? Will she remember me? Will we get to play with the turtle at our cousin's house? What if we accidentally step on it while playing? Who *is* going to feed the Haft Seen goldfish while we are away? Do you think I can jump over the bonfire tonight or are my legs still too small? I really want to, but I'm really scared too. Do you think—"

"—Shh, shh, Mooshi," he pats my head. "Don't worry, so much. It will all be fine. Yes. Yes. Why don't you go water the Haft Seen grass?"

Mooshi, little mouse, is my family's pet name for me because I speak so softly and do not like to try new things without a lot of thinking first. Maybe I am just a little mouse, but maybe I am a little bit mighty too. Mice can be mighty. I saw the cartoon on the TV once, so I know it is true. Maybe I can prove it by jumping over the bonfire tonight all by myself. The thought makes my belly flip-flop.

Instead of watering the Haft Seen grass, I find Leila to play with until something other than all this waiting starts to happen. Sometimes we collect pebbles and play knuckle bones or search for old coke bottle caps in the neighborhood to make into necklaces. She always has great ideas. Leila is in the bedroom and wants to play dolls. "You can play with my Barbie if you want to." I adore the Barbie; it is the only one we have. Leila does not like the Barbie so much anymore, not since our cousin gave it the terrible haircut. Leila had asked for a short bob to match her own haircut (and mine), but the Barbie's once long and silky blonde hair did not want to bob or bounce. It just kind of sticks out stiff like the desert grass growing outside my Naneh's home in Yazd.

When the sun finally begins to set, we all head outdoors with the neighbors. Bonfires crackle and snap in the street. We walk around and share dates and tea with each other, wishing everyone a happy new year. It doesn't matter if people are Zoroastrian, Muslim, Jewish, Christian, or— like my family— Bahá'í—everyone celebrates Nowruz. The entire country shuts down for two weeks to celebrate the new year and the beginning of spring. On this night, our street is especially loud with the sound of laughter and chatter. The communal noodle soup, *Aash*, is hot and ready to be shared. I find a bowl of the special Nowruz nut and fruit mix and grab a handful. I check to see if I have one of everything: pistachios, roasted chickpeas, almonds, hazelnuts, figs, apricots, dried mulberry, and raisins. Yes!

"Maamaan" I ask, "is it time? Can Leila and I go door-to-door now?" Maamaan looks around and sees other kids, bags in hand, knocking on doors and tells us, OK. At each house, we receive small coins or candies or cookies. Some kids eat all their candy before they get home, but I like to save mine and eat it over the entire holiday.

We return to the bonfires with full bags. I try to count my new coins but get distracted by the chanting: "*Zardi-e man az tow, sorkhi-e two az man!*" "Give me your beautiful red glow and take back my sickly pallor!" The fire jumping. I almost forgot. People chant this before they leap over a bonfire, springing from the old year straight into the new. Parents pass the smallest children safely over the fire in their arms. I do not want to be passed like a baby over the flames this year; I want to jump like my big brothers and sister.

But the fires blaze over my head.

"Mahvash!" I turn. My friend is running for me from down the road. "Look, look! A small fire. I jumped; do you want to jump?" I tell her yes, but instantly regret it. She drags me to the small fire; it is the perfect size for Leila's barbie to jump over. I think I can make it, but still, what if I don't? I walk around and around it. How to jump? Left foot first, or right? Two feet at once? The other kids cheer each other on and clap after someone jumps. I watch how they do it. The scary thing is that once you start to run you cannot just stop, or you will fall in the fire.

You have to go for it. Go all the way.

"Mahvash, it's your turn!" someone says. I mumble back, shaking my head. "I'm not ready." When you jump over the flames, the fire is supposed to take away all the bad things that happened the year before and give you a fresh start. But I cannot think of any bad things that have happened which I need taking away. Well except for, maybe, that one time my foot got stuck in the wheel of Kia's bike last summer, but even that turned out pretty good for me.

Kia loves his bike the way Baba loves the Chevy. He worked all summer at a factory the year before making spools of thread in every color imaginable to save up for it. With his very own bicycle, he could ride to the swimming pool and take me with him. The ride is very long, maybe close to one hour, but it is worth it because the pool is as big as a lake. Or, Olympic sized, as Kia says. It is owned by the Department of Water and Power, where Baba works. All the employees and their families can swim at the pool and play at the tennis courts. After my swimming lessons, I would hang out in the kiddie pool while Kia and the other teenagers practiced their laps. Sometimes I had competitions with a boy there to see who could hold their breath underwater the longest, or we would swim on our bellies in the shallow water pretending to be sharks, very silent and very sneaky like. One day as we were headed back home, Kia was pedaling hard through the busy streets, feeling strong after all that swimming. He told me to hang on tighter around his waist and to stop swinging my legs so much. "If you're tired, just rest them behind you on the caps sticking out from the wheels," he said. I tried, but my legs could not reach. I jammed my foot into the wheel by accident and the bike immediately crunched to a stop. I screamed so loud I hurt my own ears. My big toe had a gash in it, which hurt and made me cry, but I felt even worse when I saw that my summer sandal was all torn up and soaked in blood.

Kia took me to a clinic where they put five stitches in me because I am five years old. Then they covered my foot in bandages and put a big brace on it. The brace made it look like I had an elephant's foot, but the worst part was the doctor told me I could not go swimming until the stitches came out—a whole two weeks later. To cheer me up, Kia let me ride on the seat while he walked the bike home. He even said he would buy me an ice cream cone. "But," he added, "when we get home you have to tell Maamaan that you feel fine, quite fine, no big deal with the foot. OK?" I nodded. Easy. Ice cream makes everything better. We got home late and I did actually feel pretty good again. I told Maamaan so, but it didn't matter—she yelled at Kia anyway when she saw my mangled toe.

Now I am here in front of this bonfire and my foot is fine, but all I can think of is what if it falls into the flames. How long will I need to wear bandages for this time? What if I have to wear bandages forever? What if my clothes catch fire? What if my hair catches fire? Suddenly, Baba is at my side. "You can do it!" he whispers in my ear. "I've seen you hopscotch so well and jump so high for the ball when you are the monkey in the middle." He squeezes my hand, giving me some of his courage. With Baba by my side, everything will be fine. When you love someone, you don't let anything bad happen to them. And I know Baba loves me a lot, because he always tells me, like he tells Maamaan, "*Ghorboonet beram. I die for you.*" I look him in the eyes and nod my head up and down. I am ready.

Deep breath. Cheeks hot from the fire. Scared but also brave, can I be both at once? The chants and cheers sound far away now and only my heartbeat remains. My toes dig into the ground and I kick off. No turning back. I run. I jump. I land. I am on the other side of the flames. For the first time in my life, I leaped out of the old year and into the new—all by myself. A beautifully warm and intense feeling of excitement fills me up inside.

2

HOME

The heat from the morning sun warming the Chevy wakes me up. We have been on the road all night, but I can tell we are getting close to Yazd because half-fallen and cracked mud fences now dot the landscape. Last night after we left the city, we drove through rolling green hills that soon faded under a sky full of stars. Now desert and sand stretch out before us. There is no body of water for several hundred miles. "The people of Yazd are very skilled," Baba tells us. "They are survivors with a deep understanding of conservation and working in harmony with the earth. They have built underground waterways called qanats to bring water into their towns and villages for drinking and farming. Just look at their skyline. There are no metal buildings, like we have in Tehran, covered in windows that only attract and store heat." I see the houses with the domed mud roofs and beautiful mud minarets that keep the houses cool in the middle of summer heat. It is a whole different world here.

"Your Maamaan and I grew up just outside of Yazd" Baba says, "and every person who grows up in Yazd has one enduring dream—" "—speak for yourself," says Maamaan. "OK," Baba continues, "every person who grows up in Yazd, with the exception of your Maamaan, has one enduring dream—to travel north and swim in the Caspian Sea." Maamaan shrugs, "I don't know how to swim, so why would I ever want to go there?" "Well, I got my wish after I became a truck driver." Baba tells of the time one of his routes took him north through the Elburz mountain range to "the glistening green jewel" of the Caspian Sea. "Nothing" he says, "nothing— aside from the births of my four children—has so taken my breath away as the moment I first set eyes on the Caspian Sea." "Now tell us about the food, Baba!" Leila asks. We all know his stories by heart but still never tire of hearing them. "The finest food you'll ever eat!" Baba gushes, "I loved to eat my way across Iran as much as I loved to drive it. Let me tell you, the *Mirza Ghasemi* in northern Iran is not to be missed. Roasted eggplant seasoned with garlic, turmeric, tomato, sautéed in oil then tossed in an egg batter and fried. Delicious! And what about the meatballs from Tabriz? Big as a cricket ball and made with meat and rice, peas and mint, and as a surprise—stuffed with boiled egg, walnuts, fried onions, and dried plum. Mouthwatering!" My belly grumbles. We haven't had breakfast yet.

"But do you know what my favorite is?" Baba quizzes. "Dates," says Cyrus who has heard this story many, many times. "Yes! The dates from the Persian Gulf are unsurpassed. Juicy and sweet with the thin skin that just melts in your mouth! I promise, I will take you all one day and you will pick a ten-pound bunch of fresh dates—each!" "Ten pounds each? *Na baba!* We could never eat that many!" I squeal. "You don't think so, but I did. How? I don't know how. They are just that delicious. Wait until you try them, my dears. Just wait until you try them."

In the front seat, Maamaan starts to pull on her gray chador, the one covered in dark red flowers. "Maamaan, why do you always wear the chador when we go to Yazd?" I ask. "I thought we are Bahá'í not Muslim?" She turns around, looking me right in the eyes: "It is precisely because we are Bahá'ís that I choose to wear the chador when we visit Yazd, Mooshi. It may not be our dress code, but as a Bahá'í I honor and respect the laws of the land we are in, and that includes the dress code of any region. In Yazd, people are very religious and much more conservative than in the capital. The chador is important to them, in fact, I grew up wearing it! And so, I wear the chador again when I return. I don't mind," she winks, "but not until we are at least five miles away! It gets so hot under here!" she laughs now. I like to hear her laugh. It is a rare treat and a good omen for the rest of our holiday.

Everyone except Baba is rested and ready for the day when we arrive. He unpacks a mattress and retreats for a nap while Leila and I play outside my auntie, my *khaleh's*, house with the cousins. I am running really fast around a corner when I jerk to a stop, "The turtle!" I yell. I nearly stepped on him. "Everybody slow down! Time out! Time . . . out!" I fling out my arms with hands up to keep people from tagging me and stepping on the turtle. My cousins saunter up rolling their eyes. "Mahvash, we told you, the turtle's fine. Why do you think it has that hard shell?" they say knocking on its brown dome. "Look. If it gets scared, it goes inside."

The unhurried creature fascinates me but being free to roam the house and yard also worries me. "It's always protected no matter where it goes," they all assure me. Still, I am cautious. I pick up the turtle and bring it inside where it can escape the danger of being punted across the yard. The turtle likes to crunch on the lettuce I feed him, and will strain his neck out farther and farther, if I hold the lettuce just slightly out of reach.

The clock ticks down to Nowruz. The official hour of the new year is at a different time each year because it takes a full three hundred and sixty-five days plus six hours for the earth to go around the sun. This year, Nowruz happens after dinner and we will celebrate at Naneh's house because she is the oldest living member of the family. My belly growls just thinking about the special Nowruz meal we will eat tonight. The crispy white fish and my favorite, favorite rice—the green one, made with dill, cilantro, mint, and lima beans. We pile into the Chevy, all eleven of us— don't ask me how we do it—I will never know, and drive the short distance to Naneh's, balancing pots and pans of food on our laps.

When we pull up, aunts and uncles and cousins spill out of Naneh's small home and into her gardens. Her little plot of land provides everything she needs to live independently and comfortably, which she will do well into her nineties. Every day, she bakes her bread fresh in an oven dug into the ground and prepares cheese and yogurt from the milk of her two sheep. She has pomegranate trees and grapevines, vegetable gardens and chickens. The sheep provide milk, but also hair that Naneh spins into yarn for weaving. All our bed sheets and pajamas come from the fabric she spins on her faithful loom. She dyes the colorful fabrics by hand using pomegranate skins for yellow, madder root for red, indigo for purples and blues, walnuts husks for black.

Whenever we visit, I follow Naneh around and watch everything. Heating the charcoal samovar for tea from the leftover coals used to cook her meals; kneading the dough and pounding it flat; using her needles and knives to fix a jam in her loom. But when she sits in her yard, combing her freshly washed hair, I really can't take my eyes off her. Her round face is pale with freckles, and she only has a few teeth left, but oh, her hair! Her hair falls in long, fiery curls down her back. "Naneh?" I worked up the courage to finally ask her one time. "Why is your hair orange when everyone else's hair is black?" She laughed, "Oh, you. You are so cute! My hair is not really orange!" "It's not?" I gasped. "No, it is gray. Very gray. I dye it with the henna." "But why?" "Why else? I want to stay young!"

Her flaming orange hair parts the sea of family gathered outside as she makes her way toward our car. "Welcome! Welcome!" she greets us, ever smiling, always cheerful and we exchange Nowruz greetings. "*Eide Shoma Mobarak*! Happy New Year!" "Now, let us feast!"

After supper, the adults drink tea while the children play outside. I like to climb on Naneh's roof to retrieve the pomegranate skins she leaves up there to dry. I bring a handful in to her. "For you. For the fire to smell sweet." "Why thank you Mahvash. You are very helpful, just like your Maamaan. She was a good worker too you know," she says drawing me into her lap and starting to braid my hair. "I taught my daughter, your grandmother, to weave and she taught her daughters. Your mother was just a little older than you when she began dying fabrics and yarns to help the family earn a living."

I catch Maamaan out of the corner of my eye. She isn't looking directly our way, but I know she is listening. Her mouth is pinched tight. Maamaan gets angry when the family talks about her childhood.

As a child, I don't fully understand why. It would not be until I am an adult that I would come to know the whole story and understand the weight of my Maamaan's sadness. Her own father died when she was only eight years old. After having served in World War II, he returned home to work at his general store, making trips by camel to neighboring villages to buy, sell, and trade food and other supplies so he could buy parcels of land to save as future dowries for his four daughters. One day, while loading his truck in the city, another truck backed up and ran him over. Death was instant. Just like that, my Maamaan's mother, who we call Maadar, had four daughters to not only feed, but also to one day marry off. She could not lose the land her husband had worked so hard for. No one would marry the daughter of a widow unless there was a significant dowry. So, she did what she could to survive. She pulled her two eldest daughters out of school and made them and their younger sisters responsible for household chores, so that she had time to earn a living for them all.

As the girls grew older, Maadar taught them to weave, so they could also earn a living and help support the family. My Maamaan was only able to finish the second grade. She had dearly loved school and had big dreams for her future and the potential to do great things. Maamaan came to resent Maadar for the rest of her life because she pulled her out of school. The bitterness grew over the years into wracking headaches, the depression weighing her body down in bed, too heavy to lift herself up and out for days on end. I was too young then to realize that this was why Baba rose so early each morning to walk to the bakery and buy the bread for our breakfast and why, without fail, he made the tea and steamed the milk, got the quince jam and feta, and made sure we were fed before going to school; why he was the one to always tuck us in to bed at night and sing us the songs that sent us to sleep. My mother was caring, hard-working, and committed to her family, but her own pain and mental health created a wall that neither she nor we could scale, no matter how much we wanted to.

"'Everything good we have comes from your Maamaan," Baba would always tell us when we were growing up. She really was incredibly clever with the finances and flawlessly managed expenses; Baba turned every rial over to her and trusted her judgment. When Baba would come home lamenting how they could not afford to purchase a parcel of land that would make a great investment, Maamaan would say, "Well, if the land is good, buy the land." "But how? It is impossible on my small salary," Baba would argue. "Well, all the same, we do have the money." Then she'd go to the closet and pull down a suitcase filled with bags, and in one of the bags, buried beneath papers and fabrics would be a sock, and in the sock would be a wad of bills and a pile of coins. "We can sell my jewelry too if the land is good. Land is a much better investment." Baba's jaw would drop, and he would kiss both Maamaan's cheeks and praise her thrift. "Where would I be without you?" And to think theirs was an arranged marriage.

When Baba was sixteen years old, his father died. Both Baba and his older brother, Vali, had not been raised to be farmers like their father. They had been sent to school instead. Without any agricultural knowledge, especially for such an extreme and harsh climate, Baba left Yazd and went to Tehran in search for work. A new father figure would come into Baba's life a few years later in the form of Mr. Paakdel, the owner of multiple successful companies, including a trucking company. Mr. Paakdel came from a very distinguished Muslim family, but as a young adult had converted to the Bahá'í Faith, and as a result his family had abandoned him. Mr. Paakdel took the young Aziz under his wing as his helper and encouraged him to learn how to drive so he too could be a trucker one day. Being reliable and ambitious, Aziz soon made a name for himself and earned Mr. Paakdel's full trust and high regard. He eventually became a driver and earned a good salary, and perhaps most importantly, at twenty-seven years old could now be considered an eligible match for a wife. The responsibility for finding a wife for Aziz fell on Vali's shoulders and he knew of a young woman he thought could be a fine match. Her name was Monir and she was twenty-three, much too old for marriage by Iranian standards, but then again—so was Aziz.

Aziz wholly trusted Vali's judgment. He sent a ring from Tehran to Vali before ever meeting Monir. Vali then brought the ring to Monir and her mother with a proposal for marriage, she accepted the ring and the family gave their blessing. Aziz and Monir would meet before their wedding, but everything had already been arranged at that point. The wedding ceremony was simple: prayers, vows, and the signing of the marriage certificate. Monir wore a simple, white dress; Aziz, his best slacks. They trusted that they would learn to love one another in time.

Bringing his bride back to the capital, Aziz and Monir settled into marriage in a small room they rented within someone else's home in a poor and tired neighborhood. They saved their money, eating simple dishes of rice and lentils when they had enough, or a plain loaf of freshly baked bread when they did not have enough. It was there they learned what it meant to share your life with another. Soon they would learn what it meant to share it with a child. Cyrus came a year later. Before the baby's arrival, Mr. Paakdel offered a small parcel of land for purchase, on which the young family could build a two-room home. To make the purchase, they sold Monir's land, the land her father had purchased as a dowry. But it would take still more money than they had. Mr. Paakdel reassured them saying not to worry, they could pay him back in manageable monthly installments after the house was built. The walls came up, the roof put on, Cyrus was born, and the young family moved in. Eleven months later Kia made his appearance.

During those early years, Aziz spent days at a time on the road away from his family. Spending hours in lines behind hundreds of other trucks waiting to unload their cargo at seaports, then another line to load up cargo from the Persian Gulf ports, then on to drive all over the country delivering and unloading the goods before finally returning to the capital for another load. While he grappled with icy mountain roads, brakes going out and sliding backwards down passes, often repairing the truck in freezing cold weather, Monir grappled with her own mountain. There was no heat and no running water in their home back then. She went to the well and hauled water back home to store in buckets for cooking and drinking, washing and cleaning, but the water would freeze overnight. Each morning, she chipped the ice into chunks and melted it on the stove until she had enough water to hand wash the dozens of soiled cloth diapers from the day before. Something had to be done. She needed Aziz at home. He missed being there in the evenings as well. For months he looked for a new job, and finally found a government position at the city water company. He would continue to drive, but it would be a water tanker now instead of an eighteen-wheeler. The pay was less, but the work reliable; it also meant that he would get health benefits and retirement. Although, there was no way he could have known that he would end up never needing retirement in Iran. On top of the benefits, the work felt meaningful. He was to bring clean water to the city schools to refresh the students.

Aziz and Monir would live in that home for the next sixteen years, growing their family of four to a family of six. With Mr. Paakdel's help, they would purchase more land to build homes on, and rent them out for added income. When they left their original home in the Majidieh neighborhood some sixteen years later it would not be because they wanted to— but because they were forced to. But that is for later.

Today, however, is for Nowruz, and today we feel hopeful. Today we know nothing of the bombs being built across the border or the soldiers practicing their war games, or of the whispers of revolution and the threat of ethnic cleansing.

Naneh has finished braiding my hair and Baba has announced that it is time. We all gather around the *Sofreh Haft Seen*, a colorful tablecloth filled with beautiful objects that symbolize the new year. The little kids are tested on their knowledge. We love this part. Haft means "seven" and Seen means the letter "s." So, there are seven items all beginning with the letter "s" that make up the Haft Seen. *Sumac* for the spice of life, *serkeh* is vinegar for patience, and *seeb* is an apple for health and beauty. *Sir* is garlic and also good health, *samanu* is the wheat pudding symbolizing a sweet life. My favorite is the *sonbol*, the hyacinth and best symbol of spring, considered to be the scent of heaven. After a long winter, there is really nothing so delicious and intoxicating as the scent of hyacinth blooming outside the window. At last, there is the *sabzeh*, the sprouted wheat grass, which has a special purpose outside of the Sofreh Haft Seen. Work and school will start back on the fourteenth day of the new year, but because it is believed that thirteen is a bad omen, everyone celebrates that thirteenth day of Nowruz with a yearly ritual. When we get back from the road trip, on the thirteenth day, we will take our sabzeh down to the river and have a picnic; then we will toss the grass into the river and we will know spring is here, winter is over, and school will begin. At school we will swap stories about our holidays and find out who got the most money and how they want to spend it. Or if they already did! I am like Maamaan; I like to save my money for something really special and I don't know what that special thing is yet. Maybe a Chevy.

Khaleh reads from the Bahá'í prayer book on the Haft Seen table and my uncle tells a story from the *Shahnameh*, a book about the Persian kings. Kia loves poetry and finds the courage to read a poem to everyone aloud from Hafez. Some families keep a Torah or a Bible or Qur'án on their Haft Seen table—whatever is most meaningful to them. Naneh doesn't have a goldfish like we do, but she has colored eggs and she has a pretty gold mirror. None of the kids know why there is a mirror. Naneh explains, "It symbolizes the light and endless opportunities I wish for you all to enjoy in this new year."

The radio comes on and we listen to the countdown to Nowruz. Ten . . . nine . . . eight . . . then . . . three . . . two . . . one! Happy New Year! Baba is asked to chant a prayer. He has a beautiful singing voice that everyone always wants to hear. After that, it is hugs and kisses all around. Now comes the time to pass out the Eidee—the gift of money. Grownups give money; young ones receive money. I share the coins I got last night from the neighbors with my cousins, and they share coins they got with me, so I think I have about the same as I started out with. But we receive money from all the adults too, the most being from our parents. I had hoped for five hundred rials (Which Kia tells me is equal to seven American dollars. He knows these things because he is studying English to go to an American university), but I think I have more than that. When the excitement dies down, I get to snuggle up in Naneh's lap again because I am the youngest child out of all the cousins. My eyes wander to all the little black and white polaroids stuck with tiny nails to the mud walls. "What do you see there, Mahvash?" Naneh asks. "I see your photos." "That's right. But who is in the photos?" "Us." "Yes, all my grandchildren and my great-grandchildren. You know what makes a home, Mooshi?" "Sure, there's windows and floors and probably a stove." "Those are very nice, but those things just make a house. Home is the place where you cherish your memories. I cherish my family, so I keep your faces close because it is here, with you all, that I feel happy, that I belong."

I will question the definition of home many years later when I am grown and married with children of my own. I will find there is no better definition than the one my Naneh gave except that I would add: home must be a place you also feel safe—safe from terror, safe from judgment. Home is a place where you feel at peace with the world and those around you. Until I was six years old, I had a home like that. After six years old, all I had was a country that rejected me and a deep and abiding dread that I must get out—at any cost.

3
UNITY

SPRING 1978: TEHRAN

"Want to learn?" Cyrus asks me, not taking his eyes off the chess board. He and Kia are usually off playing soccer with the other boys after school, but lately they've been playing more chess together. I have been trying to figure it out on my own and already know how the bishops and rooks and kings move, but don't understand those horses. I'd been sitting on my tricycle, arms crossed on the handlebars just staring at them when he asked if I wanted to learn. Do I! I want to learn everything they know.

Just last week, Kia fetched me up to his and Cyrus's large balcony bedroom. They had friends over and were about to test their science fair experiment—a homemade volcano. They tossed a strange slurry into the center, and then the volcano gurgled and fizzed to life. Glugs of red erupted over the sides of the papier-mâché mountain. And applause erupted from the admiring crowd.

Even though I like to play with the neighbor kids who are my own age, I like my siblings and their friends even better. They teach me things and talk about interesting things. That spring I learn that castling was just as fun as tricycling and getting an *en passant* even better than perfecting my hopscotch. I race home every day after school and finish my homework as quickly as possible so I can play outside. If Cyrus and Kia are playing soccer, then I tricycle around and wave to the neighbor women as they share tea and gossip on the front steps. But if the boys are not playing soccer, then we have chess tournaments together until the sun goes down and Maamaan calls us inside for dinner. Saturday through Thursday this is what we do.

Fridays, our one day off from school, are always a fun day. I walk with my siblings to our neighborhood Bahá'í center for children's classes. We bring bags filled with prayer books, notepads, and pencils. Sometimes, Cyrus and Kia carry me—piggy back style all the way there. There are maybe thirty other children there, and together we learn prayers and sing songs.

* * *

The Bahá'í Faith is a fairly recent faith, less than two hundred years old. It was founded in Iran by Bahá'u'lláh, who had a global vision he believed all could share of world peace and harmony. Anchored in the pursuit of justice and the continual spiritual advancement of the human race, Bahá'ís believe that we can only attain maturity together, and that diversity is the bond and cause of love and harmony. Unlike other religions, we do not have preachers, it is more about living a Bahá'í life, meaning one of kindness and acceptance. There is no concept of heaven or hell and there is no belief that one must be a Bahá'í in order to be saved. The Bahá'í Faith stresses the importance of the unity of mankind. How without it, we cannot truly develop and progress. Within the Faith, members are encouraged to do an independent investigation of truth, and to not blindly accept what we are told to be facts.

I remember the day I started to really understand how connected we all are, and what my teachers meant when they quoted Bahá'u'lláh saying, "The earth is but one country, and mankind its citizens."

The teacher had taught us a simple song— "We are flowers of one garden. We are leaves of one tree. We are waves of one ocean." But unlike other days where we all sang the same melody together, that day the teacher split us into three sections. She individually taught each section a different melody to the same lyrics. "OK," she said, "now comes the tricky part! We sing together!" The song took on a whole new depth for me. It felt almost magical to my young self who knew nothing of music theory and chordal harmony. The teacher clapped her hands when we finished and told us, "What you just accomplished, that is the beauty of the human family. We are unique, diverse, all walking different spiritual paths, but when we come together, we create fantastic chords. You know what Bahá'u'lláh taught: God is One. Man is One. And all the religions agree. If everyone learns this oneness, we will have a world of unity. But as you can see, oneness doesn't mean sameness. You all sang very different notes and that diversity created the joyful song, beautiful and wonderful to the heart and soul."

Though Bahá'ís are a peace-loving people, they are also considered a heretical sect by the Muslim majority. Still, we were tolerated and welcomed, living as neighbors alongside Muslims, Jews, Christians, and Zoroastrians in Iran under the secular ruler, Mohammad Reza Shah Pahlavi, who had been the Shah since 1941. He granted Bahá'ís the same rights and privileges as everyone else—the right to marry, to attend school, to hold government jobs, etc.

The Iranian Constitution provided much more recognition and protection though for the Jewish and Christian communities; this was because Muslims revered Moses and Christ in the Qur'án as divine Figures who came before Muhammad. The Bahá'ís also revere Moses, Christ, Muhammad, Buddha, and Zoroaster, but honor Bahá'u'lláh as the most recent Prophet in a long lineage of Prophets who brought the message of peace and love and acceptance in the new era.

All my life, my faith has been a part of me, as personal and as intimate as the hairs on my head, or the smile lines on my face. It grew from somewhere deep in me, revealed itself in how I lived and spoke. It was a way of being in the world, a way that encouraged tolerance and kindness, individual investigation, equality of rights of men and women (including the importance of educating women) and treating others with dignity. It was a way of being in the world that many of our neighbors, no matter their faith system, also upheld to various degrees.

* * *

After Friday Bahá'í school, we pack into the Chevy and drive to Maamaan's sister's home just on the outskirts of Tehran for lunch. The thick, sticky air from rice steaming on the stove top warms our faces as we walk in the door. Little glass mugs line the counter, waiting to be filled with black tea from the samovar, and near them, plates of chickpea and cardamom cookies that will not be offered until after lunch. Along with the other young girls, I offer to help carry the plates, silverware, and food to the crisp white sofreh spread across the floor. Big stainless-steel pots keep the food warm, and everyone gathers around seated on the floor. Stacks of naan are passed around and we serve ourselves from little plates of cool sides like yogurt and cucumber or a *Shirazi* salad, minced cucumber with tomatoes and onions in a lemon juice and mint dressing.

With everyone talking and laughing, it is hard to make out what they are saying. My aunt offers, no, insists, on second helpings. Men politely decline, "I couldn't possibly eat anymore!" But when they look away their plates are full again. They laugh, but still proclaim that they are satisfied. My aunt insists again and finally, the men accept the food joyfully. A bit of *taarof* having just gone on. Each showing mutual respect to the other. Each not really saying what they mean to say but putting the other above themselves until equality is gained and formalities may be put aside, "Why yes, actually thank you. It's delicious. I'd love a second plate!" The most precious jewel in any Persian home is the guest. But sometimes when it is with family, we shake our heads and laugh, "Please, don't taarof with me!" And the other will swear, "I wasn't." And then we know, we are level and may speak freely. My aunt would empty her cupboards before letting anyone walk away hungry and as a guest, you feel very lucky indeed because she is an amazing cook. Someone raises a fork to their mouth and asks my aunt, "Seriously. This is too delicious. How do you do it? You must live in the kitchen!" Everyone laughs. But all jokes aside, it really is that good.

Tea and cookies are offered and after eating the sweets, all the children jump up and make a break for the backyard. Yes, there is a soccer match to play, but we also want to make sure we are gone before the pajamas come out. The women will all gather in the kitchen to clean dishes and prep food for the next meal, enjoying more tea and conversation, but the men will nap. New mats are rolled open and a dozen pillows brought from the closet. Auntie arrives with a stack of fresh pajamas and offers them all around. The men gladly accept, their own pants being now a bit too tight, the comfy cotton more forgiving to a full belly. They change clothes and then retire to the floor.

When I sneak in later to swipe another cookie, there is no need to tiptoe quietly around the men. It is clear from the roof rattling snores that nothing will disturb them. Baba snores too? I never knew! In the kitchen, I overhear the women talking of things I do not at the time comprehend.

"Khomeini is broadcasting from Paris. They're playing his message in the mosques; I've heard he is calling for the people to rise up and overthrow the Shah." "It's a wave, like so many others. It too will pass." "I don't know. There are some protests starting—small, but still. They say the Shah is anti-Islamic and has to go." "Anti-Islamic? He isn't a fundamentalist, surely, but he is not anti- any religion. I suppose it is for that the fanatics hate him—he grants even Bahá'ís rights that Khomeini would never allow."

Maamaan sees me reach for a cookie; she ruffles my hair and whispers that I better take two otherwise Leila will not be far behind.

I remember how as spring wore on and as summer approached things started to change in ways I could not put my finger on. The adults were speaking of things I did not understand. There was more whispering, an air of confusion and concern between my parents and our Bahá'í friends. The sweet bubble of unity our neighborhood and city and country lived in was being poked. How long until it would burst entirely? For all I knew though, everything was just fine. I still knew nothing of worry or fear.

Every couple of months on Friday, we would skip the Bahá'í school and the lunch and my aunt, and instead wake up at the crack of dawn to drive outside of Tehran to visit Mr. Danesh's farm—one of my favorite places. Mr. Danesh was a friend of my grandfather Akbar (my Baba's father). They were young Muslim farmers in Yazd together, who later converted to the Bahá'í Faith. Mr. Danesh continued his friendship with my Baba when he moved to this farm near Tehran. His five sons and three daughters helped him manage the farm, which sat on several acres and was home to cows and mules and chickens, fruit orchards, and vegetable gardens.

It was the cows Mr. Danesh loved the most.

* * *

We arrive to the smell of new spring grass, manure, and pear blossoms. Mr. Danesh comes running to greet us. "You've arrived just in time! Come! I have a new grandchild, come!" Baba is baffled. "A grandchild? How . . . !" "Come and see! In the barn, you will meet my new granddaughter." A fuzzy brown calf is getting licked up and down by her mother. She is the cutest thing I have ever seen. Mr. Danesh beams. "What do you think? You must admit, she is more beautiful than your daughters, Aziz!" Mr. Danesh's love for his cows knows no bounds.

In summer when school is let out, we might come visit the farm for two or three days at a time. Mr. Danesh lets me go to the barn with him while he milks the cows. He gives me a small stool to sit on. While he milks, he whispers sweet nothings to the cows and sings beautiful songs for them. I help him carry the milk pails to Mrs. Danesh, who always has fresh bread waiting for our breakfast. She pours us all a glass of the warm milk, and the thick layer of cream on the top leaves a delicious moustache behind. After breakfast we might help her use the rest of the milk to make yogurt and cheese, or we go collect the chicken eggs. The Danesh's have many grandchildren, so we play all over the farm with them, hide and seek, tag, and the boys' favorite—finding frogs to throw at Leila and me. I hate all thing creepy and crawly, slimy and slithery. We are allowed to climb the fruit trees and pick whatever we want to eat, and in the afternoons, we ride the mules bareback.

That summer I remember Baba walking alongside my mule with Mr. Danesh. I told Baba he was too close; I could handle it—I was almost six, after all. The men raised their hands in apology and took a couple steps back, but still close enough that I could hear what they were saying. "We've decided to let Cyrus leave," Baba said. "To the US you mean?" asked Mr. Danesh. "Yes, to attend university." "But how will you afford it? You should consider India instead." "We will manage." "No! Impossible. It is so expensive. He will have to cut his education short and then come back." "The growing tension . . . the protests. They're building. He should go while he has the chance and I want him to get the best education possible." "You don't think there is much weight to what they say? What can Khomeini really do from all the way in Paris?" "He is doing a lot already. What if he returns?" "Bah. A coup? It's a wave and it will pass just like all the others." "That's what everyone is saying, but I just feel . . . I don't know. It gives me relief to know Cyrus can go. We will make it work." Mr. Danesh sighed. "I know this was a difficult decision for you, and while I do not understand it, I do trust you, my friend. When does he leave?" "He's been taking accelerated English lessons for years and completes them this summer. He'll leave after that in September."

I had no idea just how far America was from Iran and what going to university there exactly meant, but I did know I wanted to join the conversation. "Cyrus is so smart. I want to be like him. He taught me to play chess, you know?"

"Chess? Sounds like this one is ready for college herself! Will you send her along with Cyrus?"

"No," I told him. "I have to go to the first grade first. I am already signed up. But maybe Baba will let me go to university next year." I didn't know why they laughed so hard.

"Mahvash," Baba said, wiping his eyes with his sleeve, "you will most definitely go to university one day and make us all very, very proud. But please, don't leave me so soon. OK? I know that none of us can escape our destiny, but still . . . I'd like to think I get to keep my mighty mouse around for a little longer yet!"

4
DREAMS

SUMMER 1978: FAMILY ROAD TRIP ON THE SILK ROAD TO TABRIZ

Once again Baba is packing the Chevy sky high with our mattresses, blankets, pillows, and suitcases. This time for a summer road trip. "Like a camel on the Silk Road!" he grunts, tightening the straps around the cargo piled on the roof. We are going to travel the famous Silk Road route through the Zagros mountain range to Kermanshah and then on to Tabriz for a wedding before returning home. The Chevy still sparkles as always, but something feels different. Cyrus is not going with us. Maamaan has not smiled in weeks. And even Kia is withdrawn, which is strange for him. Leila is as confused as I am—should we be excited about this road trip, or not? "How come Cyrus is not going on vacation?" I ask Baba. "Well, he is preparing for a bigger trip, a much bigger, much farther away trip that's to come soon. He needs to spend more time studying for his Test of English as a Foreign Language and applying to US universities."

Leila and I cannot help ourselves. Even if everyone else is acting strange, we are still excited, especially when our parents surprise us with ice cream cones to christen our departure. I am being particularly careful not to let any drip on my brand-new corduroy pants, a gift from my brothers for the sixth birthday I recently celebrated. In our home, birthdays are like any other day except that Maamaan will make the birthday boy or girl's favorite food for dinner. Presents, birthday parties, and cakes are not common or even expected, so when Kia and Cyrus placed the striped package in my hands, I was not sure what to do with it. "Open it!" they cried.

I carefully unwrapped each edge, removing the tape ever so slowly so as not to ruin the pretty paper. My brothers told me to just tear it open, but I couldn't bring myself to do that. I wanted to savor the way my finger felt sliding under the paper's edge, and the crinkly sound the paper made when I turned the package over. Inside the box was pretty pink tissue paper. I gasped when I saw what was tucked underneath. A pair of corduroy pants. I held them up in complete awe. Then I clutched them to my heart and dashed into the bedroom to try them on. Hands on hips, I ran back to model my pants for everyone, striking pose after pose, while Cyrus's camera clicked away.

I might have even spent the next few days strutting around to various doorsteps of our neighbors, hoping to dazzle all my friends.

"You know what you need to go with those great new pants?" our neighbor, Ms. Molook, asked one day while I was showing off on her doorstep. "Pierced ears." She was right. I ran off to ask Maamaan's permission. Ms. Molook has three children and no husband. She is our family friend and also the neighborhood nurse. Whenever anyone is sick, we get a prescription from the doctor for medicine, but rather than taking medicine in a syrup or a pill, Ms. Molook will come over and give it to us as an injection. She makes her living this way and the entire neighborhood relies on her expertise, along with her knowledge of bandaging and splinting, and healing muscle pain through cupping therapy. Lucky for me, she also pierces girl's ears.

"May I, Maamaan? Please?" I beg. "Well," she pondered, "seeing as most girls your age already have pierced ears, and I agree that it is a very attractive look, I suppose so. But you will have to pay for it. Do you think this is a good way to use some of the Nowruz money you've been saving all these months? "I do!" We pulled my money out of a sock in Maamaan's dresser drawer and I raced back to tell Ms. Molook the good news.

Her three kids surrounded me and told me it would only hurt for a moment and to remember to not scream or move my head. Ms. Molook sterilized the needle over a fire, and then, because we cannot afford gold earrings yet, she ran a thick piece of thread through the eye of the needle, which she left knotted in my earlobes. The pain was quick; it hurt but I did not cry.

That little knot in my ear is what I fiddle with now as we finish our ice creams before the road trip. I dream about what kind of earrings I might pick out from the dazzling gold bazaar in Yazd when I grow up.

The Chevy sets off for the majestic city of Kermanshah, winding through the lush Zagros mountain range where wild walnut, pear, and almond trees abound and where nomadic Kurds graze their goats and sheep. I spend the whole trip with eyes glued to the window, taking in everything. Leila and Kia play I Spy or Cat's Cradle and make up jokes to pass the time. Maamaan and Baba talk in hushed and serious whispers. Maamaan cries a lot, silently, but I can see her face scrunched up in the side mirror, her eyes watery and red. Sometimes Kia joins in the conversation, they talk a lot about Cyrus. Baba is not up for telling stories from his glory days on the road. I ask a few times, but he just says, "Not right now, Mooshi. Maybe later." But he does make sure to pat the dashboard now and then and tell our turquoise queen she is driving beautifully, just beautifully. Baba does not even turn the radio on for fear it will be too exhausting for the Chevy's battery. "Are we there yet?" Leila inevitably asks. "Not yet." "Well then when?" "When we get there."

When we get there, it will be late in the evening and we will go straight to bed, rolling our mattresses out on the floor of the home of our second cousins. In the morning, we tour the rock reliefs at the famous Tagh-e-Bostan, which boasts some of the best-preserved examples of Sassanid art. A sign tells us that the Sassanids, who ruled western Asia from 226 to 650 AD, chose this spot to depict their festivals, coronations, and battles knowing thousands of traders would pass by on the Silk Road and use the base of the mountain cliff as a campground and watering hole. The carvings are massive, stretching many feet above my head and even Baba's. I like the giant horse carrying a king going on a boar hunt and learning that they hunted with elephants. The elephant would retrieve the boar after it was killed, pick it up with its trunk, and place it on its back to carry home.

A couple of days later we are on the road again and off to our next grand adventure—swimming in Lake Urmia, one of the largest saltwater lakes in the world. Flamingos come for the brine shrimp, bathers for the warm, therapeutic waters. Little paddle boats line the beaches in colors like mustard, avocado, and robin's egg. I cannot see across the lake; it is that vast. The clear waters reflect the turquoise sky and creamy clouds. In twenty years from now, the lake will have been depleted by eighty percent because of illegal wells and too many dam and irrigation projects that divert the waters. It will no longer ripple turquoise, like the Chevy, but will turn a deep blood red because the algae and bacteria once living deep in its depths are now exposed to sunlight in the very shallow waters.

But on that trip, I still lived in sweet ignorance, a short season of my life where Chevys and lakes still glistened in the color of dreams.

We have a fabulous time. Even Maamaan swims! It takes some persistence on Kia's part though. "C'mon Maamaan, try it?" "But I don't know how to swim!" she insists. "Don't worry," he says, "It's saltier than the ocean. You can't sink." "I can't sink? Really?" He has convinced her. We bob together in the salty water. Kia shows both of us how to stretch our arms out wide and float comfortably and effortlessly on our backs. Maamaan points overhead. A flamingo soars above us. She smiles. I smile. Her first swim ever.

We build sand castles and paddle in boats, and everything is fun and fine until I try to swim under water with my eyes open. No one warned me not to do this. I had wanted to see if I could spot the tiny brine shrimp or the dangling toes of tourists. At home in the city pool, I am good at diving for coins at the bottom of the pool and keeping my eyes open, so I try it here. When I emerge from the waters of Lake Urmia, the air hits my eyes and they sting so hard I squeeze them shut and cannot open them again. Kia helps me out of the water and rushes me to Maamaan to rinse my eyes, telling me I have to open my eyes to let the pure water rinse them. "I can't!" I yell, fists pushed deep into my eye sockets. "I can't!" Nearby in the shade, Baba has been wiping the Chevy with wet towels while pouring words of endearment all over the car. Because of my stinging eyes, I cannot see the look on his face when Maamaan yells, "Aziz! You used up all the towels for sparkling your car! Now how are these kids going to dry off?"

For the rest of the trip, my eyes are bloodshot and dry.

"As soon as you take a bite of the famous lamb meatballs of Tabriz, Mahvash, you will forget your pain," Baba winks. "Tomatoes, saffron, eggs, plums! Is your mouth watering yet? Your eyes will water again soon, don't worry about that. Travel is good for the soul, even when it is uncomfortable." He tells me of all we will do and all we will see in Tabriz. The immense, covered bazaar with its fine silks and intricate, hand-woven carpets, walls lined with tall sacks overflowing with sheep's wool, crates of dress pants and racks of jackets stuffed into tiny alcoves, the white cheese and green pickle vendors, and the old men with their abacuses out and ready to tally your bill for you.

But before we get to Tabriz, we head to a small village called Seysan for a Turkish-style wedding of an old and dear family friend. We are all antsy to get out and stretch our legs after a long day in the car. Baba slows the car down so as not to miss the village entrance. Then, wham. I go flying into the front seat! A car hit us. Baba makes sure we are all okay before getting out to assess the damage. The trunk has jammed into the rear seat and the other car is completely totaled. To make matters worse, a high-ranking military official jumps out of the car—not from the driver's side, but from the rear seat—and comes storming over to Baba, accusing him of causing the accident. A timid woman gets out of the driver's side. Baba looks in rage at his beloved Chevy, all wrecked and bent. He demands their driver's license information; the woman does not have any. The man is furious and will not stop accusing Baba; finally, he points his finger and says if Baba wants to file a claim with the court, he can. He storms off and that is that.

We drive into the village with our spirits sagging as low as the heavy metal fender that now drags behind us.

The next day Baba goes to Tabriz to file a court claim; it takes a few days, and in the end, he returns defeated. That official had friends in high places and was able to cover up for his wife driving without a license. He even convinced the court to order Baba to pay for the damages to his car. The beloved Chevy requires expensive parts that are hard to obtain and needs repairs that are more than we can possibly afford.

After the wedding ceremony, Baba sells his turquoise beauty—the dream of his youth, the jewel of his eye—to a junkyard. We take a bus home. I wish for an elephant like the Persian king at Tagh-e-Bostan had for hunting so we could have saved the Chevy and brought it home because then—maybe, just maybe—none of the other bad stuff about to happen, would have happened.

PART II: WAR

(Schoolyard in Tehran with sandbags piled up in front of the doorway.
Mahvash is pictured in the center, looking up.)

5
DIRTY

It started with just one man chanting on his rooftop. Then it was two. Now it is at least twenty. Every night, they climb to their roofs at sunset and shout "*Allah-u-Akbar*" over and over. Far in the distance, I sometimes hear gunfire too. When I asked Maamaan why the neighbors were so happy about something called a revolution, Maamaan told Leila and me to stay inside and play with our dolls after school from now on. We also do not walk the same main streets anymore when we go shopping. When I ask why, Baba points to the television. "Protests. Strikes." The TV shows cars on fire and a theater burned to the ground. Cyrus turns to Baba, "It's been growing in intensity ever since you left on the road trip. The Shah's secret guards, the Savak, are getting more aggressive trying to stop the protests."

"I heard the prisons are getting overcrowded because they've charged so many people with violence," says Kia. It's the first time Kia has spoken in what feels like weeks. He has been walking around with his forehead scrunched up and his hands in his pockets not speaking. Sometimes though, I hear him whispering in his bedroom with Cyrus.

At dinner, he spoke again and his words surprised us all.

"Maamaan, Baba . . ." he had said looking at his plate, "I've been talking to Cyrus." Baba put his spoon down carefully. "I would like to go to the US with Cyrus, but—" Kia paused and then the words flew out of his mouth so fast, I couldn't keep up. "I know we can't possibly afford it. I know. I know I shouldn't even ask. You've done so much already, sacrificed so much. It's just that I want to go more than anything. I wanted you to know. I shouldn't have asked." He took a gulp of air and hung his head.

What my father did next surprised us even more than Kia's speech.

Baba's eyes filled with tears. He got up and held Kia's cheeks in his big, thick hands: "I have wanted you to go with Cyrus from the very beginning, but I have not wanted to say so. I didn't want to burden you at such a young age. But I believe that you can succeed in the US. I am much happier thinking of you two staying together, taking care of each other. You have my blessing."

Maamaan's jaw dropped and she stared hard at Baba. Then silent tears rolled down her cheeks, but she refused to say anything.

Now she is as moody as Kia had been.

She still refuses to talk to Baba. All she does is cook Cyrus and Kia's favorite foods. She brings them plate after plate to eat while they study for the SATs and the TOEFL. When they tell her they are not hungry, she becomes upset, "Who knows what you will eat in America? You should put on some extra weight, just in case. Eat. Eat!" If she is not cooking, then she is packing, making sure they have everything they need.

The boys finish their fourth year enrolled at a private English institute that they have been attending since middle school. Maamaan said Mr. Paakdel just showed up the day after regular school ended and took Cyrus and Kia to the institute to enroll them. Mr. Paakdel even paid their full tuition that first year. "He planted the seeds of America in your Baba's head," Maamaan explains. All they do is study, study, study, but Baba says they have nothing to worry about, they are more than prepared to pass the TOEFL thanks to Mr. Paakdel. "His four sons are all in America studying at university now, and soon, so will you!"

Baba helps them go get their passports, visas, and plane tickets. He gives them endless advice. His favorite bit of wisdom is the one he has always given us any time we go out. Pointing to the business sign of a doctor or engineer, he says, "If you want to be like me, don't study. But if you want to be like them, you must study." And that the "single most important thing to remember," he tells the boys one day close to their departure, "until you finish college, no, not even until you become the doctors you want to be, do not—do not—look any girls in the eyes!" The boys snicker at each other and Leila and I giggle, but Baba is serious. "As for you two," he says turning to Leila and me, "I am just as committed to making sure my girls get a college education too. Your time is coming, I promise. It is just as important for my daughters to be educated as it is for my sons. In fact, it is better." Baba's lessons are not easily forgotten. He repeats his promises to us all nearly every day.

Cyrus and Kia will have to finish high school in America. They would fly with Iran Air from Tehran to Paris then to New York, and from there to a place called Nebraska. Family and friends would ask, is Nebraska in America? Are you sure?" Everyone has heard of Chicago, New York, California, Texas, but not of Nebraska. "Ah, to experience the wide and windy cornfields of Nebraska," Baba grins. He's been reading up on this exotic new place. I'm excited because the boys promise to send me postcards and I have never received a postcard from a foreign country before. It helps make up for the fact that they are too busy now for chess or soccer or piggy back rides.

If only I had known I was not going to see them again for the rest of my childhood. If only I had known the men I would meet eleven years later would look nothing like the brothers I remembered. If only I had known just how far and wide the world was and just how desperate things were about to get. If only. Then again, perhaps it is a good thing I did not know and that we did not know. How could we have gone on with making the preparations? The sadness would have been too great. But I think that looking back, Maamaan knew. She knew and that was part of the reason why she grieved so hard. Perhaps Baba knew too, but he also knew there is only ever one way, and that is to push through and press forward.

In early September, we said goodbye to my brothers.

Maamaan cried about how they had never traveled alone before, how they didn't know anyone where they were going. Baba just cooed and said, "They have each other. And they are smart and capable young men." "They are only babies!" she had sobbed. They didn't look like babies to me. They looked very tall and handsome in their new suits from last Nowruz. We waved as they walked away to get in line for boarding. We waved after the ticket agent checked their passport and ushered them through the gate. We waved from the window as the plane started to back up, not knowing if they could see us or not, but waving all the same.

The house feels strange without them. As expected, school starts again and Baba reminds us to "Study, study, study! You're going to be doctors one day too, right?" "Right!" we tell him. Maamaan grumbles from the bedroom. "Quiet!" All she's done since the boys left is sob, day and night. She stays in bed and complains of headaches. Leila and I don't really know what to do except stay close together and try not to bother her. Baba wakes extra early to do chores and make sure we have breakfast before school.

At night, Baba and Maamaan watch the news. "The protests are getting bigger and bloodier," Baba says. Maamaan nods. Baba continues: "Now the ayatollahs are encouraging people to join the fight and put an end to the Shah's regime. At work, there is talk about cleansing Iran of Western influences and ideologies. You know what else this means?" Maamaan just nods. "Those in support of Khomeini consider it an insult to Islam that the Shah has allowed religious minorities—Bahá'ís—to hold government positions and be recognized. They promise a theocratic republic and promise every Iranian exclusive right to profit sharing of the oil industry; no more sharing of revenues with American and British corporations. Every single Iranian would receive a share of the profits, though I don't suppose that means Bahá'ís too." Baba shakes his head as if in pain.

The television blares something about martial law and a curfew. "What's happening?" I ask. Baba sighs. "There is an Islamic cleric in Paris who wants to return to Iran and overthrow our Shah, Mooshi," he runs his fingers through my hair. "And he is doing a very good job of stirring up discord from very far away." "Our neighbors like this man in Paris?" "Yes, Mooshi." "But he doesn't like Bahá'ís?" "I'm afraid not, Mooshi." "So, do our neighbors still like us?" Baba sighs but does not answer. He turns to Maamaan. "See? The boys left just in time. They are safely abroad." She nods her head, but her eyes are blank.

* * *

My brothers were part of a great wave of emigration during that season of uncertainty. Anyone with money or a Western education left for Europe or America. No matter their faith, if they could leave, they did. While some still clung to the hope that things would not get so bad, others, like my father's dear mentor and friend Mr. Paakdel, knew it was the hour to act. He arrived one day at our door bearing sweets and gifts for Leila and me, just as he always did when he would come to visit. We gathered on the sofreh on the floor and Mr. Paakdel happily humored me, teaching me clapping games and playing with me while he drank tea and chatted with my parents. But his face soon fell. "I'll be joining my sons in California. It's not safe. I need to exit while it's still legal to do so." Baba and Maamaan were shocked. Certainly, they were much relieved that Cyrus and Kia had left when they did, they told Mr. Paakdel, but were things really so bad as all that? "I'd like to think not," said Mr. Paakdel, "but if they get any worse, the wrath will fall first upon those of us who were Muslim and became Bahá'í." Baba nodded in understanding. Then Mr. Paakdel encouraged my parents to apply for passports for all of us. "Just in case. Be prepared." Mr. Paakdel acted fast. He was not able to take any of his wealth with him—he left everything, all assets, behind. Later, all his land and properties were confiscated and never returned.

Baba had listened to his advice and applied for passports. He'd often bring the subject of leaving up to Maamaan and they would talk it through, always coming to the same conclusion—we cannot possibly afford it. We cannot possibly leave. Every bit of extra money has to go to pay for the boys' education and housing. Period. If we leave, we might jeopardize their futures.

But by 1980, it wouldn't matter if we had passports or not. Our own futures were sealed in Iran. A column was added to exit visa applications to check which religion you belonged to.

If you checked Bahá'í, you were denied.

* * *

"Death to Shah!" "Shah must go!"" Death to America" "Salute to Khomeini!" The hot pink, yellow, and black graffiti words seem to scream from the posters of that man Khomeini. Maamaan walks me quickly past the posters and into the pharmacy to pick up my penicillin shot. When winter returns, so do my terrible sore throats. Ms. Molook, our neighborhood nurse, gives me a weekly penicillin injection—in my bottom—to help keep them away. The doctors say I should have my tonsils taken out, but my parents say they want to wait until I am older. So, each week I get the painful shot that leaves me unable to walk for an entire day. We exit the pharmacy and I realize there are many more women wearing the black chador than there ever used to be. I learned that high school students and university students aren't going to class and that workers are on strike. My parents say we must "wait and see" to understand what it all means.

In January, we begin to find out.

The Shah could not stop the uprisings, so he flees the country, a self-imposed exile. On the twenty-second day of February 1979, Khomeini returns to Iran. We turn on the television to watch people flood the streets in celebration. "History in the making," Baba says. People smile and wave banners and streamers and cry happy tears. Our neighbors even have a party on our street, but we do not join them.

* * *

News spreads fast. The revolutionaries, no longer busy overthrowing the Shah, turn their attention to religious minorities, and specifically to the Bahá'í community. Overnight, Bahá'í professors are fired from their posts for corrupting the minds of the youth. Bahá'í doctors become cab drivers. And several thousand Bahá'í students between the ages of seventeen and thirty are expelled from universities. Khomeini makes a comment about cutting off a finger that has gangrene before it can infect the whole body. He calls Bahá'ís apostates, meaning they are not protected under Islamic law and can be killed and oppressed with impunity. Then he makes a religious law that protects Jews and Christians and Zoroastrians, but not the Bahá'ís. The new Iranian constitution guarantees "justice and fairness to all" and the freedom for all Iranians to practice their religion and be represented in Parliament—as long as that religion is Islam, Christianity, Judaism, or Zoroastrian. Bahá'ís are deemed unclean, no one can touch them and anything they touch also becomes unclean. This, of course, makes it impossible for Bahá'ís to hold jobs alongside Muslims.

Baba kept his job at the water company for longer than some because he was usually out in the field, but even he was eventually fired. In rural areas, it was much worse. Bahá'ís rights were taken away, their homes looted, and their livestock and property seized. They were dragged from their homes by force and brought to mosques where they were compelled to accept Islam or lose everything and be killed. Some bowed to the pressure while others abandoned their homes to seek refuge with friends and relatives in larger cities. In schools, teachers told their classrooms that the Bahá'í children were unclean. Those children were made to sit in the back of the classroom, and the teachers instructed the other students that no one must touch them, talk to them, or play with them. Within a year or two, no Bahá'í children, except for those in big cities like Tehran, would even be allowed to attend school. That winter was cold and dark in more ways than one.

* * *

SPRING 1979

Spring is just around the corner and most of the snow has melted away. I am tired of playing inside, but when we go outside to play soccer and hop-scotch the other kids do not even look our way, sometimes they ignore us, or they run off saying they have homework to do. At dinner, Maamaan is flustered, "Aziz! They just ignore us. They never offer tea. It is like they have forgotten how many years we have lived side by side, raising our children together, how many years you brought tankers full of water so they would not have to walk to a well to get water. All forgotten." Her finger is out and pointing, "How we have shared so many dreams together, the same dreams for a better life for the working class and poor. How we have helped each other out in times of need. They have always supported us! Remember when we were first building our home and people had no reason to trust us yet, but they brought us tea and helped carry the bricks up the ladder and offered to watch the boys when you were away, and I had to fetch water from the well?"

"I remember," Baba says, looking sad, "Still, it is safer in Tehran. Their affection might have cooled in light of recent . . . events . . . but there is less violence toward Bahá'ís here." Maamaan closes her eyes and puts a hand to her temple, "Yes, that's true. They could never be violent. They are good people. We are all connected. They are just feeling a lot of pressure right now with all the changes taking place in government."

But how little did we know.

Soon we have to stop attending Friday Bahá'í school because Bahá'ís are forbidden to hold public prayer and meditation meetings anymore. Bahá'í centers have been shut down and destroyed across the country. In Shiraz, one of our most holy sites, the house of the Báb, the forerunner of our faith, was razed to the ground. They even destroyed the Bahá'í ceme-teries across Iran, digging up the graves and burning the remains. I learn all this from the television. I also learn that Khomeini insists that all Bahá'ís are spies of Israel and we should be arrested and executed unless we return to Islam. I am nervous to play outside; everyone in our neighborhood knows we are Bahá'ís. I know that we are not spies, but I do not know how to convince them of that when Khomeini is so powerful and they trust him so completely. I wish they could listen to the messages from our international council, then they might think differently. Like the message we just received from the Universal House of Justice in Haifa, Israel. It encouraged Bahá'ís to be strong and respect all the new rules of the land and recommended not fighting rules enforced by the new government. We are doing our best to be good neighbors, citizens, friends. But there are whispers.

I hear the word the kids say under their breath when Leila and I walk past. I know what they are calling us. *Sag Bahá'í najes.* Dogs. Dirty dogs.

When the new year comes around, Maamaan does not even bother to beat the Persian rugs because she says that no neighbors will come by to visit. Even though we won't drive to Yazd this year to celebrate, we do spend some of the holiday at an aunt's house on the other side of Tehran, where we play soccer with cousins and forget how different this Nowruz is from last year. Leila and I put on our new Nowruz clothes and model them to each other. We throw open the windows and wait for the heavenly scent of hyacinths to fill the home and quiz each other on the meaning of the seven items on the Sofreh Haft Seen. We listen to the countdown on the radio and Baba says a prayer like always. We get a small Eidee this year; we didn't expect much because any extra money gets sent to Cyrus and Kia. Even though rials do not go very far in America, Baba sends enough money every month to pay the boys' tuition and room and board. In a recent letter, we learned that Cyrus is a dish washer at a campus kitchen, and that Kia works nights as a campus security guard. During Nowruz, Maamaan makes all their favorite foods and then cries while we eat them. "Kia loved lamb stew," she sobs, and "Cyrus couldn't get enough of my homemade *aash.*"

The new year passes quietly, and we don't participate in the fire ceremony with the neighbors. Instead, I watched them leap over the bonfires from my window. Could that be why I still don't feel the warm red glow of spring? Will I have to feel this sickly pallor all year long?

But then, there is some good news.

"Mahvash," my father comes in smiling proudly. "I just got back from your school. I was getting them their fresh supply of water and I happened to speak with your teacher. She tells me you've done impressively this school year. So well in fact that she thinks you can challenge the second grade!" I jump up and down in excitement. Students don't automatically advance to the next grade, let alone challenge one! Each year every student must take tests, and if they fail just one or two subjects, they must repeat the entire grade. Not only had I passed all my tests in order to go into the second grade, but now my teacher was saying I could probably take the second-grade tests and skip right to the third grade! The tests are at the end of summer, in August, and we can't afford a tutor to help me. "But not to worry," says Baba. "We have something better." I give him a knowing look. We do.

We have Leila.

Leila is going into sixth grade and is always top of her class. For her, school is better than ice cream and swimming, better than barbies or hop-scotch. She is actually excited when Nowruz comes to an end because she has missed going to school. She is the perfect tutor—organized, smart, and dedicated. Since Khomeini has now made it illegal for girls to ride bicycles or swim or play soccer in public and has even outlawed music (other than revolutionary songs and Islamic religious prayers), and since the neighbor-hood kids aren't playing with us anymore, there really isn't a lot else to do this summer except study anyway.

We purchase the second-grade books and I spend all of the hot summer days reading and memorizing. Leila quizzes me on reading, writing, and math. She has flashcards and even assigns me homework. Soon I'm repeating vocabulary words in my sleep. Baba and Maamaan say I've made tremendous progress and register me for the tests. Leila clicks her tongue at my nervousness. "You can do this. You will do this. I believe in you." And she is right. I spend a full day in late August at the school under the watch-ful eye of the examiner, and when I finish, I am confident that I passed.

We get a call later that confirms it! But then the examiner tells my parents I have to retake the tests at the principal's office under her supervision. What? Why? OK. I spend another full day in the principal's office, and to my delight, passed again. We get a second call. "The thing is, we can't let her move up." "Why? Did she pass?" "Yes, but, well . . . if you want to take this to the district you can. I encourage you to do that because she has a good chance." Baba is upset when he gets off the phone. He says, "I know what this is. It's probably because they know we are Baha'is. Mahvash will now need to take the tests a third time at the district level."

My parents decide it is useless at this point for me to keep taking the tests. No matter my marks, I will not be skipping to the third grade. The district will make sure of that. Friends say we must push back and appeal to someone higher in the school district, but we don't have connections like that. Baba feels betrayed. He's always gone out of his way at the water company to ensure that the schools have clean drinking water every week for the kids, and he has long been delivering the water to our school on his own time to make sure this happens. I am also disappointed. All my hard work was for nothing, and now second grade is going to be so boring. I have already mastered the material.

I am starting to understand what this word—oppression—means and how it can start small and then, without you hardly noticing it, grow into something much bigger and more threatening.

We had thought we were safe from it. We hoped people knew us better than the lies being spread in the media. Reasoned that maybe because we were in a big city that was less conservative and religious than the small towns, we would go unnoticed and be spared the oppression.

But the writing was on the wall. Literally.

Every morning, Baba gets up to walk to the bakery for fresh bread for breakfast. "It's odd," he tells us one morning, "but I've been noticing that our walls are wet around our property even though it hasn't rained." We have ten-foot brick walls that form a fence around our home, and sure enough, every morning the walls are wet. After a few weeks of this, we get a knock on our door late one night. It's our neighbor Mr. Goodarzi. Baba goes outside to talk with him and stays for a very long time. When he returns, he frightens us with the look of horror on his face. He is pale and breathing heavily. He cannot find the words to make us understand him and this flusters him even more. Maamaan makes him sit and pours him some tea. Then we start to piece it together.

Mr. Goodarzi had come to warn us. The religious leaders at the neighborhood mosque were holding nightly sermons to discuss Khomeini's teachings and how to implement his instructions. They convinced our Muslim neighbors that they needed to take steps to purify their neighborhood of any members of the Bahá'í faith. Every night, those men had been coming over and putting graffiti on our brick walls. *Najez*, they have been writing. Dirty. "Unclean Bahá'í family must leave. Spies of Israel must go." I suck in my breath. Baba continues, "Mr. Goodarzi, he—every morning before we wake—he washes the graffiti off our walls." Baba's eyes water, his voice cracks. "But that's not all."

On this very night, the religious leaders at the mosque advised our neighbors that it was time for more action. It was time to set our house on fire and drive us from the neighborhood. Mr. Goodarzi stood up to the counsel and reminded the men at the mosque of all the neighborly things my family had done for them over the years, like how Aziz helped them with plumbing and water issues and had even driven their children and wives to the hospital in the middle of the night when they were sick with fevers or about to give birth. But the crowd was in a rage and ignored the arguments in our defense. "Fine," Mr. Goodarzi told them, "then I will stand guard at their house all night. You can burn their house down, but only over my dead body." He left the mosque and ran immediately here to tell Baba to pack up and leave. He was, at this moment, standing guard outside as Baba spoke.

We packed in a frenzy. Mr. Goodarzi stayed all night and no one came with fire. In the morning, Baba did not go to work. He went searching for a new home and found one. It was small, just a two-room apartment. A carriage house with two rooms built above the garage. But we could afford the rent and we could move in fast. The apartment was located on the north side of town, far away from our old neighborhood, in the more affluent and educated neighborhood of Yoosefabad, which meant the neighbors there would probably be less inclined to socialize or get involved in our business and would not ask about our religion. We could hide in plain sight. We left immediately.

We brought little to our tiny home. The rooms were so small that Maamaan could only roll open the Persian rugs halfway to cover the floor. She cleared what space she could in the main room for eating and sleeping. Baba enrolled Leila and me in a new school, an international school. There I would get the chance to learn English. Something new and exciting. Second grade didn't sound so bad anymore. Mr. Goodarzi stayed in touch with us and so did Ms. Molook and her three kids from our old neighborhood. And the other Muslim neighbors were more than happy to assist in finding a new buyer for our home since it meant we wouldn't be coming back. It sold in no time. "Our first home, the home we built, where my babies were born. . ." Maamaan kept saying. Finally, she went to lie down for an afternoon nap with a headache.

In our new neighborhood, there was some relief. Homes were big and fancy and people mostly drove instead of walked, so we never saw people gathering in the streets or in the alleys. No one at school ever asked what our beliefs were or what our religion was. Everyone just assumed we were Muslim like them. We did not feel like all eyes were on us for being Bahá'í. But then again, we were keenly aware that all eyes were on Iran. The whole world was watching.

The exiled Shah was allowed to enter America for cancer treatment in October of 1979 and students in Iran rose up in protest once again. They stormed the US Embassy in Tehran and took dozens of hostages, demanding the Shah be extradited in exchange. Because of this, US president Jimmy Carter announced an oil embargo against Iran and, soon after, the US froze billions of dollars in Iranian assets in America and convinced its allies to impose economic sanctions against Iran on both imported and exported goods. Khomeini had promised a monthly oil dividend to every citizen, but these sanctions crippled the economy, so instead, oil prices sky-rocketed. As did food and other goods. Shelves were barren in markets. Everyone was stocking up.

I remember the day Maamaan took Leila and me to the government office to register our household in the ration program. We had to bring birth certificates for everyone in the family. Then we were issued a coupon book and told to go stand in line to get our monthly supply of food at a discounted price. Two pounds of sugar, ten pounds of rice, four pounds of meat, four pounds of chicken, and some beans, eggs, milk, and cooking oil. The subsidized food was frozen and the lowest grade in quality. Fresh and high-quality meats and rice and oils were available on the "free" market, but we could not afford to pay the higher prices, and my parents were unwilling to engage in the new but flourishing underground economy where people traded ration cards and food for cash. Standing in line for the rations would take Maamaan all day. I often went with her so I could stand in one line while she stood in another, not so much to save time, but to guarantee that we got our food before the store ran out. Food rationing was not the worst of things.

Islamic guards eventually broke into Tehran's main Bahá'í center and turned it into a revolutionary guard headquarters. They burned every-thing, but not before they looked up all the addresses of all the Bahá'ís registered there. That was when they started to make random visits. If you were lucky, they just took what they wanted from your home, other times, worse. Within a few weeks, over two hundred Bahá'ís throughout the country were arrested, imprisoned, and later executed. Even more were consistently attacked, burned, robbed, stabbed, and violently raped. They were dragged from their homes, in front of their families, and from their businesses or places of work.

However, we Bahá'ís, we did not protest the injustice and the attacks. We did not rise up. We did not fight. Because that is not who we are. All we did was continue to believe in and practice peace. When Bahá'ís were being asked to deny their faith, it felt like being asked to deny their very being. It had little to do with doctrine and everything to do with a core way of being. How exactly does one give up something that makes them who they are? Refusing to deny your faith is not a matter of pride. It is a matter of being asked to deny the thing that has made you who you are, to deny everything you know and believe in.

Once I overheard Baba whispering to a Bahá'í friend: "But what would I do? What would you do?" he asked. "There are guns pointed at the heads of your daughters and the guards say, 'Choose.' How does anyone make a decision like that? A decision between their faith—the lifeblood of their spirit—and the safety of their family—the lifeblood of their heart?"

Baba's friend sighed: "These are impossible times."

6

BOMBS

SPRING 1980: NEW HOME IN TEHRAN, WEST SIDE

It was the spring of 1980. Women were taken to prison daily for wearing makeup and for refusing to wear the hijab. They were beaten until they agreed to follow the law requiring them to cover their heads and remove their makeup. If caught singing, they were also beaten. Baba would tell me not to worry because "none of us can escape our destiny." I did not know what he meant. Was destiny a matter of choice or of chance? I wanted to know if it was our destiny for guards to come knocking on our door to drag us away, so that I could be ready. "We can never be fully ready for anything, good or bad," he told me. "We can only pray to be courageous in the face of whatever comes our way."

I could sense Baba becoming increasingly more worried about raising his daughters in a country where things kept going from bad to worse. Even with all his courage, stress consumed him too. It manifested as nosebleeds, something he had never had before in his life. One night he bled for hours, soaking through the pillowcases Maamaan gave him, before they finally took a taxi to the hospital. The doctors diagnosed him with high blood pressure and told him that if his nose had not started bleeding, he would have had a stroke. He was given a daily medication and Maamaan cut all salt from our diet.

Eventually, we moved out of the small carriage house and into a bigger home on the west side of Tehran. From our window, we could watch the planes as they took off and landed at the airport just two miles away. This seemed like an exciting treat at the time; however, once the war started, it turned out to be the most dangerous part of the city one could possibly live in.

The first thing Baba did when we moved in was dig a hole in the backyard. "Now, please bring me all of the pictures and all the books." He meant anything religious, anything Bahá'í, including the one and only photo he had of his father. In the picture, his father held a Bahá'í symbol called the Greatest Name. The photo would be incriminating evidence against us if anyone found it, even though it was unlikely since, on that new side of Tehran, we were unknown to our neighbors. My parents cautioned us to keep it that way, to always do our best to go through life unnoticed, to not make deep connections, to be discreet and careful.

Baba handed me the photo of his father, Akbar. Akbar looked young and handsome, with the same beautiful hazel eyes and the same serious look as Baba. Baba told me the photo was taken the day his father converted to the Bahá'í Faith. "My mother," Baba continued, "never forgave him. She remained a devoted Muslim and teacher of the Qur'án in our village and forbade him from holding Bahá'í meetings in the house. There was always conflict after his conversion, and yet they remained married." Baba sighed and cradled the picture of his father, taking one long, last look before he buried it in the ground. Forever.

Soon there were many more holes in our backyard. But not to hide things.

Baba had begun to plant an orchard. "For my children. For when they return, so they can enjoy their favorite fruits." He planted persimmons for Cyrus, pomegranates and sour plums for Kia. Maamaan started her vegetable garden right away too, so that despite the food rations we could enjoy a nutritious harvest. Our sofreh was full of okra, radishes, tomatoes, spinach, cucumbers, eggplants, and cilantro. We would help her pickle the eggplants and cucumbers, cabbages and carrots to see us through the winter. "What bounty! What blessings!" Baba would say each night at dinner. Even though I could see he had added two new notches to his belt, I never heard him complain about the food rationing.

The revolution turned life upside down, bringing fear and panic, and forcing so many into hiding. But somehow, we managed. We found our rhythm again and that brought a semblance of peace. I clung to Baba's assurances that things would change, and we would be alright. He was right on one account. Things would change, and sooner than anticipated.

But not in the beautiful, hope-filled ways we had been praying for.

The day the bombs dropped is a day I will never forget. Not ever. While it was the least terrifying day compared to all the rest, simply because I did not know what war was like, it marked the beginning of the eight-year war that would end up decimating my country and my soul.

* * *

Leila and I are quietly playing knucklebones on the living room floor. We do not want to disturb Maamaan's afternoon nap. The heat of summer gets to her and she believes in the power of rest. Leila and I believe in the power of our fancy, new air conditioning unit that came with the house.

Leila tosses her stone into the air and scoops up the pebbles on the floor. As soon as she grabs the falling stone, her victory whoop is sucked away by a terrifying boom followed by a blast from outside. Jumping at the sound of another loud crack, we see the window panes splintering into cobwebs. The ground beneath us shakes. Pictures of Kia and Cyrus fly off the shelves and shatter at our feet and we scream. Then from the bedroom Maamaan screams, "Girls! What are you doing out there? Why all the noise?" She comes running out just as another explosive bone-shaking roar sends us flying into each other's arms. Maamaan freezes and listens. Then she makes a dash for the front door. People are running down the streets and yelling. They are pointing—up! Look up!

Fighter jets circle the sky.

Flames rise from the airport. Black clouds of smoke darken the sky. The bombs keep dropping. Then, a wailing, screeching sound pierces through the roar, even worse than the sound of the bombs. It makes my insides shriek, screaming and clawing to get out. Maamaan pushes us back inside and turns on the radio. "What is that noise, Maamaan?" I ask, hands pressed hard over my ears, eyes wide. "I'm not sure. Sirens?" She spins the dial around and around until she gets something. The radio message is simple: "We are in a state of war. We repeat. We are being attacked by Iraq."

After twenty minutes, the bombs stop falling and the sirens, which we find out are positioned at the airport, stop screeching. Still the sounds of panic fill the air as sirens from police cars, ambulances, and fire trucks blare throughout the city for the rest of the day and all through the night.

The next time, and every other time, those sirens sound, the hair on the back of my neck stands straight up. Now I fully understand what that expression means.

It does not matter if the Iraqi jets intend to bomb a border city hundreds of miles away because as soon as any fighter jet crosses into Iran the sirens at Mehrabad airport by our house go off. There is no escaping the ear-splitting shriek, a sound designed to make you pick up your feet and run. But to where should we run? We never know where the bombs are going to fall. Bombs do not discriminate. They fall even on bomb shelters. When that happens, hundreds of people die at once. Part of me still feels as though I will be safer in a shelter though and beg Baba to let us go to them when the sirens start. He repeats his favorite mantra, "No, we won't go because we can't escape our destiny." I am beginning to hate this message. And so when the sirens rip across the sky, instead of that god-awful sound making me feel alert and prepared to act, they have the opposite effect, my body goes cold. I am completely powerless, frozen and terrified.

The sirens sound for only a few minutes and then there is just deathly silence while we wait, listening for the fighter jets, for the anti-missiles shot from the airport, and for the bombs to drop. Sometimes they come, sometimes they don't. Either way, the adrenaline still courses through our veins, heightening our senses, quickening our heartbeats, increasing our panic, and then it leaves us. We are drowning in exhaustion, depleted and shaky. For most people in Tehran, they only hear the siren broadcasted on the radio or television, and then only if they have those units turned on. I on the other hand, live too close, to ever escape the sound.

* * *

The war took our entire country by surprise. Iraqi President Saddam Hussein took advantage of the post-revolution chaos and caught the new Iranian regime completely off guard when his troops crossed our borders, both on foot and plane. The day the bombs first dropped, Iraqi soldiers had also crossed into the Persian Gulf and burned down the border cities of Abadan and Khorramshahr, killing civilians, burning homes, and setting fire to the oil and natural gas refineries along the coast. Those oil refinery fires burned continuously for years to come, even until the cities were taken back. Iraq had struck at the heart of Iran's main economic resource.

Now, not only would our food be rationed but oil as well. While the air strikes were not successful at wiping out Iran's air force that day, around 7,000 people lost their lives in Khorramshahr, and it became known instead as Khooninshahr, the City of Blood.

On television, people argued that the US, still angry over the 1979 hostage crisis, was training the Iraqi army and supplying them with arms, bombs, and fighter jets to keep Iran in check. Maybe, maybe not, Baba said. The previous year, Khomeini had called for Shia Muslims in Iraq, whom he considered oppressed, to rise up against Hussein's secular Ba'ath government and further his own Islamic revolution on their soil. Perhaps, out of fear, Saddam sought to halt Khomeini's radicalism before it came to his borders, he did say as much, but perhaps, out of lust, he wanted to control the oil reserves of the Persian Gulf and set Iraq up as the new regional superpower. Perhaps none of these things, perhaps all of these things. As the terrors from the war grew inside me, no reason was good enough. No reason could ever justify the bloodshed and brutality, the death and destruction. No reason made sense.

Outside I watched as burlap bags filled with sand were stacked in front of glass store fronts and school windows for protection. The radio taught us the difference between the red siren, yellow siren, and white siren. Red, the most intense, for any time a jet was spotted. Yellow for if it never made it to Tehran, but we needed to still be on standby. White for the end of the attack. A citywide curfew was put into place and at night Tehran became a ghost town. At dusk, electricity was cut across the city to make it harder for the Iraqi jets to identify and target neighborhoods and facilities, such as the airport, news broadcast stations, and electrical grid. We were instructed to hang blankets, black and thick, in our windows at night to prevent any light from leaking out, and to protect our bodies from all the shattered, flying glass. Every window was taped with a wide thick "X" to keep the shattered glass together.

Darkness marked our lives.

7
CHOKING

Machine guns pummel the sky blasting away the fighter jets before they drop their bombs while sirens scream. There is no such thing as "getting used to it." There is no getting used to war. There is only the fear, a dark and close companion, keeping the body in a constant state of blood pumping, heart racing, anxiety. I grew accustomed to it, but only in the way one gets used to, say, an itchy wool sweater—it desensitizes you, but then you find yourself unexplainably irritated and annoyed at every little thing. Fear is like that, but of course much worse. On the outside, I functioned normally. I went to school, came home and did homework, ate dinner, went to bed. I moved through fear, but it was reshaping me on the inside. Changing my brain, my cells, my very DNA on a level I would not even fully realize until twenty years later when the Blue Angel fighter jets flew over Seattle practicing their maneuvers for the Seafair, and I found myself tearing down the street looking for a bomb shelter, eyes searching the sky, my body in a cold sweat. Or the moment I see the planes crash into the Twin Towers on the TV and I run with my baby to hide in the basement, certain that at any moment a war would break out and bombs would once again rain from the sky on everything I loved and held dear. Sometimes, I can understand why someone might feel it is better to die, for it is death that would bring the peace and escape from the crippling fear that sucks the life out of life.

But then again, I also understand that this is why we have hope.

Without Baba constantly telling Leila and me as children, "I promise to get you out of here. You will go to the US and study and live a full and beautiful life." I would have had no anchor for my soul. Thank goodness for Baba, he held us all together when we so easily could have—would have—fallen apart. I so desperately wanted to run away. Run like the people at the borders who fled their homes with only the clothes on their back. Those who ran with no thought of anything else but life. But there was nowhere to run to, so I set my mind on the future—on America and a great university.

My khaleh and her family in Yazd also fled their home, but not because of bombs or soldiers. Yazd was safe from bombs and sirens, soldiers and tanks, but not from Khomeini's ethnic cleansing. It was a different kind of terror that the Bahá'ís in Yazd faced. My aunt's family was forced from their home by Islamic guards to make room for Muslim war refugees from the Persian Gulf. They were not allowed to take anything. Not one thing. "What about the turtle?" I asked Leila late one night when we couldn't sleep. She shrugged. The war affected everyone, big and small. But especially the small and helpless. Children do not get a choice or a say. How I envied that turtle's hard shell. How lucky he was to have his armor to protect him and hide him, a safe home surrounding him at all times. Whenever the air pumped with explosions, I imagined that turtle and wished to trade places. I told Baba and he said we too are lucky because we also have protection—our faith in God. Every night I would wake up in a cold sweat screaming. Maamaan said I cried out to God, begging for mercy. She says I would mumble and yell about the jets and about running to shelters. I would ask about where to hide. Sometimes, a lot of times, I had my doubts about what kind of protection God could offer us. What if his best protection was for us to leave? What if he could not protect us in this place? Should we not help him carry out his plan? Is it possible to rewrite your destiny?

* * *

"There you go. Perfect!" Leila says tucking the last strand of my hair underneath the hijab and pinning it neatly under my chin. Now that I am nine, I wear the hijab too. There is an extra, triangle piece of fabric that we must pull up to cover our chins too, but only while at school.

At my new school, third grade is not as fun as it was at the international school; I miss learning English, but at least I am starting to learn Arabic. Baba says I can take summer English courses once I am in middle school to prepare me for university. Leila is a teenager in middle school now and she is upset that under the new Islamic laws she is forbidden to wear makeup. Maamaan says it is foolish to be upset about that: "Even if the government did let you wear makeup, I wouldn't! It ruins a girl's natural beauty and is just a lot of vanity." Leila huffs and crosses her arms. She and Maamaan argue more and more these days.

There is a new girl at school. Her name is Sharareh and I think we might become best friends. The first day she came to our classroom, the teacher had Sharareh stand at the front of the class to introduce herself to us. She was so very shy and was unable to look any of us in the eyes. I noticed right away that her skin was darker than the other girls—dark, like mine. You can tell a lot about where a person is from in Iran based on the color of their skin. In the south, especially near the Persian Gulf, Iranian's have darker skin and their hair is thick, black, and curly, some even speak Arabic. People along the Caspian Sea, where it rains nearly every day of the year, have lighter skin and light brown eyes. The people in the northwest have the fairest skin of all and sometimes blue or green eyes that take your breath away. From our family road trips, I learned there are many tribes in Iran with countless traditions, dialects and languages.

Baba says that people call America a "melting pot", but he says that Iran was the first melting pot. For three thousand years, people throughout Asia and Europe traveled through Iran on the Silk Road sharing their music, art, philosophy, and science. Persia was the center for the world's first empire. "Of course," Baba explains, "this land was also invaded by Turks, Greeks, Mongols, and Arabs, and that explains much of the diversity of culture and religion too. But do you know what binds us, Mooshi?" "What?" "Our common tongue. Persian." I tell him that Nowruz also binds us since everyone in Iran celebrates the new year no matter their religion. In school we are learning about the bigger tribes and the other languages they also speak—the Kurds, Lores, Baluch, and Turks. On our last road trip, the one before the revolution, I remember passing through the high mountains and seeing the colorful tents of the Kurds and stopping in for tea. The tents were so cozy and warm, with big, plush *poshties*, rug-cushions, to sit on. We were served tea in little glasses with a cube of sugar on the side, which we dipped in the tea and then placed on our tongue, pressing it to the roof of our mouth while sipping the tea slowly. Of course, this is just how it is done all across Iran, and not only a Kurdish tradition. There were so many goats and horses in the mountains where the Kurds lived, there were also many mulberry, apricot, and cherry trees. We stopped to get some white mulberries, the ones that just melt in your mouth with sweetness. Baba negotiated a price with the orchard grower and then Maamaan and Leila and I stretched a big sheet underneath the tree while Baba shook it as hard as he could to make the mulberries fall. Eating the long, juicy white mulberries is like sipping sweet maple syrup.

There is a lot of diversity across our country. In the big city of Tehran, however, that is where everyone's differences—varying skin, eye and hair colors come together. Just like Baba left Yazd at sixteen, so do many other people across the country come to Tehran in order to find work and to gain new job skills. Now with the war, people are coming for another reason—to seek refuge.

I wish I could warn them it is not that safe here either. Do they not know about all the bombs?

That day in school, the teacher had smiled at Sharareh, our new classmate, and then called on me to stand: "This is Mahvash and she's our class representative. You can go sit with her and she will help you settle in." Being class representative comes with a lot of responsibilities, but I do not mind them. It can be hard, however. My job is to keep order in the classroom each morning before classes begin, after recess, in between class changes, and any other time the teacher is not present. The other girls mostly listen, but they can get giggly and loud. All it takes is for one person to crack a joke and then everyone erupts into laughter and things get out of control. Then I have to hush them. Sometimes they start to play hand-clapping games and sing fast-paced rhyming songs. That is when I get scared—singing is forbidden now! Women go to jail for singing. "C'mon Mahvash. No one is around. Who will hear us?" they say. I just shake my head and they sigh and stop. I sigh too. There is not anything fun that we can do at school, and all of the classes are serious too—there is no art or music and only limited physical education, which we must do in our new Islamic school uniforms—long navy blue or black coats with buttons over pants of the same color and matching hijabs. Since I am always ranked first or second academically, the teacher also has me stay inside a couple times a week at recess to tutor other girls who are falling behind. So, it makes sense that the teacher called on me to be Sharareh's class mentor. I was secretly very glad. I was very curious about this tall and pretty girl. I am also tall, too tall, for my age and now perhaps, I will not be the only one in the classroom getting called "ladder" and "giraffe." Most of my good friends are shorter than me, which means we never get to sit together because the teacher assigns seats based on height.

I am always on the last bench, in the back, against the wall.

Sharareh and I stayed in at recess because we needed to make a plan for how to get her caught up in class work. She was not very talkative, and neither am I usually, but I tried a few basic questions to see what I could learn about this mystery girl.

"When's your birthday?"

"April."

"Oh, mine's in July."

"I should actually be in a higher grade. I'm a year older than everyone."

"Oh," I said again, "then why aren't you?" "There's no room in the upper class here so I have to repeat third grade."

"Oh." I coughed a little. "I have two brothers in the US and one sister, here. I'm the youngest. What about you?"

Sharareh's eyes immediately teared up and I regretted asking her that personal question. She turned away from me and I apologized. "Sorry, so sorry. You don't have to tell me that."

She wiped her eyes and looked back. "It's OK. It's just that I also have an older brother, but—" her chin quivered hard and I was not sure my ears were ready to hear what she was going to say. "—but we were separated when we tried to escape from Khorramshahr."

I sucked in my breath. Khorramshahr—the City of Blood. "You are from *there*? Were you there when the Iraqi soldiers came?" She nodded.

"They were everywhere. It was all shooting and running and screaming and shoving. We ran over dead people," she gulped. "I tripped on a little boy. He was covered in blood."

She stared off in the distance and I bit my lip.

"The flames at the refineries reached the sky. I hear the crackle of the fire, the gunshots, the screams in my dreams every night." I nod my head. I know about nightmares.

"My father worked for the oil refinery and we lived on a base nearby. We crammed in the busses and made our escape, but then the soldiers stopped our bus and I thought we were all going to die. But they just took most of the men off the bus and put them on another bus as hostages. They took my brother. You know, he had just gotten married." Her tears rolled and rolled, but she kept talking to me. "His wife, she hasn't stopped crying. She cannot leave her bed. I bring her dinner, but she doesn't eat. We don't know where he is. We don't know if he is alive."

I asked the only question I could think of. "What is his name, your brother?"

"Behnam."

I nodded, whispering his name out loud, as if acknowledging it meant he was somewhere, somehow, still alive.

Sharareh and I have started to spend every minute together at school. I try to fill in some of the voids in her life. All I feel is terrible for what has happened to her family. They were given a simple apartment to settle into, but they must piece back together all the other parts of their life. She lost everything she had because of the war, her house and belongings, her friends and most terribly her brother.

I think we are afraid to let each other out of our sight. At school, when the bombs come it is almost worse than at home because we are so far from family. The thought of dying alone, and never seeing Baba and Maamaan makes me sick. At least Leila and I go to the same school. During attacks, sometimes I try and find her in the dark hallways where kids are crying and screaming and hyperventilating. Sometimes I think, "Even if I do survive the attack, will my family even be there when I get home?"

The sirens start to scream and we all jump from our desks and race for the hallways to get away from the windows. Some kids drop to their knees in prayer, some vomit all over their shoes, while others yell with tears streaming down their cheeks. For me, it feels like the sandbags are stacked up on top of my chest and none of my screams can escape. My throat tightens like I am being choked. Then there is silence. The sirens stop, and no one says a word. We just wait. We wait for the sound of the jets, wait to feel the ground shake. Every minute feels like an hour and every movement happens in slow motion. The squeezing in my throat never lets up, it gets to the point that I stop breathing altogether, in preparation for death. The room spins and my heart races, blood pumping in my ears, but then Sharareh squeezes my hand and it is all over.

We are still here. For now. We go back to the class and try to focus, to listen and learn as if we are having a normal school day.

8

WINTER

We keep our coats and boots by our beds, ready to grab and throw on if the sirens scream at night. "Hurry. Hurry now," Baba will say as he grabs his Siemens radio and we run to the smallest room in the house—the one with the fewest windows. We sit in a tight circle and watch our breath mingle together in the air. I shiver, half from the cold, half from fright. Oil is rationed, so we only heat the front part of the house where our bedrooms are. Baba turns the Siemens on low and spins the dial, holding it close to his ear. He is hoping to find the Persian BBC to learn what is going on, to find out if there is any hope of international help. It is illegal to listen to the BBC but "they're the only ones who really know what's going on in Iran," Baba explains. Maamaan always says that radio was Baba's dowry because it was the only furniture he owned when they got married.

When the sirens stop, we wait. It could be twenty minutes before the bombing begins. The hairs on the back of my neck prick up.

The radio crackles through Iranian news reports about how many hostages were taken today and which towns are now back in our possession. The rest of the news is censored. One of my older cousins, Nader, often stays overnight in one of the spare bedrooms, so he is usually with us during the attacks. He is one of the cousins who was forced out of their house in Yazd. He often cracks jokes to try and make us all feel better, especially me. "Look, Mahvash, you should be thankful, happy even, when you hear the bombs and feel the ground shake because it means—you're alive!" I smile at his pathetic attempt and feel slightly better, for a moment.

Then come the bombs.

Boom! The ground rumbles with every explosion and my body trembles just as violently. Boom! Boom! Tears stream down my face no matter what jokes Nader tells.

The bombs stop. We are all still here. Sometimes bombs fall and sometimes they don't, but the cold fear of death is always with me.

Baba changes the radio station again, this time he searches for another illegal station—not news, but music. We go back to our warm rooms listening to beautiful Persian music broadcast from London, and our racing hearts slow to the tempo of the songs.

On Fridays and Fridays only, Baba turns on the water heater and uses a bit of our rationed oil so we can take showers and do laundry. The warm feeling doesn't last long because soon Baba has thrown open every window in the house and is on his hands and knees washing the floors.

"Are you trying to kill us, Baba?" Leila asks.

"No, I'm keeping us all healthy! If we air out the house every week, we won't get sick."

Maamaan, Leila and I huddle underneath the *korsi*—a blanket over a table with a heater underneath—and just look at each other, all thinking, "But surely we're catching pneumonia right now!" Baba lost his job months ago with the water company, but he has not slowed down one bit. Baba just smiles, sings, and wakes extra early to help with chores before heading out to look for work, such as driving other men to and from their jobs in the back of his truck, or helping people move their things from one home to another, or from one construction site to another.

A little bit of income also comes from renting a room in our house to a family friend. Under the Shah's reign, he was a high-ranking general in the Iranian military in Shiraz but was immediately fired after the revolution for being Bahá'í. He moved his family to Tehran and rents our room as a storage unit for the knick-knacks he sells on the streets, things like tea kettles, cups, and pots. "It's quite a blessing I got fired actually!" he likes to joke. "I'm so tall and my shoulders are so wide that I would have been one of the first people killed once the war started! Even the most inexperienced shooter couldn't miss me."

We do many things to save money so that after the bills are paid, we can send anything left over to Kia and Cyrus. Baba registered his truck to get gas coupons because gas is rationed since the war started. We ride the bus for personal errands now and sometimes sell the gas coupons for money. The buses are segregated now, men in the front and women in the back. When I ride a bus with Baba, I cannot sit with him even if there is a seat open next to him for his little girl, Mooshi.

When Baba needs gasoline though, he has to get in line early. Not all the stations have enough for everyone even with the rationed gas coupons. He often stays overnight and sleeps in his truck to make sure he gets his weekly allowance in the morning. Maamaan continues to spend most of her days waiting in lines for weekly and monthly rations while Leila and I continue to tromp, day after day, through the snow to school and back. In the winter, it is not just bombs falling from the sky that we worry about, but clumps of snow too. Young boys get hired to shovel snow off people's rooftops and we never know from which direction we might get struck with a shovel full. "They do it on purpose," Leila grumbles scooping snow out from her collar.

"Why don't we hire a boy to shovel our rooftop?" I asked my parents one time. "Because we can't afford it," Maamaan said. But Baba said, "I like doing it myself. It's good exercise! And it makes me feel proud to take care of our family this way, making sure we have a dry roof over our heads that won't leak or cave in." Baba worries so much about leaks that he doesn't always wait until morning to shovel. When it is a big snowfall, I wake up to the scrip-scrape of his shovel as early as four in the morning. When he finishes, he comes back inside red in the face and stripped down to just a sweaty, white t-shirt as a top layer. If we are lucky, he'll come by Leila and mine's room and whisper, "Sleep as long as you like. The radio announced a snow day from school." A snow day is the most wonderful treat we get all winter long. Two of my male cousins will come over and we build snowmen and have snowball fights, and play backgammon and chess, or even Marco Polo in the chilly rear rooms of the house. One snow day when they were over, and when it was time for dinner, Maamaan said to the boys: "Now I know it won't be as tasty as *your* maamaan's dinners—she is an amazing cook. But, we all know that 'for the maamaan to cook well, baba must bring home the good fatty meat.'"

Leila and I tried not to giggle. Maamaan is always using that famous Persian saying to excuse her cooking, blaming it on poor quality food. But the reality is, Maamaan's cooking was not that tasty even before food was rationed. That night she had made *aabgoosht* for dinner, a lamb stew with garbanzo and kidney beans and potatoes slow cooked for hours to get the broth out of the little bones. It is flavored with tomatoes, cumin, and dried lime. She cut the lamb into teensy-tiny pieces. My cousins joked, "But where is the lamb?" Baba jumped in, praising the bread and pickled vegetables instead by saying, "The fresh *sangak* and *torshi* is all you need, they're heavenly!"

For entertainment, we watch TV in the evenings.

Ever since the revolution we only get two TV channels and programs do not start until five in the evening. First, they show cartoons for an hour, then it is war announcements, followed by the call to prayer. All TV and radio programs are put on hold for the call to prayer. After, there are maybe some sports, news, or wrestling competitions. On Fridays they play movies. But they are mostly sad Samurai movies, like *Yellow Crow*, which is all sword fights and gore. They are not fun to watch because it is just more war, death, and blood. We see enough of that already. However, we particularly love The Science Competition show that plays twice a week.

Our one day off from school each week is still spent going first to Bahá'í gatherings and then to my aunt's for lunch. The difference now is how secretive we must be for everyone's safety. My children's group is very small, only three or four children instead of the usual thirty. We do not bring anything with us when we go, no prayer books or notepads or pencils. Nothing. Not even the teachers bring books or teaching materials with them. They memorize what they want to share so if they are stopped by Islamic guards there will be no evidence of their association to the Bahá'í Faith.

We recently learned that they arrested ten Bahá'í women in Shiraz. Their crime? Their religion. One of these prisoners is a courageous sixteen-year-old girl named Mona Mahmudnizhad. She was charged with teaching Bahá'í children's classes. When they searched her home, they also found an essay she had written about freedom. Her parents were also arrested on similar charges. Her father was executed shortly after. Mona and other women (including her mother), were tortured for months in prison. A year later, she and the other women were hanged. Only Mona's mother was released. The judge told her he wants her to live the rest of her life mourning the loss of both her husband and daughter.

Mona was persecuted for "corrupting" the minds of the children and youth she educated by teaching them the principles of the Bahá'í Faith, the same principles I learn each week in children's classes: the oneness of mankind, equality of men and women, elimination of prejudice of all kinds, independent investigation of truth, the common foundation of all religions, the essential harmony of science and religion, universal compulsory education, universal peace upheld by a world government, a spiritual solution to the economic problem, a universal auxiliary language. I don't understand why it is wrong to learn these messages. I am scared that someone will come to take my teacher or me and my sister away and hang us, like they did to Mona.

Last week we learned a new prayer. I handwrote it on a piece of paper to help me memorize it, then my teacher helped me burn the paper before I left. Prayers give me something to hold on to when my mind races with worry about bombs and blood and death. The prayer we learned was a unity prayer by `Abdu'l-Bahá' that goes like this:

O Thou kind Lord! Unite all. Let the religions agree and make the nations one, so that they may see each other as one family and the whole earth as one home.

May they all live together in perfect harmony.

O God! Raise aloft the banner of the oneness of mankind.

O God! Establish the Most Great Peace. Cement Thou, O God, the hearts together.

I now say this prayer every night at bedtime. Sometimes I say it ten times, because as the darkness settles over Tehran each night, and the terror of bombs fills me, I become so desperate for the Most Great Peace.

9

POMEGRANATES

FALL 1985

Winters come and go. Summers, spring, fall, all of them pass in the same way year after year. I am ten, I am eleven, I am twelve, I am thirteen. On and on we go. We study hard, we pray for peace, we wait. We wait for many things, the end of the war, the end of our lives, the end of our time in Iran. We are always just waiting for our new life to begin, but how it will come and in which way will it arrive—who can say? There are questions I no longer think to ask, desires I no longer know how to feel. Like what is life? Life is survival. It is getting from point A to point B safely and back again. It is going through the motions of routine that are meant to simply keep us fed and alive. Alive for what? So we can greet death head on when it comes raining from the sky? Or greet it in the face of the Islamic guards come to persecute us for our faith in love, peace, and unity of humankind? But I do not want to die even though I live in despair, it is just that I am not sure what it feels like anymore to actually live. Can one live when one is not truly free? My lungs take in oxygen. My heart beats and pumps blood to my brain. My digestive system processes my food. This is life, is it not? Perhaps at its most basic functioning, but are we not made for so much more? Is the heart not good for more than just pumping blood? Does it not also dream? Does it not know how to soar to great heights at the sound of music and throw wide its gates to welcome truth? Is the mind not made for more than to worry about the future? Is it not full of sacred, far reaching spaces full of imagination? Does it not know how to create the music that moves the heart and the stories that lift the soul? We have had so little of such things that I don't even know what I am saying. It is a vague hope, something in me that seems to know this to be true, but I can't fully feel it in my bones. Maybe one day. Maybe when I go to America (how and when? How and when? I ask God daily). Maybe then I will learn something about beauty, truth, and love that this war has made me forget. Or maybe, it will give me the peace and time and space to make sense of the little beautiful things that are still here in my life and in my heart. I cling to them when they come; they are just so hard to hold on to once the bombs start again. It seems like the stress erases everything good that was starting to gain a foothold. One minute I feel some semblance of peace, the next minute I do not know the word.

I am changing. I know that much is true, but into what, I am not so sure.

Here are things I am beginning to understand: I understand that Maamaan is depressed and has always been depressed. I understand that this is not something we can talk about because this is not something people in Iran ever talk about. I understand that as hard as it has been on me to not understand why I cannot get close to her, I realize that living with depression is even harder for her. Depression and mental illness are considered a sin. People judge you and your family, avoid you like you are contagious. Those who suffer from depression use the little energy they have just to hide it. I understand that there are more people walking around depressed than we acknowledge. Because in reality, who is not depressed anymore? If it's not for the war or the oppression or the little shrines we see at every street corner for the young men who lost their lives in the war, then it's the fact that we do not hear music, we do not dance, we do not do anything fun. We are all feeling depressed, understanding it better than we have before. The color has been wiped from our lives. We look around and what do we see? Every woman is clothed in a black, brown, gray, or navy-blue hijabs. When color comes, I cling to it. Like my cool, new Swatch watch with its colorful band, a gift from Cyrus for my middle school graduation. With it came a box of the most delicious candy called Almond Joys—and what joy they did bring!

I understand that we must cling to these small moments of joy even in the midst of our suffering. They remind us that there is still goodness and sweetness out there. They remind us to hope. These are the thoughts I am thinking of often these days, and with them comes other insights, like how I understand that faith has the power to open eyes but also the power to blind if we lose ourselves to doctrine and forget the simple tenets of love, upon which I believe all great religions would agree is the foundation for their faith.

But mostly, I understand that there is still a lot I do not know, though I desperately wish to know it.

Here is something I haven't stopped thinking about: Last Nowruz, I noticed that Maamaan and Baba have not bought new clothes for the new year ever since Kia and Cyrus left. Why didn't I realize it before? Because I was young. Because I didn't see. I didn't see their shirts were thinning; I didn't see the holes in the bottom of their socks. But now I am seeing more and understanding more and what I see and understand mostly scares me.

Other things fill me with gratitude and perseverance. Like the way Maamaan and Baba sacrifice for us and never tell us of their sacrifice because, in their mind, they do not even see it as a sacrifice. For them, it is their one true way of being. To be any different wouldn't be truthful, it wouldn't be their nature. What is my nature? It is not as optimistic as Baba's and yet for all that I do not give up. Ever. Even if I have doubts, I keep moving. I have learned to just focus and do the next thing, the thing I can reach for, the thing I can control now. I cannot change the revolution, the persecution of Bahá'ís, the hate, the fear, the war, the Iraqis, the rations. I cannot change Maamaan's depression or Baba's unemployment. But I can wear hand-me-downs. I can stop whining about what we don't have, and I can study hard at school. So in attempt to be more grown-up, more helpful, and useful, I told my parents: no more Nowruz clothes for me. I am happy to wear Leila's hand-me-downs. Leila on the other hand is a teenager, she is horrified by Maamaan and I in our old clothes. She is especially embarrassed when Maamaan shows up at her school wearing her sister's old jacket. "What?" Maamaan asks, "It's a good jacket."

Even though I don't buy anything, I still enjoy going window shopping with my cousin. The last time she wanted to go shopping, the bombs started to fall just as we were on our way out the door. They don't fall every day but when they do there is often a pattern to them. Lately, they drop around two p.m. and then don't fall again the rest of the day. This goes to show just how crazy it is to live in a war zone. We waited for the bombs to stop falling as casually as I would wait, many, many years later, for the rainstorms of Seattle to pass before taking to the streets again. But whereas an umbrella could shield me from the clean, life giving rain of the Pacific Northwest, there was no umbrella wide enough or strong enough to stop the downpour of death in Iran. My cousin and I had shopping to do, and so, we waited for our hearts to stop racing, and then proceeded with the day's plans as if nothing had happened.

Strolling through the boulevards, we passed a shoe store. "Oh, these are so great, don't you think?" my cousin asked, reaching out to grab a shoe and hold it up in admiration. "Wait a minute, how'd you pick up that shoe . . ." I said. It took us a second to register the strangeness of the moment. We were on the street, just then realizing we were standing amidst glass. She had just reached through a blasted-out window to pick up the shoe. "Oh!" she said, quickly throwing it back on the display before anyone could charge us with shoplifting.

Outings like these help me stay sane, but it turns out poetry is my favorite place to find refuge from the stress of war.

For years now, I've been studying Persian poetry in school and it is the highlight of my day. I look forward to my poetry class, but also to my Persian literature class and calligraphy classes because I find that there is something poetic within literature and calligraphy as well. I've learned that if I combine poetry and literature with calligraphy, then I have the best of both worlds. I covet our old and worn copy of the *Shahnameh: The Persian Book of Kings* by Ferdowsi, a book of 50,000 couplets, the longest epic poem ever written by a single poet. It took him fifty years! Is it a history book? Is it a fairy tale? It is part myth and magic and another part history and fact, but it is all parts fantastic and glorious. My fingers trace the lines down the pages until I find a passage I can't resist, then I pick up my bamboo pen and dip it in the ink pot. Delicate curls and ribbons, dots and tendrils decorate the blank space and I lose myself to the beauty that whispers from the page. Baba has taken up the practice too. From the moment I brought home my first pen, he was curious about my interest in the slow, deliberate twists and turns. He is always checking my pen tips and tut-tutting: "That one's no good! Here, allow me." Then he whips out his pocket knife and whittles away until it's perfection again, but instead of giving it back, he writes a few lines himself and smiles with satisfaction to show me how it is done. For a man whose thick hands have known hard labor—carrying bricks up the ladder and mixing cement to build his own home, working on engines and getting covered in oil and grease, changing giant semi tires, planting trees, trimming branches, scrubbing floors, shoveling snow—how is it that his big, calloused hands can hold the thin bamboo pen and move it so delicately across the page? I will wonder the same thing again many years down the road when my Baba is a grandfather to my three children and I find him expertly combing and braiding my child's hair after her bath. Her black locks shiny and swaying like the natural curves of the Persian script I will remember practicing on long winter nights. The short rope of her braid just barely grazes her shoulder, and I am in awe of the smile on her face as she thanks Baba and asks for her bedtime story—her smile is a perfect couplet to rival all of Ferdowsi's. Baba will know this too, and so will always ask for a kiss from her in return for a story.

But these thoughts would have felt impossible for me to imagine as a teenager living in a war zone. Another life full of safety, full of love, and with my own children seemed impossible. And yet it would be true, and so it was also somehow inevitable. Is that what Baba meant when he said you cannot escape your destiny? The impossible inevitability of our lives? The impossible inevitability that life will persist? That it will unfold, evolve, and take root once again, sprout, and grow? But I get ahead of myself. I was understanding more and more, but that mantra, at that time, I understood less and less. I firmly set myself against it, refusing to believe in destiny when the reality in front of me was so grim.

So here I am, still thirteen, still a child wanting to play, but finding myself more mature than most of my peers and getting called on to assume more and more responsibility. I am on the verge of giving up childhood altogether, but I do not know it quite yet and despite my desperate yearning to know all, sometimes it is better to not fully understand your path until you must walk it. Only then will you find you have the strength for the climb.

* * *

During the month of Ramadan, the bombs never drop. For once, we can predict a peaceful month ahead. For once, I get to sleep. Yet even though the bombs are gone, the nightmares remain. I wake up screaming, "The jets are coming! The jets are coming!" and fall back exhausted onto my mattress in a feverish cold sweat. Maamaan comes over and hugs me, holds me in her arms while the hot tears fall silently, until my breath returns. She reminds me that it is Ramadan and the war is on hold.

At school, we never participate in the Islamic call to prayer simply because every student goes home now before afternoon prayers. Khomeini's new ruling says boys and girls must be educated separately, but there are not enough schools to accommodate the decree. The solution is a block system, girls in the morning, boys in the afternoon. This has its benefits for Layla and me—no one discovers that we are Bahá'í by our refusal to join in the Islamic prayer. But during Ramadan, when fasting is observed during the day, we also choose to fast from lunch and from snacks at recess. To enforce the practice of fasting for young, school age children, the school's water supply is shut down as well. The teachers and students assume everyone is Muslim and so, thankfully, the schools in Tehran have not enforced any religious questionnaires, as the schools in small towns do. As Ramadan comes to a close, summer vacation begins and that means more opportunities to get out of the city and away from its war-torn streets.

When school ends and vacation begins, Sharareh and I visit our good friend and classmate Setareh. Her father is the gardener at the soccer stadium about four kilometers north of our neighborhood. They actually live in a small house inside the stadium and her family is the groundskeeper. The midday sun is hot, it is late June, and we are excited for what awaits us at the end of our thirty-minute trek. Setareh greets us at the gate and then, shedding our dark Islamic uniforms and sweaty head scarves, we run into the stadium and into the cold spray of the sprinklers watering the soccer field. We squeal and laugh. We are free. Someone finds a soccer ball and we pretend to be in the World Cup. We run up into the seats to watch the penalty kicks as we take turns scoring on the wide-open goal. We scream wildly to celebrate our goals. For a precious few hours, we taste the joy of childhood, of innocence, of freedom from fear. For a short time, we are given back the life we have been cheated out of. When the sun starts to set, we put our Islamic hijabs on over our wet clothes and ready ourselves again for the reality of life outside the stadium. We thank Setareh for the experience and ask when we can come back. She says she will let us know when there isn't a soccer match. Sharareh and I walk home grinning from ear to ear. Today, it was fun to be a kid. Little did we know, that women would be banned from entering this stadium for the next forty years to even watch a soccer game, let alone ever taking part in a match on the very grounds that we freely roamed.

Every year in June, I get the same phone call from my cousin Farzin. "Hi Mahvash," he begins. "Hi, Farzin." "So, it's four this year." "Oh," I say, "We have our work cut out for us." His mother makes him call to tell me how many classes he has not passed. He is just three months younger than me, but much shorter. Ever since I was ten years old, his family invites me to visit for three to four weeks over the summer to tutor Farzin, so that he can retake his tests in August and move to the next grade. Without fail, every morning Farzin will pretend to fall out of a tree and "break" his arm, or "accidentally" lock himself in his room and lose the keys, or who knows what other kind of excuse. He is a very creative boy. I bargain with him. We can spend the mornings playing if we spend the afternoons studying. He always comes around. I deeply love my time with Farzin; it is a vacation from the pandemonium of Tehran. There you cannot hear the sirens from the airport, just Farzin's bees buzzing happily in their hive boxes and the animals bleating and braying in the fields. Bird songs become familiar to me again, and I find myself humming and singing along while we feed the chickens and collect their eggs. Ping pong tournaments and swimming in the pool fill our days. Sometimes we walk down to the river and buy ice cream from the vendors. And just like our scoops of ice cream in the summer heat, my fears start to slowly melt away.

In the fall, Farzin's family rents a pomegranate orchard in the foothills of Tehran and invites us and the rest of the family to join them on Fridays from September through November to celebrate the season. Between first and second cousins, there are at least twenty kids to play with. We all wear special clothes dedicated for these days because, with any luck, we will be covered in the sweet, red juice by the end of the day. Pomegranate seeds will rain throughout the orchard as we play catch and pitch them at targets. Sometimes the targets are each other. We spend hours climbing trees to pick as many as we can. Then we roll them until they are soft and squishy and make a tiny slit at the top to suck the sweet juice out from the inside. While we play, the women all gather to prepare huge vats of food. If they are not making lunch, then they are preparing foods to last through the winter. They make a pomegranate paste to use in a famous dish called *Fesenjoon*, a savory meal of walnuts, chicken and saffron slow cooked for hours, so rich and filling in the cold winters.

When I get too tired from running around, I visit the women tending the fire pits and cooking. I will stand over the giant pots of tomatoes bubbling down into a paste and feel my face get all warm and steamy while I breathe in the earthy smell. Sometimes I stay for a bit and help stir the sauce with a huge wooden spoon that is half my size. Other pots are full of pomegranate seeds and also being turned into pastes that we will use in our cooking all year long. The women also dry herbs—mint, basil, parsley, cilantro—and vegetables in the sun. In between backgammon games, the men bring freshly chopped firewood to keep the fires going and the pots bubbling. At the end of the day, the pastes get jarred and split between all the families, and everyone goes home with a big basket of pomegranates to last until the following Friday.

Pomegranates—my country's longest love affair. There is nothing about this fruit we do not prize. We use the skin, the seeds, the juice in all our favorite dishes, and even as we boil them into and sprinkle them onto our cooking, we are singing their praises just like we have done for centuries. Pomegranates in poetry are nothing new. Even the Qur'án says the pomegranate tree grew in the garden of paradise. Pomegranates have found their way into the embroidery on the robes of kings, into the intricate stitches of Persian rugs; they are etched in walls and painted on urns and plates. My favorite book, the *Shahnameh* tells the story of the intrepid Esfandiyār, who, after being given pomegranate seeds to eat, gains superhuman strength and becomes invincible. Like I've said, how much of the *Shahnameh* is fact and how much is fiction? A little make-believe gives my mind an escape from its war-torn thoughts. Am I fortifying myself with some elixir of life? With every handful of pomegranate seeds I eat, am I building up my resistance to this war? Strengthening not just my immune system, but also my muscles to be able to outrun and outlive any attack? The pomegranate tree is evergreen, and the fruit filled with what seems to be an incalculable number of seeds, and so the pomegranate has become a beautiful symbol of immortality. Sometimes I allow myself this illusion of immortality if, for no other reason than just for a moment, it gives me a reason to smile. But when I look out across the hilly orchards, the trees exploding with their big maroon orbs, I also feel hope. They remind me there can be sweetness even in winter, and a burst of color even in the midst of gray days. When the fruit is all picked, and the trees are barren for months on end, the evergreen leaves become another sort of anchor for my soul, reminding me of the joy of the harvest past and the fruit of the future yet to come.

10
DARKNESS

In my dreams, I walk among broken things. Twisted metal and ruined concrete, a brown leather shoe, a plastic sandal, torn burlap bags and sand wet with blood. There is no one else. No animal. No bird song. There is no sound. Just a warm breeze flapping the curtains inside a home. There are no window panes on this street. The glass trail leads me to a family resting, peacefully, face down, limbs splayed, on their red Persian rug. Then I see him, to the left. The Islamic guard in the alley; he points and yells. *Bahá'í najes*! Dirty dogs! I turn to run but my feet stick fast; I am desperate, straining and willing myself to move, but I cannot. He gains on me. Then a loud boom stops him in his tracks and he turns and runs the other way. I look up and see a doomsday constellation, black missiles scattered across the sky. I make a wish on every falling bomb: Please don't kill me. Not tonight. Not yet. Please.

First come the explosions. Then come the screams. When I wake up, I realize there is no difference between my waking and my sleeping anymore. Outside or inside, everything really is broken.

Even the street names are changing. What used to be Elizabeth Boulevard is now called Keshavarz Boulevard. We used to walk down 5th Ave Bimeh to get to the bakery, but now it is called Martyr Ahmad Gilani. Even the alleyways are being renamed to honor the heroes—the men and boys who lost and will lose their lives in the war with Iraq. Little shrines fill the streets with twinkle lights and photos of deceased young men and sometimes child soldiers. For up to forty days after the death of their child, parents stand by the shrine and hand out Persian dates to everyone who passes. They smile at me, offer a date and say, "My child was worthy." I don't know what to say back. Am I supposed to smile? I cannot. I have been good at hiding behind the hijab, and being silent about my faith, but it is much harder to hide my feelings from my eyes. The deaths disturb me. I want to hug the families and cry, but they want me to celebrate their death and praise Allah for the heroes who followed their religious duty to protect the revolution and defend its values, something that those, they say, of the materialistic West will never understand. But I can't understand it either. Perhaps I am not made of the same type of courage.

The shrines for these children, they are the children I see on TV being sent to the front lines. They run through minefields to clear a path for soldiers to follow. The TV anchormen praise the children, "They volunteered!" One time a mother said in an interview, "I have three sons who died, and I have a little one now who I can't wait to grow up, so he too can be a soldier of Islam!" One of my friends at school said she heard that during the religious sermons on Fridays, the ayatollahs give the children plastic keys to hang around their necks, "These are the keys of heaven!" they tell them, "if you die on the battlefield you will ascend straight to God." I don't know if this is true, but what is true is that children are dying by the thousands with hundreds more coming home mutilated. Some girls in my class paste photos of a boy named Mohammad Hossein Fahmideh on their notebooks. When he was thirteen, he pulled a pin from a grenade and then leaped with it under an Iraqi tank. He died, but he also disabled the tank, and so the girls say he is a legend. The deaths are all so devastating to me, but if you are Muslim it is the greatest honor to die for Islam.

I learned the depth of this when we went to visit Ms. Molook's son, Jamshid, in the hospital. He had signed up to go to war immediately after finishing high school. He was actually exempt. His father had passed away, so Jamshid was considered the breadwinner for his mother and sisters and didn't have to go. All the same he insisted. "It is my calling," he told his mother. He went to war and was injured by a landmine. When Ms. Molook came to our house to give us the news, we got the hospital's address and immediately went to visit him. My parents hugged and kissed Jamshid. "We are so grateful," Baba beamed at him, "that this is just a limb injury and that you were not killed." Maamaan nodded her head in agreement, tears in her eyes. But Jamshid frowned at the words and looked at the ground. His voice trembled, when he said, "I wasn't worthy of being murdered for Islam." I stood there stunned by his words. "Please," he asked, "if you pray for me, pray for a quick recovery so that I might return to battle."

Eventually, that is exactly what he did and a few months after, he was killed. When we went to visit Ms. Molook to give her our condolences, there was a little shrine with twinkle lights set up in the alley and the name of the street was now Martyr Jamshid Karimi. Ms. Molook was devastated.

But she could not stop him.

* * *

As the war intensifies, so does this summer heat. Sleeping indoors is suffocating because we don't run our fancy A/C unit anymore, in part to save money but also because most of the time the electricity is cut anyway. Before the war, we used to sleep outside on the rooftops in the summer. Some neighbors say it's still a good idea because there are no broken bricks or shattered glass to fall on you in an attack, but others say that's ridiculous—outside we are exposed to the explosive shock waves that can maim and kill. We have all heard the story of the woman who stuck her head out of her kitchen window to see what was going on outside during a bombing. Her body was found crumpled on the kitchen floor; her head, a few blocks away. I pass people on the streets who are missing arms. The unfortunate ones who didn't make it indoors in time and had a limb left dangling from a window in a building, or from a car, right before or after an explosion.

No, sleeping outside on the roof doesn't sound fun anymore. Though, Leila and I did try it again a few times just for some relief from the heat and because there seemed to be a break from the bombs. But anytime something moved in the sky, a bird or a bat, a passenger plane or a shooting star, I thought it was an Iraqi fighter jet approaching. It was a troubled sleep. Nothing like how it used to be.

I remember in the summer, when Kia and Cyrus were still here, all the neighbors would come outside around dusk to sweep their rooftops and balconies or to spray water on the bare ground to cool it—all three areas being a great place to camp out under the stars. The boys would kick their soccer balls across the rooftops to each other and the girls would play hopscotch, and the maamaans would always call up, "Be careful! Be careful!" There are no railings on rooftops and the only way to get on top is to climb a ladder. Broken arms or legs from falling off roofs were just part of a good summer vacation. We'd go to a neighbor's roof or they'd come to ours and we'd share fresh lemonade, sour cherry drinks, and watermelon slices. In those months, Baba always made a trip or two to the vegetable bazar of Tehran to fill the whole car with watermelons and bring them back to us. They have always been his favorite. He even has a special watermelon spoon because everyone from Yazd has a special watermelon spoon. Every morning in the summer, we could hear him slurping away, finishing half a watermelon himself before the sun had risen.

Late in the night, once the sun had gone down and the air cooled, we'd roll out the wool rugs and *poshties*, huge handmade rug pillows, on the roof and spread the sofreh on top for a light supper of fresh bread, feta, crunchy melons, cucumbers, herbs, walnuts, and the special mint yogurt drink called *doogh*. Little lanterns would be lit from underneath the mosquito netting and twinkle around all of the families gathered on their rooftops, laughing and enjoying their dinners. Then Maamaan would unroll our sleeping mattresses and sheets and prepare a cozy nest for us while we brushed our teeth. I remember it was easy to fall asleep back then. We'd count shooting stars and identify galaxies, all while our "nighttime story" aired on the small, battery-operated radio at 10 p.m. sharp each night. The air was fresh, the night was cool, and our dreams were full of color. "What a bunch of slackers," Maamaan would tease in the mornings, after we'd slept so late that the sun was high in the sky.

But no one plays in the streets or on the rooftops anymore. There aren't soccer matches or hopscotch tournaments. No one crunches watermelon and laughs with their family on the roof. Teenage boys do not chase teenage neighbor girls on the rooftops anymore. Young girls do not sit under the stars singing love songs and twirling their hair. The only sounds I hear rising from the rooftops now are the men chanting *"Allahu'akbar"* at dusk, showing their support of the Islamic regime and all its accomplishments at war, all its victories enforcing Islamic laws. This they never did before the revolution, then it started with just a few people, now it seems every man, everywhere is on his roof in the evenings chanting the same words for twenty minutes, *"Allahu' akbar."* They are more constant and reliable than the shrieking sirens.

At first, when Leila and I started sleeping outside again it felt like a good distraction from the constant fear of being killed by a bomb, but then I realized it was really just denial. When we learned about a scud missile landing on a six-year old's birthday party, killing the entire family and all their guests, it shook us up so badly that we put an end to our campouts once and for all. The danger is real, and we can never know from which direction it will come.

Inside the walls of our home lives another sort of darkness, subtle and seemingly less dangerous, but toxic in its own way. Its name is sadness.

Maamaan waits outside every morning for the mail to arrive. Letters from Cyrus and Kia are few. When a letter does arrive, it is postmarked nearly three months earlier. There is no direct mail route to Iran from America anymore, so multiple postmarks on the envelope show us its circuitous journey through Europe and the Middle East before finally reaching our own front door. But it's rare to get a letter. That, however, means nothing to Maamaan. She still waits, every day, just like she always has for the mail carrier and when she sees him, she calls out, "Sir, sir! Do you have a letter for me? Are you sure? Look again. From my boys. Look again." Every day she does this.

When we can scrape together enough money to send them a package, she fills it with their favorite cookies and sweets, and sweaters and scarves she's knit herself. She has me sit and write while she dictates a letter that includes every single detail of every single family member's life all the way from great-grandparents to third cousins. My hand cramps long before she's through. Then, she is angry when she learns it took months for the boys to receive the package, well past Nowruz, well past their college graduations, well past whatever ceremony she wanted to celebrate from afar with them. We got rid of our land line to save money because selling our number helped pay for another semester of their tuition. Every now and then we try to call them on a pay phone. The lines for a pay phone wrap around the block, and when we finally get to make a call, it's a gamble. Often it is so scratchy and garbled we barely hear anything my brothers say. Only the most important words are repeated, "Safe, safe. . . good, yes, good. . . love, all my love." "*Ghorboonet beram, ghorboonet beram,*" Maamaan repeats over and over, hoping the phrase speeds through the static and reaches her babies' ears. "I die for you. I die for you." The Persian way to express the deepest, most profound sort of love possible. When I look at my Maamaan, all I see is endless loss. This is a weight I don't know how to bear.

I really don't know how much longer I can take any more of this darkness inside me or resist all this darkness outside me. Death and the fear of death consume every hour of my life, waking or sleeping. I have my tricks to try to ignore it, to find some relief from the adrenaline constantly coursing through my veins, speeding my heartbeat, but in the end that's all they are—tricks. And so I also fear that the effort it takes to keep up a spirit of determination and hope in the face of this monstrous tidal wave of death and destruction will one day run out. Then what will I do? Where is the line to stand in to get my monthly ration of courage? Losing myself, my body, to the bombs is one thing, but losing my mind and my soul, to this darkness is another. These thoughts, the fear, are all worse at night, made more oppressive by being locked up in our home with the windows blacked out and taped up, the streets eerily silent.

Since the first day the war began, since I was a little girl, every night before I fall asleep, I have wished for a spaceship. I don't want to visit the moon or roam the galaxies, culling their mysteries for new cultures and worlds. All I want is to climb inside my little pod and travel to the other side of the Earth, to the side where the sun shines bright and warm, and I will not come back until the sun is rising in Iran again.

All I want is to live in the daylight forever.

11
FOCUS

Leila is further and further away these days. She sits often on a cushion in the corner, knees hugged to chest. I recognize the distant look that grows in her eyes.

Last week Leila learned she will not be allowed to take the college entrance exams. In the back of our minds, if we're being honest with ourselves, we always knew this day would come. We always knew that eventually being Bahá'í would catch up to us and we'd be denied our education here in Iran. But it did not feel real until now. Somehow, we heard the words, but we didn't believe it could ever be true for us—until it was. School has been our saving grace all these years. We've focused all our energy into our studies. Leila has only ever been disciplined, focused, and committed; always coming out on top in her class. She is the one who has spent hours tutoring her classmates over the past ten school years, and yet they are the ones who—though they still suffer through their studies—have all been accepted to colleges. It's hard for her not to feel bitter. "I spent my recesses helping *them* and now they're going to college, but not me," she says.

Now that Leila is graduating, what will she do? Maamaan hasn't even taught us to cook because it would have taken time away from doing homework. She would say: "You're going to be doctors not chefs. I'll take care of feeding you, you take care of your studies." Studying is all we know.

It's so unbelievably unfair that Leila's only option is to go to hair-dressing school. She tries it out rather than staying home and being upset, but it feels like a waste of her brain, a waste of her talents. I think that I too should despair knowing this is also my future, and yet—I can't. Things might change. They might. And even if they don't, there's always America. I can study there. The only question is—how exactly do I get out of Iran?

Bahá'ís are denied exit visas; they are not even allowed passports.

Kia and Cyrus got out just in the nick of time; this is why Leila is so mad. Why did we not all leave? Why did my parents not foresee this future? Why did they build up our hope of education all these years when all our dreams were only ever going to be crushed? If she does talk these days, it is only to argue. Maamaan and Baba are patient and they stick to their story: We will find a way to get you out of here. Leila just yells, "How? We have no money. You've given everything to the boys."

During the last two years, numerous families have reached out to my mother to arrange for their sons to meet Leila. Marriage is on the minds of most sixteen and seventeen-year-olds, but not Leila's. Most of my cousins were married at that age or are currently engaged and preparing for mar-riage. Their parents never made school a priority. My parents are different; they never even considered a backup plan—they never saved for a dowry because what was the point? We were always, only, ever going to go to uni-versity. We have always been on a different track, with a different mission. College has been our singular focus. Maamaan even clucked her tongue at all the would-be suitors, sent them on their way, saying, "No thank you, she's still just in high school."

But now Leila is not in high school anymore, and the boys know it. The doorbell has been ringing again and this time Maamaan tells Leila, "Maybe it's not such a bad idea. Maybe you should give them a chance?" Leila screams at her, slams her bedroom door in Maamaan's face. She wants nothing to do with boys. Through the door Maamaan tries to persuade her, "These are good Bahá'í boys from good Bahá'í families!" Leila will have none of it: "If you love them so much, why don't *you* marry them?"

Her disappointment devastates me. Maybe it is foolish of me, but if I don't keep my focus on college then I don't know what I will do. I can't survive here. That much I know. I grit my teeth and tell myself it will all be different in a few more years. I do empathize with Leila though. I understand her. I don't want to get married this young! I don't want to be a homemaker. Every part of me resists that. Maybe one day, but not for many, many years. It's ridiculous then that, secretly, my favorite class is home economics. Of all the things we are forced to take, this one makes no sense to me. They could give us art or music, but they don't because art and music teachers are being charged as criminals under Khomeini's rule. Instead, they give us pastries and pajamas.

"Today we're learning to sew buttons. Tomorrow, we knit scarves so you can make them for your children," they explain, "This is all to make you very good homemakers." In class, I roll my eyes, but at home I take a certain delight in following the patterns and practicing my stitches. I don't do it because I believe this is what makes me a desirable woman and great future wife. I do it because I love to learn, because I actually enjoy arts and crafts. I do it because it's something new. Day in and day out, all we ever do is math and science and some history. Classes are complicated, serious, and tedious. Home economics is kind of, dare I say—fun? Besides, the competitor in me says I have to finish anything I begin, and I have to do it well—doesn't matter if it's calculus or basketball or knitting. I'm going to ace the test, sink the shot, and knit the best sweater you ever saw.

Maamaan is good at this stuff too and a great help because the sewing machine was a complete mystery to me before she showed me its ways. Leila has already taken these classes, so she helps me decipher the clothing patterns, which I find more complex than the periodic table. Maamaan tells me, "You'll never realize how useful knowing how to sew is until one morning you wake up and the buttons on your surgeon's jacket have all popped off. It's just the sort of thing that happens, which makes you glad you know how to sew buttons *and* suture head wounds."

Keeping my grades up is still worth every bit of energy, but I have to admit I grow weary of it at times. The high school vice principal is so strict. Leila had warned me about her, but now I see it firsthand. She stands outside our classroom door in the morning waiting to inspect every girl who walks in. She digs through our bags for cassette tapes and makeup and anything Western and keeps a measuring tape at the ready in her chador to measure our pant legs. Never mind that our school uniforms are long jackets in black or navy blue that reach well past our knees. The pants we wear underneath must also be in code with her standards. But her standards change depending on whatever is fashionable in the West. For the longest time, all through middle school at least, Leila and I always wore loose fitting or sometimes baggy pants. This wasn't a problem then. But apparently, baggy jeans are coming into fashion in the West which means now they are "out" here, and we have to wear tight-fitting pants. The vice principal has sent many girls home for having pants just a centimeter too loose around their ankles. It's frustrating trying to please her when we're all just trying so hard to stay focused on more important things. We're at war. My thoughts turn more to staying alive than to which of my two pairs of pants I'm going to wear today. But this past semester I had two encounters with the vice principal that were exceedingly aggravating and even Maamaan lost her cool.

During a normal morning makeup roundup, the vice principal searched my bag, found nothing, but then shoved her face close to mine and squinted into my eyes. "You're wearing mascara," she hissed. I was taken aback by the accusation. "I'm not. No, really." She threw her shoulders back and told me to, "Go home. Take it off." "I can't take it off. I'm not wearing mascara . . . I just have long eyelashes." She laughed and told me that if I wanted to attend class today I'd have to return with my mother. My mother returned, dragging me by the elbow into the principal's office. She didn't yell, but her voice was stern with an authority I've never heard before. "You think she has makeup on? You think she is lying? Mahvash never wears makeup. I never wear makeup. There isn't any makeup in our home. Look at her. You think she has on mascara? Then you try to take it off her if you can. These are her real eyelashes." I got to return to class but the episode left me feeling a little ashamed, as if I had broken some kind of rule. The vice principal has a way of unsettling us all.

But worse than the mascara mix-up, was her proclamation against my new shoes. Cyrus sent me an amazing pair of brand-new, Adidas sneakers from America. I can't remember the last time I had new shoes; it was such an unexpected treat. They are so comfortable, and they would have been great for PE and sports since I run track and play basketball and volleyball. The first day I wore them to school I was positively glowing, but then I saw the vice principal staring at my feet from down the hall and in my gut, I knew my shoes were doomed. "I'm afraid you'll have to go home and return with different shoes, Mahvash." My heart sunk. "But why?" "Those three white bands at the top—they're too . . . flashy." "Just because of the bands?" "Because of how flashy they are. They're inappropriate and a distraction." When I got home, Maamaan tried removing the bands, she was so upset. She wanted me to be able to wear my new shoes. My parents would go naked if it meant their children were well dressed. My other shoes were worn out from all the sports and even though I don't complain, my mother noticed, and she knows that Leila would have been embarrassed. She doesn't want me embarrassed either. But the bands wouldn't come off, so that was that. There was nothing Maamaan could do to change the vice principal's mind about the "flashiness" of my American-made sneakers. The one relief from being sent home that morning was getting to escape the morning line up in the school yard where we repeat after the vice principal, whose voice booms over a microphone: "Dawn to USA. Dawn to Israel. Death to anti-Islamic forces and groups. Allāhu akbar." But the silver lining is short lived. Between strict teachers and Leila's grief, I've been a bit distracted.

Distraction lets despair creep in and then despair suffocates all hope. When I need a dose of positivity, I know where to look—Baba's garden. He listens to me go on and on about school and my studies and my frustrations and fears, all the while humming and every now and then interrupting me to tell me how many blossoms on the persimmon or the cherry tree will turn into fruit—an old ritual of ours. He's done this since I was a child. I don't know what I hope he will say or what I will get out of it by venting. Am I just complaining? Am I just adding to his burden? But he finally turns to me, sighs gently and says, "You know, I really do mean it. I've always meant it, always believed. You and Leila will get out of this hell hole." It's not often I hear my father swear. It's the certainty of his voice, the seriousness in his eye that does it. I find my resolve. I understand—our time is coming. I just need to hold fast and stay focused. Honestly, there really is not much else for me to do unless I want to ride the waves of depression too.

Thankfully, Baba is always on the lookout for ways to cheer us up and keep our spirits high. He announces a road trip to get away for a little during Nowruz. "After all," he begins—and we all know what he's going to say next— "travel is good for your soul!" Happy to put books and study aside for a couple weeks, we pile in the truck and make our way to visit Maamaan's cousin, Vafa, and his family. I remember visiting them in the historic city of Bam some years ago. Beautiful date trees lined the street and, in the middle of the road, a wide boulevard full of orange trees in full bloom greeted us upon arrival. Baba rolled down the car windows and the fresh citrus filled our lungs. But Vafa no longer lives in Bam. He and his family have been exiled for ten years to a small, rural village not far from the port city of Bandar Abbas. Back in Bam, Vafa was a teacher, but he has been fired from his post for corrupting the minds of Muslim children with Bahá'í teachings. In the new village, Vafa must report every morning to the Islamic authority guards. Come rain or shine, sickness or health, he must personally appear before them and sign a paper for the next ten years. The only work he's been able to find is driving people between villages. His small wage is just enough to pay their meager expenses. "Because he cannot leave the village," Baba says, "we must go and cheer them up!"

It was a good trip, not just to get away, but mostly to give me perspective again. Things are bad in the capital for us, but they could be worse.

We could be cramped in a rustic hut and forced to live within just a small circumference for the rest of my childhood and early adult life.

12
EMPTY

It's 1987 and Leila has gone to Turkey. Her complete withdrawal from people and life finally convinced my parents that something had to be done. She was done with the beauty school and only attending her private English classes to stay busy. I don't think it was as difficult or as emotional of a decision for my parents to let her go as when they sent Cyrus and Kia off at ages sixteen and seventeen. Leila is nearly twenty and it was time for her to get to a place where she could finally live her life. Since we've been living off my parent's savings though, and because the rial is so devalued outside of Iran, my parents are not able to send money to the boys or to Leila because it wouldn't go far. With the financial help of Cyrus and Kia, Leila can begin the process to seek asylum in the US. Despite our limited income, somehow my parents still find a way to send me to private English classes in the summer. "You're next," Baba keeps saying.

The house is lonely without Leila. Baba plants a cherry tree in our backyard orchard, Leila's favorite. He still hopes that one day his children will return and get to enjoy the fruits. Cyrus's persimmon tree and Kia's pomegranate tree have grown enormous after all these years. I walk the gardens with Baba. I ask Baba if he will plant a *toot*, a mulberry tree, for me when I leave? We pause, feeling awkward. "Say, remember the time you tried to teach Leila to drive?" I ask slyly. Baba smiles, "And she backed the truck into the grape trellis and never wanted to get behind the wheel of a car ever again?" We laugh. Poor Leila, it wasn't a big deal and Baba wasn't mad at all. But Leila has always been shy and reserved and doesn't like to make mistakes. I wonder how she will be on her own for the first time and in a foreign country. I don't want to leave and have Baba plant a tree for me. I would rather that we all leave together, and soon.

Instead, Baba plans another road trip. This time to Isfahan to visit Maamaan's sisters and mother. The youngest sister has always lived there, and the oldest moved there with Maadar after being forced from their home in Yazd. We try to go every summer. Even Great-Grandmother Naneh is going to go for a visit this year. I don't even know how old she is anymore; I'm not sure she knows. She's in her nineties, certainly. Maybe it's because she is so old, or maybe it's because she's always worn the hijab and lived quietly, but no one bothers her in Yazd. She has lived safely and happily all these years tending her gardens and goats and doing her weaving, always weaving.

Isfahan never fails to take my breath away. Ancient Perso-Islamic architecture speaks to the glory days of this great city in its many mosaics and mosques, minarets and monuments. Once the capital of Iran, Isfahan is full of green gardens and opulent boulevards. When I arrive, my cousins immediately take me down to the Si-o-se-pol bridge—one of my favorite spots. Thirty-three arches form the bridge that stretches across the Zayanderud river. We rent a boat and take it out rowing, letting our hands float in the cool water, while we watch the sun set over the city. At dinner, somehow the topic gets turned to the war. I am so sick of thinking about the war. My aunts are appalled because the city was bombed just a couple days ago. In all these years, Isfahan has only been bombed maybe twice. They are worried and stressed, and I think to myself that they can't even begin to imagine living in Tehran. Naneh chimes in and I'm curious to hear what she has to say. Her back is so crooked she sits with her head permanently bowed. To speak, she must cock her head to the side, and look at you with only one eye at a time. Still, that one eye says a lot. "They weren't going to kill me in Yazd! But I show up here and they've got bombs! We'll see about that. I'm going back to Yazd tomorrow!" We try to convince her to stay, telling her how unlikely another bombing is, but she is stubborn and insistent. She's going back to where she knows she is safe. "She's resilient, that one," Baba says to me later, "like you. Lived through a lot—both world wars, now this, and still she smiles." Baba is sweet to compare me to her, but no matter how much I admire Naneh, I still can't will myself to smile. She might be able to walk around unphased by the chaos, but I struggle daily not to let myself drown in it. Our vacation comes to an end and we make our way back to Tehran, back to another school year, back to our old routines.

When the year passes, we are still no closer to leaving Tehran. Leila is still in Turkey and communication with her is rare. Worse, the night bombings have intensified once again. There are so many empty desks at school that I don't know if my classmates have fled the city or if they are dead. Tehran becomes a ghost city.

By January all the schools shut down. That is how unsafe it has become. Bombs fall on schools and hospitals and other public places—killing hundreds of people at a time. Without school, I have absolutely nothing left to distract me, nothing to focus my attention on except for the emptiness all around me. No homework. No electricity. No friends. No Leila. Just the anticipation of when the next bomb will strike. I can no longer sleep. I borrow banned books from a cousin—*Dr. Zhivago, Jane Eyre, Papillion, Napoleon Bonaparte and Josephine*—these are my only companions. This is the first time I have read western novels; they are nothing like the history books and Persian poetry and old Arabic writings I am accustomed to studying in school. I'm devouring them, mesmerized by them, amazed that books can be read for pleasure and entertainment. Everything I read for school had some element of pain embedded within it—wars throughout history and the suffering of imams and prophets. But these novels show me another world. A world of love, romance even. I am a Bahá'í, so I understand that men and women are equal and valued; however, the reality is that I have only ever seen people persecuted for acts of affection.

Just having feelings for someone of the opposite sex is a crime. Men can go to jail for being seduced by the voice of a female singer and women are beaten and jailed for seducing men with their voice. It is illegal for Baba and Maamaan to hold hands in public. I came across a Persian novel called *Blue Bus*, and it was pure romance—it showed me that we Persians have romance in our soul too. There was a time when Iranians did not have to censor these beautiful, natural human tendencies. I've never really witnessed what it means to nourish a relationship. All my life I've seen men and women segregated, but in these books, they come shoulder to shoulder, face to face, and create amazing stories together. The books help, but only so much. My home country feels like a prison. Can I even call this place home anymore? Has it even been a home since Khomeini seized power and made it clear that Bahá'ís were not welcome here?

I am following in Leila's footsteps now. I too have taken up the banner of dissent in the family. Most of my days are spent fighting and arguing with my parents to get us out of Tehran. I do not want to be here anymore. I *cannot* be here anymore. Baba tells me I cannot escape my destiny, and I tell him this isn't about giving up. I argue that we can't just sit back and let destiny be in charge. I tell him, for the first time ever, that I want to rewrite my destiny. We have to take control and contribute! If anything, I am fighting for myself now more than ever—it's a personal battle. I will get out of this hell hole. They resist and resist and resist despite my tears and all my begging.

But by March, to my surprise, I seem to have worn them down and they finally cave. We will move to Yazd they tell me. The cloud has lifted. Sunlight streams through. I am thrilled, and utterly relieved, to move to Yazd. Bombs never fall in there, so it sounds like a veritable paradise. And, Yazd is famous for its sweets. Diplomats and royalty come from all around to go to Yazd confectionaries. There, I can find and indulge in my favorite ice cream every day if I want to, *bastani akbar mashti*, a heavenly swirl of saffron and rosewater custard flecked with toasted pistachios. It's perfect. Why didn't we think to move there sooner?

Oh, how naïve I was.

PART III: REFUGEE

(United Nations photo of Mahvash)

13
DESTINY

SPRING 1988

Now I understand why my parents were so hesitant to move away from Tehran. Yazd is a whole different nightmare. Bahá'ís have been persecuted here even before the revolution; since the revolution, it's only become worse. The town is highly conservative and highly religious. I don't mind that I have to wear the long, dark chador over my school uniform and cover myself from head to toe, that's a small inconvenience really when I think about it, a fair trade off. Wear the chador but sleep easy because there are no bombs. On the other hand, there's the realization about just how unsafe it is to not only be a Bahá'í in hiding, but also a woman. I am not allowed to leave the house without an escort, my father. My parents must chaperone me wherever I go, including walking to school every day and even just down the road to the bakery. I am not free to move about on my own, which is suffocating since I've been independently taking busses all over the city to get to classes since I was twelve years old. The girls at school don't like me; they mock my accent and make comments about "wild" girls from the capital. They all know I am Bahá'í because my parents spoke with the principal to explain why I won't be participating in the Islamic prayer during the lunch hour. It's only a matter of time before I get dismissed. I hear the whispers again. Dirty dog.

There is a sense that something worse, far worse is going to happen.

I'm not sure what's next for us. To distract ourselves from the rising stress, Maamaan and I go to the bazaars. The long, winding, and narrow mudwalled passage-ways are always full of bustle and excitement. "Isn't it glamorous?" Maamaan whispers through her veiled chador. We're in the jewelry section where delicate works of art in eighteen-carat gold displays sparkle under lights. Then we go to the spice and herb bazaar where cumin and curry, saffron and teas fill the air. We watch old women picking through baskets of dried flowers to use in medicinal remedies and then picking out henna for their gray locks. The fabric bazaar contains bolt after endless bolt of handmade cotton sheets in every color and pattern imaginable. We wander through the veggie and fruit bazaar and the sweets section, the irresistible spicy smell of cardamom cookies making my mouth water. The baklava from Yazd is world famous and sometimes we buy a couple pieces. But then it is on to the brass bazaar for a cacophonous finish to our stroll. Here young men hand-carve and hammer designs into brass pieces all day long. Hammers pound at tin and the clang bounces off the walls and rings in our ears. We browse decorative trays and practical pots but buy nothing. Our joy is in the witnessing, the reveling.

Every now and then we pass wedding parties, the matriarchs—mothers, grandmothers, aunts—of the family shop in large groups for all the final necessities that make up the bride's dowry. Maamaan explains arranged Muslim marriages to me. It's a very business-like negotiation, and while the bride's family is responsible for the dowry, the groom's parents pay for everything else including the wedding. Before any of that happens, however, they must first negotiate the *Shir Baha*—the fee paid to the bride's mother for the "nursing of the bride as a baby." It will be a gift offered in gold coins or cash. If the groom's family offers too small an amount though, it could be seen as an insult to the bride's mother and the entire wedding might be called off. There is an art and finesse to offering the Shir Baha. Then there is a second negotiation called the *Mehrieh*, a mandatory payment or promise of payment to the bride, perhaps in money, gold, land, or other possessions that will legally become the bride's property in marriage. I tell Maamaan it all sounds so exhausting. "Ah, so you are glad I didn't start filling a room in our house with spoons and bowls and curtains for your dowry when you were just twelve years old?" "Certainly, I am glad. I have other plans." But even as I say it, I sigh. Life has still been plenty exhausting even without needing to plan a wedding. At least these couples know that all their efforts will end in a joyous celebration.

I, on the other hand, am not sure what all my efforts have been for or how this is all going to turn out.

* * *

I am staring at my parents speechless. They had just picked me up from school and walked me home when they pulled me into the small room we rent and whispered that we needed to have a private conversation. And now the thing they have told me has left me speechless. They have a way to get me out of Iran.

For months, I've been trying to make them feel guilty for sending their three oldest children on and holding me back. For months, I've pressured them to get us all out of Iran. But now that they tell me there is a way out—I don't believe the words I am hearing. But I also don't hesitate with my answer. Yes. I am up for it. Yes. "Are you sure?" they press. I gulp and replay their words in my head.

Baba had started. "You remember Bahaar and Kamran, Mr. Danesh's daughter and son, and their two families?" I nodded and he continued. "They're leaving Iran and we're considering sending you with them."

"But we're hesitant because," Maamaan looks at Baba and back at me, "remember their older sister, who was smuggled across the border but caught?"

"Yes, I remember," I whispered, "she spent three years in jail." My parents nod their heads.

"But," I ask, "if we do choose to go, how will we afford it?"

"Well," Maamaan said, "No one in their right mind would buy a house in Tehran during a war, so since we can't sell the house yet, your father and I will stay behind."

My insides went ice cold. "You mean I would leave without you?"

"Yes. You are fragile from this war, emotionally and mentally, your wellbeing depends on getting out of here. But we also know you have an inner strength that will see you through, and we trust God to give you safe passage."

Tears sprung to both their eyes. "It's your best chance for escape and you know how much we trust this family. Are you up for it?"

"Yes, I'm up for it."

"Are you sure?"

There is no way I can let my parents know how scared I am about getting caught at the border and sent to prison. There is also no way that whatever hardships lie ahead that they could possibly be any harder than the life I've been living in Iran. I must find the strength to meet their eyes, to answer boldly and let them know I want to take this risk to change my life and end this miserable existence in Iran. "Yes. I'm sure. What happens next?"

Next happens faster than I expected. We immediately turned in the keys to the house we were renting a room in and the next day I dropped out of school. Baba had already bought bus tickets to get us back to Tehran where we could pack my belongings and he could sell his truck. "Sell your truck, no? You can't!" I had said. "It's the only way, Mooshi. We have nothing left to sell and we need $1,500 to pay the smuggler, but it's OK." "But it's how you make a living. You can't survive without it." "Look, when you are gone then our expenses will be even lower and we can get by on the government's monthly food ration just fine the two of us," he assured me. "Besides, the war will likely end soon, and we'll sell the house and be right behind you." I wasn't so sure, but I had to trust he was right.

There was one thing I'd wanted to ask Baba for a long time, and it seemed like as good a time as any. "Baba, I have one request before we leave Yazd." "Anything. What is it?" "I want to meet your sister, my Aunt Safa." His eyes dropped, and he frowned, "Oh. I don't . . . no, that is not a good idea." "But I might never have the chance to meet her ever again." He looked at the ceiling and sighed. "As you wish. We'll go in the morning."

Baba's father converted to the Bahá'í Faith when his children were still young and his mother remained a devout Muslim, who taught the Qur'án to the people in the village. Once Baba and his brother turned sixteen, they could choose which faith to follow and so they also chose to become Bahá'ís. Baba's sister, Safa, followed in her mother's footsteps. The conversion was a source of so much conflict. When my grandfather died, my Aunt Safa was just fourteen and my widowed grandmother arranged for Safa to marry a cousin, so she would always remain in the Islamic religion. She had never associated with our family, but I'd been long curious to meet her. Before going to her home, we stopped at Yazd's most popular sweets shop and bought Safa's favorite pastries, then we walked the winding alleys until we came to her door. Baba knocked. We waited. "Who's there?" came a voice from inside. "It's your brother," Baba answered. Safa opened the door in amazement. And I stared back in amazement.

She looked so much like Baba. Just shorter and a bit overweight. She was covered from head to toe in the Islamic hijab, but we kissed her on her cheeks, and she welcomed us in to her home and showed us a place where we could sit on the floor. Then she announced, "I'll return in a moment. I just need to go wash my face and do the *ghosl*." When she left the room, I whipped my head around at Baba and he just shrugged as if to say, "See? I told you." The ghosl is a prayer that Muslims say while washing their face and hands whenever their skin comes in contact with something unclean like a dog . . . or as I was then realizing, even their Bahá'í relatives. We saw Aunt Safa go to the pond in the middle of her courtyard to perform the ritual cleansing and then heard her yell out to her daughters, instructing them to "cover up before entering the room because there is a man in the house." A man! Not just any man, their uncle. My cousins came inside and said hello. They brought us tea and then engaged in polite small talk. How old are you now, Mahvash? How are your brothers doing in the US? Aunt Safa mostly grunted at my answers and seemed eager for all the pleasantries to be over. When we finished the tea, she pointedly told her daughters to keep our cups separate for proper washing. That was enough. Baba, uncomfortable and embarrassed, offered our good wishes and good byes. We walked home in silence. I was confused and a bit heartbroken, more for Baba then for myself. Only years later would we speak of that day, with Baba quietly saying, "It's OK. Safa is just ignorant. If she was wise, she wouldn't have acted that way. It's all OK."

Back in Tehran, the truck sells quickly, and I begin to pack my small backpack. I pick up the old barbie doll with the spiky hair that Leila and I shared. "You'll have to stay behind." I trace the photos of friends and families with my fingertips and roll a pawn in my hand from the chessboard Cyrus and Kia taught me to play on. Nearly everything I pick up I must put back down. Maamaan helps me make the hard decisions of what must be left behind: albums, cassette tapes, shoes, school yearbooks. She reminds me that new and beautiful mementos are waiting for me. I must dig deep in myself to find the strength to look at the bigger picture; it's heart wrenching but none of these things in our home have any true value. A bomb could drop tonight and burn it all to the ground. A bit of hope, that is all I want to put in my backpack and all I need to carry in my heart.

Maamaan surprises me with just the bit of hope I need. "If you have room, I'd like to give you these. I've been saving them for you." First, she places a beautiful gold ring with a black stone in my hand. It has a Bahá'í carving of the calligraphic symbol for the Greatest Name; and she tells me it belonged to her mother. Next, she drops a pair of small gold earrings in the shape of a flower into my palm. Finally, she dangles a small gold chain with a butterfly pendant above my hand. I have only tears, no words. Maamaan hugs me tight against her chest and tells me everything is going to be just fine. Then we get back to the task at hand.

After repacking several times it's down to this: two t-shirts, one set of pajamas, one pair of light pants, and a couple pairs of underwear and socks. Toothbrush, toothpaste, floss (courtesy of Baba who is adamant that I maintain good oral hygiene no matter how dire the circumstances), a comb, some feminine pads. I sincerely hope I don't have my period during the trip across the border. But even if I don't, my nose is sure to bleed. Extra tissues and cotton balls get stuffed in every crack and crevice of my bag. The nosebleeds started back in fifth grade, and always as soon as the weather got hot and dry. They were so bad and so constant that the doctors even tried cauterizing the veins in my nose numerous times, but that still didn't stop the blood. The only thing that sort of helps are Vitamin K injections. Every week I go to the clinic for shots. Every summer the needles leave tracks and bruises on my arms. Embarrassed, I have found an odd relief in Iran's conservative dress code that keeps my arms hidden away from sight and judgment. Into my bag go a few family photos, an address book with contact information for my brothers, for Leila, and for a cousin in Pakistan. I take a blank notebook and pen for new memories and an old notebook full of notes and memories from school friends. I can't bear to part with the Seiko watch that Cyrus sent me for my fifth-grade graduation or with my favorite watch, the colorful Swatch the boys sent me for my eighth-grade graduation. I reason that since it snaps on my wrist, it doesn't count as packing since it won't take up any room in the bag.

"Maamaan, I've been thinking. Is it possible for Rana to come with me?" Rana is ten years older than me but has always been like a big sister. She was expelled from university with other Bahá'í students before she finished her degree to become a teacher, so instead, she took her natural talents in fashion and became a successful bridal gown designer. Over the years she's turned down numerous marriage suitors and has often said she wants to leave the country. Maamaan thinks it's a fabulous idea and calls up Rana to discuss it with her and her parents. My Aunt Zinat and Rana come over and the conversation does not go as I anticipated. First Maamaan explains the situation, the smuggler's fee, the plan, the family I am going with, etc.

"I'm thrilled! This is the opportunity I've been waiting for, and it will be so good to be going with Mahvash!" Rana says. A wave of peace washes over me; I really don't want to do this alone. Aunt Zinat says, "I mean, it certainly sounds reasonable. Risky, but life here is risky too. So when can we meet the smugglers?" "Oh," Maamaan says, "we have no idea who the smugglers are. We've never met them; that's part of the safety plan." "What? Are you insane, Monir? You're handing your fifteen-year-old daughter off to men you've never met?" "We trust the family who is organizing this." "But don't you know how they rape girls along the way?"

Just like that any peace I had is gone. Terror rises in my throat. Aunt Zinat turns and looks directly at me now. "And what if you get caught? You'll go to prison," she pauses, unblinking. "They rape girls in there too." I'm sure I am as white as a sheet. Aunt Zinat takes Rana's hand and stands up. "If I can't meet the smugglers, I certainly won't be handing my daughter over to them. Monir, don't be crazy. Reconsider." Rana turns and embraces me for what may be the last time. Then, she takes my cheeks in her hands, and says, "Until we meet again." "Until we meet again," I answer, choking down tears. When they are gone, I'm not sure which I fear more: getting raped or Maamaan changing her mind.

On my final night in my home with my parents, the other families I am journeying with come over. We will all leave together in the early morning. There's Bahaar and Kayvaan with their three children ages fourteen, eleven and seven; Kamran and Roya who have a six-year-old, and Roya's younger brother who is a little older than me at nineteen. That makes ten of us in our caravan to freedom. Bahaar and Kamran are siblings and the children of our dear Mr. Danesh. Our home bustles with small children and anxious, excited energy. When Maamaan is nervous, she cannot stop talking, but that makes her a great hostess; she makes the rounds chatting with everyone. Baba retreats to a corner and watches, smiling in silence. People start to laugh but end up in tears or start to cry and end up laughing. As I walk through every room of the house, saying goodbye to memories—both good and bad—I feel all the same fear mixed with excitement as the others do. It is almost more than the mind can handle. This house holds the ten most terrible years of my life, but now that I am saying goodbye once and for all, it's not so easy to release. There have been good times here as well, and some of my memories are only unlocked when I look at things like the poshties we use to take to the roof in the summer, or the lamp shade I punctured running into it during a game of Marco Polo, or the corners Leila and I sat in and studied late into the night by candlelight. I catch sight of Baba in the corner, sipping tea from his cup, and I am transported back to when I was small enough to curl up in his lap. I'd stay up late, waiting for him to get home, and he'd let me sit in his lap while he drank his tea from that very same cup he sips from now. He would stroke my hair and tell me sweet things until I fell asleep. Tonight, it's impossible to sleep. We are just hours away from our lives changing forever.

When night turns into morning, Baba walks to the bakery for warm fresh bread and makes me breakfast just as he has done every day for as long as I can remember. I watch him heat the milk, make the tea, and set out the feta cheese and quince jam. Then he joins me on the floor. We sit on the sofreh, the handwoven one, a gift from Great Grandma Naneh. It's just the two of us. It is my favorite breakfast, one I know so well, but today we eat it seasoned with the salt of our tears. When the others wake, it's time to say goodbye.

Maamaan has insisted that she stay with me for as long as possible, so the smugglers have allowed her to fly with me from Tehran to the Zahedan airport, the city a few hundred miles away from the border of Pakistan where I will meet the first smuggler. Her instructions are strict though; we are not to say goodbye, hold hands, hug, kiss, or shed any tears once we come off the plane. She will end up speaking nonstop the entire plane ride, whispering advice to me, and saying a long goodbye, but right now it is Baba's time to say goodbye.

He chants a beautiful prayer for our protection, then he holds his prayer book up high and I walk under it. "You are in the hands of God," he says then hands me the little prayer book he has found refuge in every day of his life. "And every day I beg God to look after my little girl and keep her safe." I kiss the book and slip it in my backpack. Baba holds me so tightly against him, and I can't breathe his scent in deeply enough. I don't want to forget any part of him, not the scratch of his unshaven face against my cheek, not the feel of his thick fingers holding my hair, or his lips kissing my forehead. "You're going to the United States now," he whispers. "Just like I always promised you would."

The short two kilometers to the airport feel like two hours. The streets are empty and I watch the sun start to rise over the city. I press my cheek against the cool glass of the taxi. It feels good against my skin. As the world turns in slow motion, the unbearable pain I've endured here feels so wrong, like I was born at the wrong time and raised in the wrong place. All the same, this city is familiar to me and I ache thinking of how it has been destroyed and wondering what destruction still lies ahead for it. I take it all in, knowing it is the last sun rise I will ever see in Tehran.

If people are talking, I can't hear them. It's just me, the dawn, and my heartbeat.

14

ESCAPE

ZAHEDAN, IRAN: MAY 1988

I had been thrilled to take my first airplane ride ever, but now that the plane is on the ground, all my excitement has turned to dread. My back stiffens against the seat. I see my hands clutching the arm rests, but I can't release my grasp. I am cold. Maamaan is talking, but what is she saying? Her voice is far away. I hear zippers closing up bags, people clearing their throats, and my heart beating in my ears. But Maamaan's words. I can't make sense of anything. I know that I must move. I must pull myself together, remember the smuggler's instructions—don't look scared or emotional or lost. *Don't look suspicious.* I force myself to release the arm rests and then everything happens in slow motion. I rise from my aisle seat. I get my backpack. I take one last look down at my mother. Our eyes lock and then hers overflow with tears. I force my tears into my throat. Her mouth moves silently, "*Ghorboonet beram,*" and she nods once, slowly. Just like that she's given me permission to walk away—to walk away and not look back.

I am walking. I am quivering. I throw my shoulders back and try to look like I've done this before. This. Walking away from everything I know and everyone I love and straight into a great and terrifying unknown. I exit the plane and scan for my traveling companions. There. I hurry over and try to blend in, just another daughter. A young girl alone at an airport would be highly suspicious. *Don't look suspicious.* Whatever casual looks like when every nerve is on edge, that is what we do. I am certain we stick out like a sore thumb, but then again, no one seems to take any notice of us in all the normal airport bustle. We begin to make our way toward baggage claim and I can feel her eyes on me. Maamaan. Maamaan! My heart cries back to her. I do not turn around, but I know she is watching my every step. Watching until the very last moment, when I am finally swallowed up in the crowd and lost from her sight.

There is nothing for us at baggage claim. All we possess is on our backs, but we need to exit through the doors near the baggage claim con-veyor belts and start looking for a blue Paykan—a modest looking sedan. There are a few. But there's only one with a bearded man leaning against it wearing a white skull cap and khaki-colored Balochi clothing. That's our man—tall, skinny, thirty-ish. Go.

We greet each other casually, just enough to look like acquaintances, not enough to arouse suspicion. His face is serious, giving away nothing. He points to a second car, and the ten of us quickly split up into two groups. My hand is on the door and a rush of thoughts flash through my mind. Is this man for real? Is he a fraud? If I open this door and climb inside, my life is in his hands. Do I trust the words of a stranger? I think of all the people trying to escape who have been left halfway, or robbed, or caught. Some people get smuggled on the backs of motorcycles and others make the journey on foot. This sedan—this is the deluxe version of smuggling. All I can do at this point is trust; I take a deep breath and climb inside.

We're inside and we're moving. The airport is fading from view and the roads lead us out of town. Fewer and fewer cars, fewer and fewer peo-ple and finally a quiet alleyway. We pull into a driveway and the car parks. Tall, solid metal gates close behind us, and a wall of bricks surround the courtyard and home. We get out and follow the driver into the large home and into a living room. The entire floor is covered wall-to-wall with Persian carpets and against the walls are poshties. Some people find a seat on the floor. Most of us stand in uncomfortable silence. What do we do now? No one wants to ask. The two drivers ask to talk to the adults in private. The kids are to go play on the other side of the room. I look at the kids walking away, and I look at the adults around me. I know I am only fifteen, and two of the other oldest children are eleven and fourteen. But they have their parents. I am on my own. Two weeks ago, I needed my parents to walk me to school in Yazd. Today, I am in charge of my life. So I stay.

"Bathroom's down this hallway, kitchen's out that door on the left. Make yourselves comfortable," the driver tells us, "but don't spread out too much. You're on standby at a safe house. You need to be ready to leave at a moment's notice. Don't unpack, just use what you need then put it back." "How long will we be here?" "Can't say. We've sent our men out to scout the roads. Not all are safe, some have security checkpoints and roadblocks. Some are easier to get through with a bribe than others. We want to be certain that our *connections* will be at each checkpoint when we're there."

The two drivers continue to speak. They avoid looking at me and only talk to the adults and I don't understand everything they say. Do I even exist? Am I here? Everything is hazy, surreal. I look over at the kids playing on the other side of the room and it hits me: I've taken my place with the adults. My childhood is over.

"Just keep busy or the anxiety will get to you." They leave us with backgammon and chess sets and playing cards to take our mind off the ensuing waiting game. Later we are given food and water, but we're mostly left to ourselves. In the evening, they return with mattresses, sheets, and blankets. It's awkward; I'm to sleep in a bedroom with all the children. The adults stay up late, pacing the floor, drinking tea, discussing. They can't sleep, but neither can we. The scratch of chess pieces moving across boards and of dice slapping the backgammon box over, and over, and over go on long into the night.

The next day it is the same. We are getting anxious. When the drivers arrive, we mob around them but are told, "Be patient. We're making sure the checkpoints are safe before we get out of here. Because once we're out . . . there's no turning back." On the third day, I realize there is only so much chess you can play. Like the adults, I pace the floor. I study the carpets. I stare into space. It is late afternoon when a man on a motorcycle drives into the yard. He jumps down without turning it off, runs into the house to where our guides are. He's covered in dust and speaking fast, trying to catch his breath. The guides rush into the living room and tell us we must leave at once. "We're going to prepare the truck. You have five minutes."

Waiting these three days was torturous, but I'm not sure the sheer panic I feel now is any better. Everyone is rushing everywhere at once. I grab my toothbrush from the bathroom and pull on my school uniform, wrap a scarf around my head, and run toward the door for my boots. Parents are yelling at kids, "Look around, don't leave anything behind!" I wonder, what's left to leave at this point? But then again, when you have little, the little you have becomes even more precious. Our guide runs in, out of breath, "It's time. We've got gasoline and water. Let's go, let's go, let's go." My heart beats in my palms, my neck, my forehead, my chest. I am a single, throbbing pulse. "This way!" He takes us to the back of the house and when we see the giant SUV truck we break out running for it. "Get in the back. Hold your bags on your lap. Sit low and find something to hang on to. It's going to be dark. Things will get thrown around." We nod.
"And you must be silent. Make sure the kids don't make a sound. Do you understand?" We understand. But he hasn't told us all. He saves the worst for last.

We put the children at the rear with their backs against the cab, the rest of us line the sides and the gasoline and water cans are placed in the middle. The tarp is pulled out, but before they throw it over us and pin it down, our driver gives the final warning: "I don't know how many days it will take to cross into Pakistan. Safety is crucial, so if conditions aren't safe, we wait somewhere along the way. If we're caught, we all go to prison, and . . ." he pauses to look me up and down, "perhaps worse. You're very young and very pretty." I break out in the familiar cold sweat. Not this, not again. The terror starts to claw at me; I swallow hard forcing it back down. "It's possible you won't see me again. We might get separated. If you are left alone, you must stay put. Stay silent. Trust that someone will return for you." I've gone ice cold and in my ears is the sound of bombs dropping outside my home. The terror is here; it has me at the throat and I am screaming the silent scream that dies inside. The other driver has turned the engine on and the rumble of the truck shakes me back to my senses. There is no way but through. I bend my head over my knees, my backpack secured between my legs, and the smelly, thick canvas comes down over our heads, sealing in the darkness that has long been my life. I kiss the Bahá'í ring on my finger and tell myself there is daylight on the other side.

The truck is backing up and I am clutching the butterfly around my neck and whispering the prayers that Baba loved. *Is there any Remover of difficulties save God?*

Then Baba's voice is warm and clear in my ear, "Mooshi, don't worry so much. Don't you know? You can't escape your destiny."

15

BORDERS

ZAHEDAN TO PAKISTAN

At some point my nose begins to bleed. The sticky warmth reminds me I am still alive; something I've been less and less sure of with every mile after rocky mile. Between the ragged jolts and thumps, I somehow manage to unzip my pack and find cotton balls to stuff up my nose. Such a small action, but it helps pinpoint my mind—in the darkness I've slowly started to lose track of time and reality. Everything hurts. Everything's bruised. I am acutely aware of bones I never before realized I had. But for one thing I am most grateful, despite the suffocating heat of May, despite the brutal bumps, despite everyone's deepening nausea—no one has vomited. I fear if one person loses the contents of their stomach the smell will be too much. I will break. Or I will vomit too, a chain reaction, a sort of filth I don't like to imagine. Yet I am imagining it. Because what else is there to imagine? The worst thoughts keep coming to me and I keep pushing them back, holding them off. Hour after hour after hour. I am exhausted, body, mind, spirit. All.

Suddenly—praise be to God—the truck stops. My heart leaps. The cab door opens then slams shut. Footsteps crunch, hurrying . . . away from the truck. My stomach drops and all is silent. Under the tarp, we barely dare to breathe. We wait and wait some more. How long have we waited?

An hour? Two? I can't stand it anymore. I try to peek out, but the tarp is strapped down so tightly that I only manage a couple inches. Mountains. The sun has nearly set. Still we say nothing. Finally, the footsteps return and with it a voice. "I'm loosening the tarp now." We gulp in the fresh air. Fill and empty our lungs again and again. Stretch our stiff necks and reach our arms high above our heads. Our eyes slowly adjust to the darkness. There is light from the stars. We're in a narrow valley sandwiched between tall rocks and . . . we aren't alone. Flashlights blink in the distance and voices echo through the canyon. The driver brings us bread and water. We circle up, sharing the bread and cup. The first person to take a sip of the coveted water coughs and spits it out. The second person does the same. "Tastes of gasoline," he spats. The driver tries it and agrees. "In our rush, we must have put fresh water in containers previously used for gasoline." My heart sinks. No water? A new sort of panic sets in. Desperation. Like I've only been able to just hold onto my sanity because I knew eventually, I could at least quench this thirst and wash the stifled screams stuck in my throat away for a night. The driver tries the other water containers. There is only one that's still pure. But at least there's one.

"Time to rest. We'll stay here for a few hours. There's still a long journey ahead." The desert night is cold but it's also peaceful and still. My body tingles and begins to release the tension from the ride as I curl up next to the others on the steadfast earth. We fall asleep sitting up, slowly sinking onto each other's shoulders and laps as fitful dreams overtake us.

"Wake up. Time to go. You can go to the bathroom behind the rocks over there, and you really should try to because there will be no breaks before we reach our next stopping point." The bit of morning light brings warmth to our stiff and cold limbs, but more than that—hope. I stare straight up at the sky and into the rising sun. I know we must hurry, but I need this. I need a few minutes in the light. Now I can see where the voices were coming from last night. Down the valley is a line of the biggest SUV trucks I have ever seen, thirty at least. Our truck is about in the middle. Is each one smuggling refugees? The thought is a comfort. Here we are surrounded by others with the same intrepid spirit, the same broken dreams but fierce hope, the same will to live, to survive, to thrive. But then, I am alarmed. Every single truck has machine guns set up on top. Someone else asks my question out loud: "What exactly are those trucks smuggling?" "We're in a caravan; they're smuggling gold, Persian rugs, drugs, other illegal items. Items the US won't allow exported because of the trade embargo against Iran." "But what about the guns? We don't have a gun." The driver looks uncomfortable, he hunches up his shoulders and gives us a sympathetic look. "We're the only truck smuggling people." In other words, some cargo is valuable enough to kill for if threatened or robbed. Other cargo, not so much. "Don't worry though, it really is safer for us to tag along with them. A gunfight isn't likely and we'll separate from them soon enough."

We sit in the truck bed and eat the bread from last night; it's cold and hard to chew, harder even to swallow. The truck engines start to turn on one by one and then each heads out, leaving a thick trail of dust behind them. "Time for the tarp to go back on." I take one last look at the sun still making its way over the mountain peak and whisper good morning to Baba and Maamaan. Then everything is black again.

It's like being on a fast-running bulldozer tackling every cliff and rock in its path. Again it is hours of this and again my nose bleeds relentlessly. Again I am exhausted. When the truck stops, the driver jumps out and rushes to the back, leaving the engine running. The tarp peels back. Sun! "Grab your bags. Run. Hide behind a rock. Iranian guards are nearby. Wait here until another truck comes for you. Don't move. Don't make a sound." We ask no questions. Bags, run, rock, hide. I race for a three- or four-foot tall rock as parents panic to get their kids out of the truck and scramble to find a good hiding spot. We watch our driver jump back behind the wheel and drive away as fast as he can to catch up with the other trucks. We watch the convoy fade out of sight. We look at each other in silence, the fear in our eyes speaks for itself. What just happened? Have we been stranded on purpose? What if no one returns for us? The sun beats down and the desert sand heats up. It's the middle of nowhere. Nowhere. Just hills, sand, rocks, and more rocks. Nothing lives here. No plants. No animals. How long can we last here? The complete silence of the desert is ominous. Every so often we check in with each other. Just a head nod and a wave. Everyone is here. Everyone is ok. Everyone is managing.

I am running out of cotton balls and tissues at a frightening pace. In this heat, there is no stopping the blood. One hand holds the tissues to my face, squeezing my nose, the other tries to fan myself with my scarf. Still, the blood drops in spots all over my clothes. The sun burns hotter with every passing hour and there is no relief. We are completely exposed. I hear Roya trying to hush her whining, tired child. Poor thing. We are all so hungry, thirsty, hot, and tired. I lean my head back and close my eyes. What if the trucks forget about us? What if they don't come back? How long will we wait? A few hours? Days? What if, what if, what—

A truck pulls up in the early evening. The engine is left running and a new man jumps out but with the same instructions we are now used to. "Get in the back, stay low, hold on tight." I welcome the change, and in the truck bed we find water bottles waiting for us. Nothing has ever tasted so sweet. The tarp descends, the engine revs, and we're going at the same break-neck pace of our previous driver. Getting more of the same bruises on all our same bony spots. Hours later we come to a stop again. The engine turns off, door opens, slams shut. Tarp comes off. It is just as dark outside as under the tarp. The driver holds a flashlight and tells us to follow him. My feet sink in soft sand as we make our way to a squeaky wood door of what must be some abandoned shack. "Get comfortable. Get some rest. Wait and don't make any noise. I promise—someone will return for you." Our lives rest on so many promises; promises of men we don't know and will never know. Who are these men? How did they come to be here? Why do they do this? Do they have families at home? Are their wives saying prayers for them even now? I should pray for them too. I will pray for them. I will make myself remember them. If I make it out of this desert, out of this country, I will make sure I remember these men and pray for blessings upon their lives.

He's gone, but he's left us with water. My arms reach blindly for the walls. Mud. I find a spot on the floor. Earth. But soft and sandy. It smells foul—of animals and urine. I don't care. I lean against the wall and find the crackers in my bag. My body says to stuff them in my mouth, chew hard and fast; I am so hungry, but I resist the urge. I nibble softly, slowly, so as not to be heard. I am not up for sharing. Am I actually settling into this crazy routine? Getting used to the transitions—do as they say, don't ask questions, act fast, be silent, stay patient. Still, I have no idea where I am or what the plan is for tomorrow. I didn't even know what the plan was for today. My eyes start to water. I just want to cry. No, I want to sob. Here I am sitting in some disgusting shack, probably surrounded by rattlesnakes and scorpions and other creepy crawly things that have always horrified me just to think about, and I feel so alone and so far from anything, everything— my home and parents yes, but also my mind, my heart, my very self. I don't feel like myself. Who am I anymore? Will I even get to answer that question? Will I even like who I am if I make it to the other side of this journey? This is horrible. Everything about this journey is horrible. Everything about war is horrible. It is horrible that this is what humans must resort to—to being smuggled like illegal goods. I am human. We are all human. How can I be illegal? Does illegal mean dangerous? Me. The little mouse. What was I thinking saying yes to this? I was thinking this: It is horrible to live always in fear. It is horrible to live among bombs. It is horrible to have your rights taken away from you. It is horrible to have religion forced on you or be forced to change your religion. If another country is willing to accept me for who I am, they will not be disappointed. I will bring my best. I will bring my all. How can I not? How can I not work every moment of every day to build a good and true life for myself and everyone around me? I've seen too much. I know too much to ever take life, and home, and community for granted. I know how precious they are and how easily they are lost. But they won't be lost on my watch, not if I can help it. I slip in and out of a troubled sleep.

The door creaks open and a man in baggy clothes with a big mole on his cheek walks in. "Get your things and get back to the truck as fast as possible." We're up fast, shaking the dirt from our clothes, creating a cloud that makes it hard to breathe. Cracks in the walls and roof let in the early morning light. The shack is barely holding itself together, kind of like me. We step out into the bright desert sun, and I raise my palms face up to soak up every bit of daylight I can before we are pinned beneath the tarp again. At the truck the man with the mole tells us we've come to the most dangerous part of our journey. "We're near the border of Pakistan, in Afghanistan, not far from the guards post." What! We still aren't in Pakistan? Even after almost a week of traveling? I can't believe it. "This area is under close surveillance, and if we are caught, we'll be sent to an Iranian prison. So pay attention and follow my rules exactly, OK?" Every head bobs up and down. We have no other option.

The truck flies across the desert. We get cooked under the tarp and feel sicker and sicker as the day heats up. I have bruises on my bruises at this point and I'm not even sure the skin on my back is still there. Certainly not on my spine. That was rubbed raw miles ago. We've traveled so far already; it had seemed like we'd made good progress, and yet it could all be for nothing. At any moment it could all be over. We'll get caught. We'll go to prison. Everyone is saying prayers, even the children, for our safety. My mouth keeps getting drier as the panic sets in. There is nothing I can do but put trust in God's hands. I focus on my prayers and not the pain, not the panic. Even though I don't know how or where this journey will end. Even though I don't know what life will look like on the other side when I finally meet my brothers in the US. Even though there is so much unknown ahead, still I know I must not give in to my fear. I thank God for Cyrus and Kia and all the piggy back rides they gave me; for Leila for studying late into the night for exams with me, for being brave enough to follow her path; for Maamaan who always hopes for us, even if she can't hope for herself; for Baba . . . Baba, who's big hands stroked my hair, who sang me to sleep, who has never, ever, ever doubted in the goodness of

God. I am always so full of doubt. Baba has always said, "It is not wrong to be full of doubts, it is only wrong to succumb to them." It's so hard Baba; it's so hard. You don't know what it's like under this tarp . . . in this blackness. You don't know.

The truck finally comes to a stop and there's the comforting sound of the cab door opening and slamming shut, and the tarp peeling back. "Congratulations," our driver smiles, "you're on Pakistani soil now." We kiss and hug each other and cry freely, and we don't care that our faces are tear-stained, blood splattered, crusted in salt and dirt, or that only moments ago we were the most miserable we had ever been. We've crossed over. "Grab your stuff and follow me." He leads us through a large yard fenced in by trees. It is dusk and there's electricity here—warm lights flood from the windows of multiple, small, one-room structures. He leads us to one of our own, the walls and roof are made of mud, but it has glass windows and is cleaner than the shack we stayed in last night. "You'll spend the night here. The journey isn't over though. Still a long way to go, a few more days at least before we are safe. But at least," he adds casually, "on this side of the border bribes go a long way to help with that." The adults raise their eyebrows at this statement. "It's true. They won't deport you if you bribe them," he says and then walks out.

I wonder if this is a hint of things to come.

16

BEYOND

Using a bit of water and the corner of a scarf gets me only somewhat cleaned up but still feeling fresher than ever. There is no toilet, just a hole in the ground in the back, but it serves its purpose. Inside we wait while someone, elsewhere, prepares us dinner. Our bodies buzz, draining all this excess adrenaline, energy, emotion. It's hard to wrap my mind around where I am and what I've been through, how my body has been transported so many miles away from Tehran. Smiles break out, sighs of relief, and we find ourselves shrugging and shaking our heads in disbelief as if to say, "Wow, did we just . . .? We did." There are no words.

Soon, our smuggler returns with jugs of water and after that some other men bring us dinner. Warm bread with spicy daal and perfectly steamed rice! Such a luxury after days of cold, hard road snacks. I eat it more quickly than I'd like and wash it down with lots and lots of water. A full belly makes for a happy heart. I wander to the window, still so grateful to be able to stand up tall and stretch my limbs. A party seems to be taking shape out there. A large group of men smoke, talk, and drink tea. They are quiet when they eat their dinner, but afterward the noise picks up again and then several come toward "our" safe house. Suddenly we have half a dozen faces pressed against our windows. Old men, young men, some missing teeth, some fully bearded, wearing turbans or small white caps. We are unnerved as is, and then it gets worse. The men start spitting. Another burps into the glass and the rest find that hilarious. Laughter ensues and more burping all around. Other men come and take their place to get a look at us and join in the burping fest. I look at Bahaar and Roya, there's uncertainty in their eyes. We do not know if we should be alarmed. This is disgusting and irritating behavior, but it's also frightening. Hamid gets up, finds the light switch, and turns it off to cloak us once again in darkness. There. We are hidden from their eyes. Now, without being seen by the men, he tries to discreetly lock the door. I don't know if he succeeds or not because within minutes there are flashlights beaming through the glass and into our faces. The men keep laughing and spitting and belching. They do this for hours, robbing us of whatever bit of peace we thought we'd found and stealing our ability to fully relax and actually get some sleep. Eventually, they tire and move on and we do, finally, get some rest on the bare floor.

In the morning, there are just a few men around and all are working in the yard, cleaning up the garden or attending to the trucks. We are given bread and tea for our breakfast and by noon the smuggler is back. It's back to the normal routine. Into the truck. Heads down. Tarp on. Maybe it's because I ate a full meal and got some real sleep, or maybe it's because I've got thicker skin now, but the drive doesn't feel as bad. This driver is no different than the others—he's cruising over hard bumps and landing in every pothole. That's it for the day, a rough drive straight to another safe house. This one, thankfully, looks a little more civilized. There are women and children here and that is a comfort. After another warm meal and water, we clean up and lounge for a bit before a new man comes in and gives us instructions about tomorrow. "OK," he says, "tomorrow is going to be the most challenging part of the journey yet because we've hit a number of roadblocks." He puts a hand up to start ticking off problems on his fingers. "First, we couldn't find a safe route. That means we will have to risk going through a security checkpoint. Two, we don't have any contacts at these checkpoints. Three, that means we have to get through without any lookouts or bribes to smooth the way." "Well that certainly doesn't sound promising," one of the men whispers. "But," the smuggler continues, "we have a big van prepared for you. We've removed the seats and created compartments for you to hide inside. We'll put some merchandise on top of you to hide you further. However—" he scanned the room. "I need one female to accompany me in the front seat and pose as a passenger—a family member—when we cross over. I'll leave it to you to choose that woman."

In a flash, all eyes are on me. Oh no no no, I shake my head. "Please, don't make me . . . please," I beg. "Mahvash, we have to stay with the kids to comfort and quiet them," argues Bahaar. "And besides," adds Roya, "Your skin is darker than ours. You are a more believable candidate for a passenger from this region." The men agree, so I really don't have much choice. "OK," I tell the smuggler, forcing myself to be brave and look him in the eyes, "I'll do it." But I'm truly terrified and spend the rest of the night worrying about what will happen tomorrow. How will I convince armed guards that I'm this driver's sister or cousin or who knows what? What if I fall apart right in front of the guards? If I fail to do my part, we all get deported. We all go to jail.

So tired. I'm just so tired. Can I really carry one more thing on these worn out, tiny shoulders of mine? My body feels weak and limp. There's no fighting it, I'm sick with fear, and yet there's still no turning back.

In the morning we are treated to warm bread and tea again. It's nourishing to have had two regular dinners and breakfasts in a row. After breakfast, the driver hands me some Pakistani clothes. "That's the *ghamis*," he says handing me a dress, "and these are *shalvar*," he hands me baggy pants. "And a shawl to cover your hair . . . and preferably, your face." I perk up at those last words. "My face?" "Yes, sorry, I know it's going to be so hot, but—" "—I don't mind! Really. I'll do it happily." Oh, thank you God. I much prefer to hide behind the shawl then to bare my face and expose all its emotion to the guards at the border. My new outfit is so fresh, so colorful and clean. I stuff my blood stained and dirt covered clothes in my backpack and then make my way with the others to the covered barn where the van waits. Everyone else get situated in the little compartments designed for them, some lying down flat and others hunched over. I take my seat in the front next to the Pakistani smuggler, not daring to look him in the face.

Our drive is smooth compared to the past week. We're on a fairly groomed dirt road and driving at a reasonable pace for once. The sun is out in full force and the van is without an air conditioner. When I go to roll down a window, the smuggler raises a hand and says, "Better not." He points to a big dust cloud forming on the road ahead from all the traffic. The van heats up like an oven and I swear the engine must be directly under my seat because my bottom is getting absolutely fried. I shift back and forth trying to relieve the burning heat. The smuggler shifts the van into a lower gear, and I look up. There's a long line of pickup trucks, vans, and SUVs ahead of us. "This is it," he says. I gulp. My heart pounds hard in my chest and my pulse throbs in my neck. I start to sweat even more than I already was. "Speak minimally and only if necessary when we encounter the guards. I'll do the talking. You really only need to say hello in Arabic," he explains. I nod. I can do this. I can do this. "It's better if you avoid eye contact too and keep your head low." I pull the scarf up more to cover my hair, head, neck, and face as much as possible. I can feel my cheeks flush red hot under the fabric and I see my body trembling under the colorful folds of the ghamis. I clasp my hands in my lap to steady them.

Every vehicle stops and the drivers talk to the guards before they pass beyond the checkpoint. As we inch closer and closer, my breathing gets heavier and heavier. I stare at my feet; I just want to curl up, be small, and cry. But I know if I lose my head, I put everyone in danger. They are hidden back there, probably breathing hard and sweating with fear too. Their faith is in me and my faith is in God. I say a silent prayer for protection and then it's time.

"Pull down your window and say *salaam alaikum*," the smuggler says, jolting me into the moment. My fingers slip on the handle and I rush to correct myself and roll the window down fast. "Salaam alaikum," I say but I don't think the voice is my own. "Salaam alaikum," the guard says, then crosses in front of the van to the driver's side. The two men speak and

then the guard circles the van and asks the driver to step out for a few minutes. When life dangles in the balance, time stands still. Sometime later, the
door clicks open, the smuggler steps in, turns the key in the ignition and
pulls forward. The gate lifts and we pass through without a word between
us. That's it. Is that it? I don't know if it's over or not, but I think it's over.
The driver is going fast, and I realize I've been holding my breath and am
hyperventilating now. I feel nauseated, and my body goes limp as a wet rag.
My nose starts to bleed all over my clothes, but what can I do? My bag is in
the back. I don't care anymore. Soon we're in a village with mud homes and
short, half-broken fences and crumbling walls. One fenced yard is for us.
We drive in and a gate closes behind.

"Alright. That's it. You can get out now," the smuggler directs. My fingers barely have the strength to turn the door handle, but they do, and I slip
down from the high front seat into the green yard. I take a few shaky steps
before I have to sit. In my peripheral, I see the shadows of the others being
helped from the van, but then everything goes completely black and silent.

The air is sweet and cool on this shady balcony, and there's a lovely
thick carpet beneath me. I see a blue sky behind the climbing vines and
close my eyes again because I don't want to wake up from this dream.
Oh, but it's not a dream. I hear the voices of my companions and immediately sit up and look around. They are here with me, with big smiles.
They say I wasn't passed out long. In the air is the smell of freshly baked
bread. The night continues as the past two have, but here it feels even safer,
and certainly more civilized. The smugglers return later in the evening
with satisfied smiles, "Everything has gone as planned and has been very,
very smooth." What would it have been like if it wasn't smooth, I wonder?
"Tomorrow is easy, and you'll reach your final destination." The rest of the
night I pace, antsy for it to be morning, ready to leave this journey behind
and start my new journey as a refugee.

We pile into the truck bed the next morning and hunch over for the
last time. I won't say it's bittersweet. It's not. We are all ready to live in the
light and be treated as humans again. A few hours under the tarp and then

we start to hear motorcycles revving, cars honking, and people shouting. We must be in a town of sorts. The truck comes to a stop and metal gates shut. Tarp comes off. This time we follow the driver through a narrow and smelly blue-tiled hallway. The floors are sticky and crusty with dirt. He leads us out into a motel reception foyer. Behind the counter is a man in a cloud of smoke, he takes a final drag on his cigarette and then stubs it out in a glass tray piled high with old butts and gives us a wide, crusty smile. Our driver speaks with him briefly, gets a key, and motions for us to follow him. The man lights another cigarette, sucks in the smoke, and watches us each as we pass.

Our room is small, but big enough to hold ten single beds. I toss my backpack on the one at the end and lie back, exhausted. Sharp springs poke my bruised body and the thin mattress smells heavily of tobacco. I can already feel a headache coming on triggered from the smell, but at least, we are safe. I listen from my bed to what our driver is saying. "You're in Quetta, the largest city of the Baluchistan region. We're near the Pakistan-Afghanistan border. This town is a trade and communications center between the two countries." My headache is in full force now, shooting pain up both sides of my temples. "In the morning," the driver continues, "the motel administrator will call you a cab to take you to the United Nations camp for the next phase of your journey. You'll need to have your pictures taken before you go though. It's late in the day, so I'm not sure who we'll find, but we're going to try to get someone to come to the motel tonight to take photos." I stand so I can thank him properly with the others before he takes his leave. He assures us he'll call his contact in Tehran who will let our families know we made it safely across. I can only imagine the sleepless nights Maamaan and Baba have endured while they have waited for this phone call. It's been nearly ten days now of not knowing, not hearing, just trusting.

On the way out the door, the driver casually remarks that, "You all need to blend in. You should start wearing traditional Pakistani clothes and get rid of your Iranian clothes." He points to another man we don't know, but who has been at the motel seemingly waiting for us and the driver, "He can help you get the clothes. I have to go prepare a van for another group." This new man tells us about how much clothes cost and we pick through our pockets trying to come up with enough money. Then he tells us he needs a woman to volunteer to go with him to the bazaar to buy the clothes for the women and children. Silence. No one volunteers. I feel all eyes on me—the most obvious candidate. I wait for someone to make a case about my dark skin or lack of baggage. Finally, one of the fathers starts to say, "Well, how about Mah—" I cut him off right there. "No. I'm not going. Absolutely not. I refuse to be separated from the group and go out alone with a man I don't know who has just taken a bunch of money from us." It feels good to say no with such strength. "I've come this far and I'm not going to throw it all away and walk away with a stranger. OK? I'll take my chances and wear my Iranian-Islamic uniform to the interview tomorrow." I cross my arms and sit down hard on my cot.

The adults look around at each other, but no one else volunteers. The man says fine, he'll find a woman from his household to go with him, "But," he warns, "You're really taking your chances. This adds extra time and stores are already closing, and I don't know sizes of the children and women." "I don't care," I say, to no one in particular. He offers his final warnings, "Don't leave this room. Keep quiet. Do nothing to draw attention to yourself. Don't even stand in the hallway," and then he walks off with all our money. For all we know, he might never come back.

The next time the door opens it's to usher in the motel receptionist who is accompanied by a short, dark-skinned fellow with a limp and a camera around his neck. He quickly lines us up and snaps our photos one by one. Taking pictures with no head scarf? This is new. There is little conversation except when he states his fee. Money is going fast all of a sudden and there was so little to begin with. At least the smugglers already paid the motel fee. Soon after getting our pictures, the other man returns with our clothes. "I've done my best to get the right sizes," he says, and then heads out. He's done a surprisingly good job. As we all try on our new outfits, we giggle and talk more than we have all evening. Giving sly compliments and striking poses for each other. "How do I look?" "Like a Pakistani princess!" "Mahvash, you look like a tall, refreshing glass of lemonade!" I laugh, my outfit is bright yellow, like a daffodil in the sun. At last, everything seems to be going smoothly.

Suddenly our door bolts open and we gasp. Two Pakistani guards stand in the doorway with batons, the motel receptionist behind them. "Passports," they say. Kayvaan smiles warmly, "We don't have passports. We are going to the UN in the morning." The guards turn to the motel receptionist. The three speak Pashto to each other, even though the receptionist speaks Persian to us, and the guards had spoken English to us. We're all frantically trying to understand each other before the guards make a rash decision. It becomes understood that they want to take us to the police station and deport us for illegally entering the country. The receptionist goes pale, and the rest of us stare blank-faced. Our dreams are crushed. It's all over. We're getting deported. The guards bark orders and tell us to hurry up. The receptionist gets the guards to speak with him outside the room for a moment. We slowly pick up our belongings, returning bags to shoulders, children to hips. The receptionist rushes back in. "Quick! Don't you have any money or jewelry or something to give them?" It all clicks. "They won't deport you if you bribe them," our smuggler had said a couple days earlier. We drop our bags and go through them for the few precious items we might have left, filling the receptionist's hands with gold bracelets and a few coins. He races out of the room again. A few minutes later, he is back, breathless. "You have to leave the motel right now. Those guards will be back or else they will be sending their friends over all night." "But where will we go?" asks Hamid, "And how did they know to come here anyway?" "I suspect the photographer turned you in. He wasn't one the smugglers have used before," he explained, "And you can stay in my basement storage area until I find somewhere else for you. Come on. We must move."

Down, down we go, down steep stairs and into a damp and foul-smelling storage room. "Now stay put and keep quiet," the receptionist says. As if we didn't already know. "And don't turn on any lights," he orders before shutting us in. We hear him lock the door from the outside. I'm sorry I complained about the smoky mattress and sharp springs in the cot. I'd rather have that than this dark dungeon that smells of rats and sewage. No one dares to sit down in our new clothes. Pipes creak as they warm and cool. Muffled voices filter down from high above us. Our breath labors on.

A key finally turns in the lock. "I'm so sorry about what happened. I have a van and a sedan outside for you now. They will take you to a new place to stay. Come." We follow the receptionist out of the building. Before the doors slam shut, he waves and wishes us good luck. Our final destination is another motel not unlike the one we've just come from. Maybe worse. The new motel employee here also instructs us not to make any noise or turn on any lights in our room. Only the children sleep that night. The rest of us wait up desperate for the morning.

Morning comes and with it a substantial room fee. The motel employee puts a cigarette between his lips and smiles a sly wide grin I recognize. "An additional fee," he says, "you know, for keeping you all safe until morning."

17
REFUGEE

The long line of small flags waving in the cool morning air let us know that we have finally, finally arrived. When the gates of the UN close behind our taxi, my spirit feels like it is lifting right out of my body, ready to lift me up off the ground even and send me soaring. I am free. I am safe. I am free! I press my palms to my eyes and run my fingers down my wet cheeks, laughing. I have never known tears like these before. A weight is lifted, and I am light as a feather. We are ushered into a large tent where many people are seated. A UN representative hands us clipboards and pens. "There are many before you, so just fill out this application and hopefully we can get to you today." I hear her words, but I refuse to acknowledge them. No way am I going back to that motel. This is our day. We just have to be seen today. No going backwards.

My name is called in the late afternoon. An interpreter introduces me to a UN man and woman who will conduct my interview. We sit at a small table across from each other and they immediately start to ask me all the basic questions that I just answered on the application. Full name, parent's names, date of birth. Then they get into the deeper questions. Why am I here and what do I want? Why did I leave Iran? I take a deep breath and tell them all about my family's struggles as Bahá'ís in post- revolution Iran. "Wait a second—" the interpreter interrupts, "Where are your parents now?" "Back in Tehran." My interviewers look at each other, puzzled.

The interpreter asks again, "They want me to clarify. Your parents were in Iran *then*, but where are they *now*?" "They are still living in Tehran. They didn't escape with me." Everyone's eyebrows raise. The interviewers shuffle through my papers and whisper to each other. The interpreter responds, "But you are only fifteen? You are underage?" "Yes." "You left your country alone, without your parents? What about your siblings? Are you joining them here in Pakistan?" "No, my brothers are in the US and my sister is in Turkey waiting for a US visa, and I am hoping to join them all in the US."

The conversation takes a gentler tone after this. Understanding that I am still a minor, they treat me with more tenderness and it feels good to be a child again, if only for a few minutes. We discuss the details of my family and my grand plan for reunification. Then they smile and ask me to wait in another room. Soon, a woman calls my name and hands me a piece of paper. "This is your temporary travel document until the UN can verify your story and make a final decision on whether to grant your asylum request and to issue a permanent acceptance card." "Thank you," I tell her, noticing the paper includes my name, birthdate, and the photo from last night that nearly got us deported. "Keep it safe," she smiles and tells me to take a train immediately to Lahore where there is a Bahá'í guest house ready to receive refugees. Refugee. That's me now. But what about my traveling companions? I find them outside and wait for the last few to be interviewed, then we all take our temporary travel documents and catch the next cab to the station.

The train is just about to pull out but thankfully we have all found seats in the same car. We sigh audibly, happily, and settle in for the twenty-seven-hour ride ahead. A man in uniform comes down the aisle punching tickets. He stops at our group and takes us in. "Tickets?" The two fathers in our group show him our tickets. "Passports," he says flatly. Kamran speaks for us, "We don't have passports yet, but we do have these," and hands over our UN travel papers with a smile. The man in uniform smiles back, takes the papers, and glances at them only briefly. "Get off the train. This is not official." Now both Kamran and Kayvaan start talking, arguing over the paperwork with him. The man isn't giving our papers back, he is folding them up and threatening to rip them. He holds them high and just as he says he's about to tear them all down the middle, Kayvaan says, "Stop!" and pulls out his wallet. The papers come down, the guard takes a stack of bills from Kayvaan, and hands us back the papers with a satisfied smile. Then he steps off the train and blows his whistle. All aboard. The train starts to chug and haltingly picks up speed as we sit panic-stricken. When we can breathe again, our anxiety and exhaustion give in to the rhythm of the train clicking as it moves down the tracks, and we fall asleep.

We wake up in the dark, hot and parched. The train stops at several small stations, without a soul around. Even though we'd really like to buy water, we're happy that we've made it through several stations without needing to bribe anyone else. Eventually, the train starts to slow as it enters a station, a big one this time. Karachi, reads the sign. We stick our heads out the windows, the city is bustling even at this late hour. It's noisy and the air is thick with humidity. Below us are a couple of boys, barely ten years old, running along the tracks holding up paper tubes. When the train squeals to a stop, I see someone else pay for a tube and am thrilled at what's inside. Watermelon! Fresh, juicy, sweet watermelon. Exactly what we need. Kayvaan counts coins and cleans out the boy's supply. The boy beams. Other boys rush over and try to sell us the treats in their tubes—mango, nuts, candy—but we only want our watermelon. The train pulls out of the station and we drool as we pull out the juicy chunks. But when I sink my teeth into a piece, I nearly gag. Oh, yuck! What is this? It's . . . spicy! So so so spicy. I inspect the watermelon. Chili flakes pepper the cubes. Everyone agrees—this is truly disgusting. Why would you ever put chili on watermelon? I guess we've had our first encounter with the Pakistani palate. Our Persian tongues aren't equipped for hot spices. From now on, we only buy water and nuts from the boys running along the tracks.

A day passes and then we wake up in Lahore, sweaty and hungry, and with a lot less money in our pockets, but thankful we didn't have to bribe any more guards. The friendly and familiar faces of refugees from the tent at the UN compound greet us on the platform. We see signs in Persian welcoming newcomers, so we go, tentatively, over to them, to ask if that might apply to our group? It does. The Lahore Bahá'í Center sends a team to the train station daily to receive all the new refugees. They take us to the center and give us a tour of the guest house complete with bunk beds, bathrooms, and a kitchen. Housing is limited to one week so as to accommodate all the waves of new refugees who arrive daily in Lahore. Everyone is so kind, so hospitable. There are large and happy groups of women cooking meals in the community kitchen.

Over the next few hours, I notice hundreds of people coming and leaving the center. All they do is gather around several bulletin boards. Cheers or tears follow their inspections. I am curious to know what's going on, so I ask a woman to explain the papers on the board to me.

"They're lists. Lots of different lists. There's the short list. That one has the names of the lucky few who get accepted by the UN for asylum and granted aid and protection from deportation immediately after their border evaluation. Don't expect your name to be on there unless you need immediate medical treatment or have a special circumstance that puts your life in immediate danger. Then there's the long list, filled with the names of those summoned for a second or third UN interview. That list tells which day to report to the official UN office in Islamabad."

My kind acquaintance continued for a while. There really were so many lists. A third long list included the names of people confirmed as Iranian Bahá'ís and who could now receive an official Bahá'í ID card. Then, a fourth list confirmed people who were granted UN aid after their second or third interview. Other lists were broken down by country for all refugees who had requested to be settled, or were assigned to settle, in a particular country; it showed who was scheduled to go for an interview with the officials from that country. And the best list of all, the names of people who had been approved to travel to their final destination country.

"So basically," the woman explaining the lists said, "if your name is on any of these lists—you cheer, because you are moving up in the world."

I keep probing others about the procedures involved with moving "up in the world." Apparently, there can be many obstacles that get in the way. Some of the disappointed faces come from men and women who have been waiting more than three years now.

"You're lucky you have family in the US," I'm told. "If you have family anywhere in the West, you get priority to join them. If you don't have family anywhere, you simply have to wait for a country to say it has an opening for refugees."

Even if I run into obstacles going to the US, I have options. I have cousins in Australia, Norway, Sweden, and Germany. I wonder how long it will take to see my name on that long list, the one summoning people for their second interview.

"Mahvash! There you are," Bahaar clasps my arm, and I turn toward her smiling face. "Listen," she says, "we wanted to confirm it was alright before we officially asked you, but you know how Kayvaan's brother's family lives here and is awaiting flights to Australia?"

"Yes, he is coming to the center to bring you to his home, right?"

"Right, and we'd like to have you join us at his home. Do you want to go?"

Without a doubt. "What a gracious offer!" I say, "But, Bahaar, it will be crowded even without me. Are you sure you won't mind?"

"We don't mind if you don't mind!"

"Then yes! Thank you. I hope to find a cousin of mine who is also here in Lahore, so you don't have to worry that I will overstay my welcome."

"Do I look worried?" Bahaar asks, "It's a plan."

We leave the Bahá'í Center and step out into the streets of Lahore, on our own. No smugglers. No trucks. Just us and our freedom. As long as we dress in acceptable attire and respect the Pakistani laws, no one will ever stop us again. If the streets had seams, they would be bursting out of them. People and vehicles burst from around every corner, flowing in an endless wave of lively chaos. Public busses pass by with all the glass windows removed. The overflow crowd hangs themselves out the sides and from the backdoor handles. Vendors on bicycle carts line the streets, shouting their wares. Motorbikes carrying entire families cut through the busy traffic. "Look at that!" I yell over the din, pointing to three-wheeled little vehicles splattered in a rainbow of paint. "Those are rikshaws," Kayvaan's brother explains, "They are a bit more expensive, but much more comfortable than hanging out a window in a bus!" "Let's take them!" I say, because it feels like a new adventure already, and a fun one. We take two and still have to pile up in them to fit.

The rikshaws drop us in a middle-class neighborhood called Officer Colony. The house is three stories and has about fifteen other Persians living there. The owners live on the first floor, and the rooms on the second and third floor are rented out, with three or four people living in each room at any given time. The unit we are staying in has two rooms and the kitchen is communal with all the other tenants. This is a common setup, the brother explains, young, unmarried refugees go to the Bahá'í Center to find roommates of the same gender. Banding together, they then knock on people's doors in the community and ask to rent a room in the house. I take mental notes of all he says since this might be exactly the position I find myself in soon. Over the next couple of days, I will go back to the center to see if I can get some basic household items like dishes, pots, blankets, a pillow from a departing Bahá'í family.

A glass of cold mint tea washes away the last of the great anxiety that has stuck in my throat these past few weeks. My bones still ache, but my heart beats with more hope than it has in years. I am offered a mat and a pillow to stretch out on the floor for an afternoon nap. I need no blanket, for peace has finally come to cover me.

18
GROWTH

I call my brothers first because Maamaan and Baba don't have a home phone. My brothers ask for the number of my house and call me back because it's cheaper, but we don't talk long. Still, it's long enough for my heart to swell a hundred times. It's good to hear their voices so clearly, they already sound closer than they did last time we spoke back at Nowruz. It's so good to have good news to share with them. Whether it is intentional or not, they don't ask about the journey; it's enough to know I'm safe. "OK, Mahvash? What's next then?" I tell them about needing to find a place to live and about the paperwork and the lists on the bulletin boards. They tell me first thing, open a bank account, and they will wire me money to take care of rent and food and anything else I might need. "We'll give your number to Maamaan whenever she calls us next, and then she and Baba can get in touch with you." "How's Leila?" I want to know before hanging up. "She's in Vienna now; she finally got out of Turkey. She's doing well. One step closer every day. You'll both be here in no time." The phone clicks after we say goodbye and I let out a big sigh. I hope they're right, but either way, I have a good feeling that I can relax a bit here and settle into a new way of life.

When Maamaan calls a few days later, it is the final load off my back. I am so happy to relieve them of their suffering—they've been waiting weeks to hear from me and to know I am safe. "Every phone call, every knock on the door," Maamaan says through tears, "brought me the shivers of dread. I thought for sure it would be news that you were caught at the border and that I would be coming to visit you in jail." I'm safe, I tell her. I'm happy, I tell her. I do not tell her about the trucks with the guns or the shack or the motel. Another time, maybe. For now, I just want them to be proud of me and all I've accomplished.

Ruhi is the name of the older sister of my goofball cousin Farzin, who I mentored every summer. She and her husband and their two young boys have been in Lahore for nearly two years waiting to be resettled in Australia. The next time I go to the Bahá'í Center I ask around about them and am surprised at how quickly I find someone who knows them and can give me their number. Ruhi invites me to come stay with them for a few days while I look for a place of my own to rent. I thank Kayvaan's family for their kindness and generosity, and then I'm off. Ruhi also rents two small rooms in someone else's house. There are many other rooms and she says the occupants change so frequently that just as soon as one family leaves a new refugee rents their room and buys their belongings. Her own furniture, sparse though it is, was also passed down a long chain of refugees. "Some days I think this furniture will forever be mine because there's no way we are getting out of Pakistan," but she rolls her eyes when she says this, then shakes her head and laughs. Ruhi can't be truly pessimistic to save her life.

Ruhi and I could talk all night. She's ten years older than me, but we've grown up together—and flung our share of pomegranates at each other—so she's essentially another big sister to me. After a bit, she eyes me up and down and asks: "Is this your only Pakistani outfit, Mahvash?" "It is, for now." "I'll show you all the markets and we'll look for fabric then I'll make you your own clothes, so they'll fit the best. We'll do two. One with light fabric, one with heavy, for the different weather." I tell her that Kia and Cyrus are wiring me money, so I can pay for the fabric and her time. "Nonsense. Don't pay me. Just play with my wild boys while I sew, and we'll call it even." Her boys are just four and six and so cute. They've changed so much since the last time I saw them two years ago. Playing with them sounds like a great exchange for a new wardrobe.

Finding a room to rent proves easier than expected. Two sisters across the hall from Ruhi were looking for a third female roommate to help them share the cost of living. I learn they've been here a year and a half already and are waiting to join their brother in Texas. They think it will take one or two years more before they get there. My eyes pop. I'm excited to be in this new land, but not for three years! Could it take that long for me as well?

Nasrin is the older sister and Vida the younger. They receive a small monthly stipend from the UN, but money is still tight. Vida earns extra money styling hair at a salon nearby and loves it. She's learned some new skills like painting with henna, which is especially popular among brides. She promises to take me next time a wedding party comes in. "Because," she says, "it will be by far the most entertaining part of your week."

By the middle of June, I'm not sure it's possible to survive if it gets any hotter than it already is. Some days, it's so hot the bottoms of my flip flops melt on the asphalt, sticking to the ground then slapping back up against my heel. Twice a day, at noon and in the late afternoon, we remove everything in the house from the tiled floor, sweep it, and throw water on it to cool it down. The outdoor shower in the backyard is a great way to cool off too, as is buying sugar cane juice from the street vendor who makes it on the spot with a small grinder and lots of long sugary sticks.

Vida, Nasrin, and I have worked out a routine for ourselves. Each morning, we wake up, put away our mattresses then have a breakfast of hot tea and bread and cheese. After, Vida goes to work and Nasrin and I start thinking about lunch and what to buy at the markets. We don't have a refrigerator, just a hot plate, so we must buy our food fresh each day. "Let's catch the *imamzadeh* today, I don't have much money," Nasrin tells me. The *imamzadeh* is the crazy, overcrowded bus that is decorated on the outside and has all its windows removed. It's the cheapest option for transportation and the most unpleasant. The cushions are either ripped or missing completely from the seats and half chewed gum is dried all over the backs of the seats in front of us—if we're lucky that is. Because sometimes it's on the seats we're sitting on. Garbage on the floor and chickens hanging from bags on people's shoulders make for a smelly ride. The bus gets packed as tight as possible, which gives easy opportunities for sleazy men to take advantage of the situation and press their sweaty bodies hard against you, sometimes nearly wrapping themselves around you. And it is because of this reason—not the garbage or the chickens—that we pay the extra money and take the rikshaw whenever possible. Other times we might take a van; it's the next cheapest option after the rikshaw, but it's a wild ride in its own right. We can always hear the van before it even turns down the street. The van blasts the loudest music and drives so fast we can hear the tires screech as it turns corners. Boarding the van takes a certain skill because it never exactly stops at the same place and you never know where exactly it's headed. As a van zips down the road, a helper will throw wide the van's sliding door and shout its destination while it goes through a traffic circle. Then, people from all sides of the street start running. The van stops briefly for passengers to jump off, and new ones to jump on. And, just like that it's off again.

The chaos continues at the market, but I find it all very amusing. Motorbikes weave in and out of the throng of men carrying large baskets of citrus on their head. No one seems to notice or to mind. Large carts piled high with perfectly stacked towers of fruits or veggies take up residence in the market with no rhyme or reason to their set up, white plastic chairs sit scattered around boxes of fresh produce, or blankets lie on the ground to sit on while the vendors wait for customers. Oranges come in dozens of varieties, the mulberries are long, the mangoes huge, and the tangerines even huger. Cows walk freely through the city, up the sides of roads, and through alleyways leaving large manure pies everywhere they go. They are gentle enough, but every now and then I'll see one take a stab at a person with its massive horns, so I've learned to give them a wide berth, just in case. The cows are sacred to the Hindus of Pakistan, so you'll never find beef for sale in the market. But cages full of live chickens and other birds? Yes. Goat and lamb carcasses filleted down the middle, their ribs exposed to passersby? Certainly. Buckets of livers, intestines, and tongues? No problem. But never beef. The first time I came to the market I asked for a chicken and ever since then I've been a vegetarian. The seller pulled a live chicken from a cage, weighed it and told me the price. I handed over the money still trying to figure out what I was going to do with a live chicken, when all of a sudden, the vendor grabbed the chicken's neck and popped its head off. He started peeling back the skin with the feathers still attached, blood squirting down his arms while I watched, horrified. The cruelty was too much. I'll take rice with chickpeas and lentils from now on. Besides, the already butchered meat and dairy products sit out in 100-degree temperatures all day with flies swarming on them. It's not exactly appetizing to begin with. Bread, fruit, and veggies—those are a safe bet.

We buy fresh milk from the milkman who delivers in our neighborhood. Each day he rides the streets with aluminum milk containers hanging from the handles and in a little bucket on the back. "*Shir! Shir!* Milk! Milk!" he calls, and people wave out their windows to grab his attention, sending their children down to purchase a glassful or two. From the milk we buy, Nasrin taught me how to make yogurt. We blend it with citrus or mango for creamy, cool drinks that take the edge off the hot afternoons. Another trick is to make mint tea. Ruhi taught me to always boil the water before drinking it to avoid any strange stomach bugs as this would save me from a lot of unpleasantness, and any extra costs incurred from needing to see a doctor. First I boil a whole pot of water, then I take fresh mint from the market and steep it along with a Darjeeling tea bag and a bit of sugar. I let the mixture cool and then we enjoy mint tea for the rest of the day. When I am out and about Lahore in the heat though, there is no way to quench my thirst except to drink from the large fifty-gallon water barrels placed for people at intersections. Each barrel has its own little plastic cup for public use. I tried for a long time to avoid using that cup. How many hundreds of lips had sipped from it that day already? I watch people approach the barrel with very obvious skin infections, open sores oozing or cracking down the sides of their faces and mouths. As they drink, they chant verses under their breath. Prayers? Mantras? Talismans against disease? What will I do if I get a nose bleed? I'll have to use that cup. I worried for days over this dilemma, but then a miracle! I stumbled upon a true treasure at the market—a small, plastic folding cup that fits into my purse. Now I too drink from the barrels. Of course, it wasn't boiled water, so indeed vomiting and diarrhea were close companions for several weeks. But then I was restored and nothing has bothered me since. I like to think my immune system is stronger than ever.

The sisters and I take turns cooking meals and I can't help but notice that everything I make, even though I'm using the same fresh ingredients, just doesn't taste any good. I pose my question to Ruhi, who scrunches her face up and says, "But in Iran, did you cook food that you liked eating?" "In Iran I never cooked at all!" I tell her. This is the first time I've learned to cook; I was so busy studying I never even watched my mom fix a meal. "Hmm, that's incredible," Ruhi murmurs. "OK then, tell me what you do, step by step, from the beginning." Simple. I explain the chopping and the oil and the cooking and how nice and colorful everything looks plated, but how boring it is once we eat it. Her laughter takes me by surprise. "You don't use any onions? Or spices? No wonder!" I crinkle my nose at her. "I hate onions." "Oh indeed," she says, "You and every other child say the same thing, but we sneak them into every Persian dish. They're essential." She explains the finer points of sautéing onions as the very first step and then shows me turmeric and pepper, coriander and star anise, and promises to take me shopping tomorrow to buy me my own. "Believe me, this will help and if nothing else," she continues, "at least use some salt!" She laughs again about how I've been leaving out all the spices. Sure enough, following her advice my cooking improves and I take even more pleasure in the process, but the absolute best thing Ruhi teaches me is how to make *tahdig*—it is rice, but the kind that leaves that oh-so crispy and crunchy rice layer at the bottom of the pan. Leila and I always fought over who got to eat that part, and now—I can make it for myself, as often as I wish, and eat it all myself too! I smile, but then I'm sad and long to have Leila around to fight with over the tahdig. She'd probably be pretty proud to know I've mastered the perfect crisp.

Even Bahaar and Roya are impressed with how much I have learned and so quickly. Bahaar even asked me to take her oldest child, who is just a year younger than myself, to the markets to teach him everything I know. It seems I've become a sort of role model. On the day I took him, there was a tropical rainstorm. These storms never last long but they always flood the streets because the irrigation systems are so poor. For the locals, a little water is no problem at all. They just hoist their baggy pants up over their knees and wade through in their flip flops; its business as usual. But I refuse. Dog droppings, cow droppings, who knows what other detritus is floating around your legs? What if there's a cut on my foot? I can only imagine how many pathogens bloom in those waters waiting for any little open sore to come around that they can infect. Maybe I'm worrying too much, but I've seen it happen. Vida got an infection from a tiny pimple on her neck that she couldn't keep from picking at. The pimple grew to be the size of a walnut and we scrambled to find a doctor for her.

So, clearly, the boy and I decided not to go swimming in the murky cesspool at that moment, and just postponed our market trip for a couple hours until the waters receded. Our trip had to be cut short, but it was enough time to show him how to navigate the public transportation and which stop to get off at, how the weighing process works—fruits stacked on one side of the scale while the vendors pile little weights on the other side until it is even, then they multiply the weight with the price. I explained what a good price is for different fruits, and how the exchange rate works, why I don't recommend buying meat, and how to stay clear of the cow horns. He seemed determined to take it all in and make sense of it, but I could tell he was thoroughly overwhelmed. "Don't worry," I said, "It just takes coming here a couple times on your own and you'll get the hang of it in no time." I believe this because it has been true for me. If I put my mind to something, I can accomplish it. This past month has been a whirlwind of newness and busyness, but I am making it, and I dearly welcome the change of pace. How vast the world is, I realized, now that I am not stuck behind sandbags and blanketed windows, now that I am on the other side of the border, on the other side of my fears. Everything has been fairly peaceful and easy and for a moment I even wondered about what it would be like to stay and make a life here. But that thought vanished as quickly as it came, and I knew, full well, that I was and am making the right choice to seek a place to live where I am respected as a person and a woman. That place is not here. I learned that just the other day when I was out with Ruhi.

We went to the fabric bazaar for new material for my Pakistani clothes and we were both feeling as light and breezy as the colorful fabric we bought. Until we walked to the bus stop. A young man in front of me, and headed in the opposite direction, passed by us and as he did he reached out and grabbed my breast and squeezed it. I stopped, shocked. What just happened? Was that intentional or just an accident? Oh, come now Mahvash, no one gives a squeeze like that by accident. Tears sprung to my eyes. I was angry, so angry! Why was I crying? I was shocked, I wanted to do something, yell something, but there wasn't anything I could do. I just felt violated and so vulnerable and the only response was tears. I don't know what the laws and rules of Pakistan are, but if a man did that to a woman in Iran, the woman would be blamed for tempting the man. That man harmed me, unsettled me, but more than that—it scared me that he put me in a position to be blamed, to be beaten, to be jailed. At least that's what would have happened, in Iran. Ruhi clutched my arm and told me I could walk closer to her the rest of the way home.

So, I know I'm making the right choice to leave this place, to go somewhere—anywhere—where my religious beliefs are respected and where I don't have to hide my identity. I don't want to fear my neighbors or bombs or the way I dress. I don't want to fear that men will take advantage of me and that I'll be the one blamed. Is it so much to ask to live one's life unafraid? Is there really a place like that? Is that the American dream?

19

JOURNEY

Every Tuesday, Baba and Maamaan call to check in and I let them know that even though I visit the Bahá'í Center a couple times a week, my name has not made any lists and probably will not for several more weeks yet. But the center has several classes they offer like English classes and Bahá'í literature, so it is a good place to socialize and fill my time. I write my parents long letters describing my friends and the culture, like finally getting to go to Vida's hair salon to see Pakistani wedding preparations.

Early in the morning, the bride and all the women in her family come in carrying multiple suitcases. Vida starts with their hands and arms, painting them in delicate henna. While the thick, black henna dries the women proceed to have their eyebrows threaded and shaped and their widow's peaks removed. Many of the older women get their chins and moustaches waxed as well. Then it is on to the hair. Vida is masterful at weaving and braiding and knotting their long, thick locks into gorgeous arrangements piled on top of their heads or with a few curls left cascading down their necks. Nasrin and I giggle in the corner while we watch them. We can't understand any of the Urdu they speak, but they are clearly teasing each other and laughing so much that it's hard not to join them. They like to show off for us, displaying their henna or hair. We clap when Vida presents each freshly coiffed woman. When all the hair is complete, the women remove the smallest bags from their suitcases—the jewelry bags.

Beautiful pendants are pinned in the hair with gold strands that sway over the forehead. Dozens of gold bracelets decorate the arms both above and below the elbow. Long earrings dangle and shiny jewels bedeck the nose. But they still aren't through. There are still toes and fingers to adorn with rings before the nails get shaped and painted in whites, and pinks, and reds.

It's a good thing Nasrin and I brought snacks. This is like going to a movie.

The transformation isn't complete until the makeup is on. Vida's steady hand turns the wedding party into porcelain dolls; they choose such bright colors for their eyes, and cheeks, and lips that I barely recognize them. They really do look beautiful. Now the silks and finely embroidered fabrics that make up the bridal gown come out of the suitcases. Under all the layers of gorgeously patterned fabric, the bride wears the traditional baggy pants. Every time she turns, the long silks ebb and flow around her like a slow, warm sea tide. By the end of the afternoon, they all head off for a big party. I have sometimes passed these parties in the streets. Wedding celebrations last a whole week and the family closes the entire alleyway where they live to erect big tents for the parties to go around the clock. They fill the spaces with large, decorative pillows and special thrones for the bride and groom. Women cook food all day and all night to feed the family and friends that are always coming and going. They call the celebration *Shaademoney* and on top of the continuous stream of food, the music, the dancing, and the prayers also never cease.

I also tell my parents about the friends I am making and how we go to the parks in the evening when it has cooled down to picnic on bread, cucumbers, walnuts, cheese and spicy potato samosas that we get from the street vendors. "The spice is actually quite nice I'm finding, and it helps with all the heat and humidity!" I tell them. They don't believe it. I am reminded of the watermelon flecked with chili peppers and realize I would probably find it quite a refreshing treat now. Our picnics in the park mean so much to me. I had forgotten what parks were like since the Iranian Revolution had sucked the simple pleasure from my soul. Many of the friends I make are refugees in transition and while our interactions are innocent enough, playing cards and telling jokes, there is a fair amount of flirtation too. I've already seen shy smiles turn into covenants of love. For refugees who have been here a long time, marrying someone who's paperwork has already been processed means a faster exit for them as well.

Speaking of fast exits, my brothers also check in regularly with me and let me know they have sent a request to the UN to be my private sponsors; this will, apparently, help speed up my processing. They told me I am eligible for a private sponsorship since I am a single, female, minor in an Islamic country. Sponsorship means they partner with the UN to assume some of my expenses, like half of an airline ticket. After all the years that Maamaan and Baba supported my brothers, it is incredible that they are now able to support Leila and me. Cyrus earned his Bachelor of Science in respiratory therapy and is now in his third year of medical school in Texas. Kia moved to California after receiving a Bachelor of Science in electrical engineering, and now works full-time with Hitachi in the Silicon Valley while completing his master's degree in computer science at Santa Clara University.

I haven't told my parents or my brothers about the street assault. Ever since it happened, it makes me embarrassed to talk about it. I've become more restless and anxious to get out of here, even though I know it has only been a few weeks and I really am making some beautiful memories with friends and my roommates, and Ruhi. It was still so jarring that I struggle to remain focused. But then I get the most unheard-of news. I am one of the lucky ones.

On the way home from the bazaar, someone who I know vaguely through the Bahá'í Center stopped me and told me they thought they had seen my name on the bulletin board. It couldn't be! It was much too early for that kind of confirmation, but I had to know for certain. I hailed the next bus, sleazy men be darned, and went straight to the center. Time slowed down as I walked up to the bulletin. The air around was hot and sticky with humidity, which made it hard to breathe. My eyes did not have to scroll far through the names. Sure enough, there I was. I couldn't believe my eyes. My name was up on that very, very short list. The list of people who are accepted by the UN after their very first interview at the border! A huge smile spread across my face and I turned with joy to those around me, ready to shout in celebration and share the news with anyone, everyone! But the many frowns and tears I saw of people who still hadn't made any list made me reconsider. I erased my smile, clasped my hands tight in front of me and looked at the ground. All I wanted to do was jump and dance and celebrate, but that would have felt like bragging. What torture it is to feel the delicious bubbling over of joy and not be able to share it with anyone at all. The only people who would care to know were my family.

I couldn't wait to tell my parents and my brothers, but we only talk weekly, and we just had our call. It was the longest week of my life trying not to bust at the seams holding in the good news. When we were finally able to speak, they each went right to work to tackle the next steps for getting me out of Pakistan.

First thing was to confirm I am a member of the Bahá'í Faith. This was tricky. All documents had been destroyed after the revolution to protect Bahá'ís from religious persecution. Still, Baba and Maamaan worked on my behalf in Tehran to try to supply the UN with the information they needed. Somehow, my parents' persistence paid off and the Bahá'í representatives in Tehran were able to produce the confirmation I needed. Then, it was Kia who got even more promising news two weeks later. Since Leila had been in Austria already for a few months, the Bahá'ís of Austria agreed to request a visa for me to get me out of Pakistan as fast as possible and to join her there.

Everything is moving at such a quick pace now and each victory in the process feels like a gift beyond imagination. What should have taken months has been reduced to weeks. My joy abounds, but I temper it around my friends. I know they want to celebrate with me, and they do offer sincere smiles and hugs, but I know it hurts. It hurts to be left behind, again. It hurts to see someone so new get moved up in the process so fast.

My next steps are revealed the next time I speak with my brothers. The Bahá'ís in Austria have been successful with their visa request. Now, I need to go to the Austrian embassy in Islamabad as soon as possible for an interview. I've never been to Islamabad and I've never taken a bus that far alone. Ruhi has taken the eight-hour bus to Islamabad several times for her interviews and after the incident in the bazaar doesn't think I should take the overnight trip by myself. She arranges for a young man she knows, a friend of her husband, to accompany me. We meet briefly at the Bahá'í Center and make arrangements to take a night bus the following evening. His name is Jamshid, he is quiet, kind, and exceedingly respectful. He also has made this trip to Islamabad numerous times—he's been here close to three years already—and has been rejected numerous times for a visa, for one reason or another. Through full eyes, he tells me: "I've seen thousands of people come and go and I really don't know if I will ever be able to leave." His willingness to chaperone me is yet another gift, and a humbling one. I promise to pay for his tickets, accommodations, and food.

The bus is called a "flying coach" and not only is it roomy and clean—it's air conditioned. Nestled by a window seat, with Jamshid to my right, I'm thankful for his presence, a barrier from the many men standing pressed, tightly together, in the aisle. It doesn't take me long to figure out why it's called a flying coach. Our driver is aggressive, speeding through lanes of oncoming traffic trying to pass other vehicles, quickly veering back into his own lane, racing over potholes, and ignoring the honks from other vehicles. I throw my back against the seat and dig my fingernails into the cushion to brace myself and hang on for dear life. Outside the window, I see accident after accident. *Is there any Remover of difficulties save God? Is there any Remover of difficulties save God?* Jamshid hears my mumbled prayers and comes to my rescue with conversation to take my mind off this wild ride. He speaks softly, and his voice is immediately comforting.

I learn he was the only boy in his family and when he finished high school, he didn't want to serve in the war, so he escaped to Pakistan. He grew up in a port city and I find his southern accent kind of silly and charming.

"I don't have family in the West for sponsorship though," he explains, "so my chances for exit are less and the process much longer." He tells me he is the anchor lease holder on his place, his roommates come and go, but still he stays. He's helped so many people find houses, get roommates, complete paperwork, buy or sell furniture, get to their interviews. "Like me," I say, understanding more clearly just what life has been like for him here. He nods. "I've seen people get married, have babies, get divorced, get sick, get hospitalized, and even seen a few die." "You've been through a lot." "Well," he smirks, "I can at least be proud to say I've probably been here the longest of anyone!" His smile disappears, and he stares ahead, "Of course it's sad, and disappointing." Then he looks back at me and there's his smile again. "You know, I've never seen anyone leave as fast as you may be able to. That makes us a special pair." "Oh yes?" "Yes, we're the record holders for shortest and longest stays!" I tell him about what it was like living through the bombings in Tehran, about my journey across the border. "I feel like my whole life has been one big waiting game. And now that there's some movement, I finally have hope. Things really are changing. I really can have a chance at another life." He sighs. "You can. And you will," and then says, "We should probably try to get some sleep. We'll get to Islamabad's twin city, Rawalpindi, around six a.m."

In the morning, we head first to the Bahá'í Center to get some breakfast and for me to freshen up for the interview. The streets look like Lahore even here: the milkman on his bicycle, the samosa sellers, and the mules pulling produce wagons. The sun comes up fast; it's going to be another hot and humid day. Another van gets us to Islamabad and here the city is a world away from anything I've yet seen in Pakistan. "Beautiful, right?" Jamshid says noticing the drop in my jaw. There are boulevards with manicured lawns, flowers, and sculpted shrubbery in the medians. To say nothing of people's lawns. Not a trace of garbage is to be seen anywhere. "It feels like I am in a different country," I gasp. "Everyone feels this way the first time they come to Islamabad. It is so different." "Why?" I ask. "Because most of the residents are foreign diplomats or have high-power jobs that allow them to live in big, gated compounds and drive big, flashy cars, and hire full-time gardeners to keep everything pristine."

We exit the van in a traffic circle to hail a cab. This is because the embassies are in a restricted area. Jamshid surprises me by speaking Urdu to the driver. Soon we're passing through a large, guarded gate and we arrive at a beautiful building. Inside the embassy it's crisp and cool. We wait and wait and wait before we are able to speak to someone behind the counter. I hand her the paperwork I've already filled out, and my letters from the United Nations. She closes the sliding glass window. A few minutes later she returns: "OK, looks good. Passport please." "But I don't have a passport." She smirks. "OK, well your request for a visa to Austria was received, but how exactly do you intend to travel without a passport?" My cheeks burn. She laughs, "Where exactly would you like me to stamp your visa?" I don't know what to say. After a few awkward moments, I ask her what I should do. "I don't know," she shrugs. I'm at a loss, staring through watery eyes at this calloused woman. "Look," she, rolls her eyes, "Go to the United Nations and ask them for help." Then she slides her window shut and leaves.

Jamshid and I take another cab to another restricted area. The UN building here is also very impressive with beautiful gardens, but by the time we arrive they tell us to come back tomorrow morning as there are no appointments left today. A fog of disappointment consumes me. Jamshid tries to cheer me up. "You've made so much progress in such a short time. I've seen thousands of people come and go through the immigration and asylum process and you are quite an exception to the process. This is just a small hiccup in the road for you." "A hiccup?" "Look, I know how it feels to be so invested in getting out, in being reunited with family and friends only to be rejected," he says, and I know his words are true. If anyone understands me right now, it's Jamshid. "You're young, you're in the most productive time of your life, yet you get stuck here doing nothing for months or years. A state of limbo, often without hope. But you, Mahvash. You have hope. Don't discount that so soon." He's right. I know he's right, but I feel like wallowing a little longer. "All around me I see young people like you getting addicted to cigarettes, alcohol and other drugs, just to cope. No one—no one—ever had a visa ready for them before they even had a passport!" He's really on a roll. "Every time I get rejected from an embassy, they tell me to pick up the pieces, choose a new track and a new country and move on." I look him in the eyes and nod; I really am so very lucky. I don't have to change all my plans around. I just need to get a passport. How hard can that be?

We stay at the Rawalpindi Bahá'í Center and the next day rise extra early to try to be the first at UN headquarters. When we arrive, there are hundreds of people in line before me. It's early afternoon before I get an appointment. The woman is nice and chatty, thumbing through my papers while explaining that, "Yes yes, a passport takes a while. It could be months before you leave for Austria or the United States. Don't worry, my dear. You know there are an awful lot of people ahead of you who—" she stops short, thank goodness, because her words are crushing my heart. "Wait a second. You're only fifteen?" Oh, praise God. "Well, my sixteenth birthday is in a couple weeks," I say. "But you're just a kid! This changes things. Hmm, still the process could take months . . . unless you have a private sponsor." "I do! My brothers will sponsor me!" "But, will they pay all your resettlement and travel expenses? Most sponsors only pay a portion, but if they relieve the UN of that burden we can definitely expedite your paperwork." "I don't know if they can afford that, but I can see. What do I do?"

She explained that should one of my brothers sponsor me then he would need to go to an agent of the International Rescue Committee in San Jose, California. There he could initiate the paperwork he'd need to sign for his responsibilities. Then, "There will be more visits for you here, in Islamabad. Once sponsorship is approved, you'll get fingerprinted, submit new photos, complete more paperwork and finally get a temporary travel document that is as good as a passport. And then, you'll go back to the Austrian Embassy for your interview and visa." There's so much still to do.

I breathe deeply and settle into the idea that I will still be here for a number of months even if things are expedited.

Navigating immigration is like groping through a labyrinth in the dark, but here I am. Here we go. I have my next steps and I have a faithful chaperone willing to return with me on all these subsequent visits. "It's all going to work out just fine," he says, giving my hand a squeeze. There's so much on my mind that I am unphased by the reckless driving of the flying coach on our way back home. The next day, my parents call and I tell them everything. Baba tells me, "My commitment to educate my daughters as well as my sons still stands. I will call your brothers right now and tell them to step up and do what they must do for you—now!" And he does. Kia calls me later in the day and tells me, without hesitation, that he will take full financial responsibility for me from then on.

Over the next six weeks, I take my weekly trips to Islamabad to move the process along to the next step, applications filled, pictures submitted, interviews, finger printing, everything unfolds just as the chatty woman at the UN told me it would. When the Austrian visa is finally stamped on my temporary travel document, I let out a huge sigh of relief. This quadruple folded piece of paper that isn't even a real passport is my ticket to get one step closer to living a peaceful life, to a reunion with my family. All that is left is for Kia and the UN to arrange my plane tickets.

Goodbyes are bittersweet. My traveling companions from Iran are clearly uncomfortable. "My goodness, but you're leaving so soon." "Yes." "That's . . . terrific." They try to hide the hollowness in their voices, to fight their own angst to get a move on with their life and to try to feel happiness that I will be safe and with family soon. "As it should be. You should be getting out. We have our spouses here with us, but you have been doing this on your own. It's good. Really. We are happy for you," the women say. I know how frustrating it must be for them; they are still waiting on their second interviews. The men's jokes take me by surprise. "But did you bribe someone? Is that why?" Kamran lets loose a stream of expletives, saying it's just not fair, and that money buys everything. This embarrasses me deeply;

I feel their pain and I don't want them to lose hope or feel like no one cares for them just because the process is taking longer. I stop saying goodbyes to people and just give away the few things I've acquired while here.

Jamshid travels with me to the airport in Islamabad where I have a flight straight to Vienna. As we part ways for the final time, he hands me a small prayer book. "Pray for me," he asks, "Pray for me to leave this hell hole and not to waste away here, to find my purpose and follow my best path in life." "I will," I tell him, "Thank you for everything . . . you've been a dear friend." We look at each other for just a few moments, tears welling in our eyes, before he nods his head, signaling that it is time for me to go. He turns, pauses, and walks away. I watch him go and I'm glad I do, he turns back and gives me one last smile and a wave. And then it's just me and my backpack.

A UN representative meets me and hands me a large envelope with the official UN seal on it. Inside are all my travel documents, my visa information, and a name tag which I am instructed to wear around my neck "at all times."

Four months ago, I took my first airplane ride with my mother, terror coursing through my veins. Today, I fly again, but this time I feel only freedom and peace flowing through me. My throat clenches with emotion again, but not in panic. This time in deep love and gratitude. I cannot stop the tears as I step aboard my flight toward Leila. The flight attendants worry about me, thinking I am afraid to fly, but I tell them no, it isn't that.

It is because I am just so happy.

20
SISTERS

I step off the plane and into my sister's arms. We cannot stop laughing and stroking each other's hair and wiping each other's tears away. One and a half years since we have seen each other, and even longer since I've seen her smile. She looks so good and her joy bubbles over. I tug at her short haircut, it was past her shoulders last time we were together. She has always worn it long and curly. "Short, huh? I like it." She points to my face, "Pimples, huh? Puberty is catching up with you!" "That or all the greasy samosas," I say. "Oooh, well no samosas here, just plenty of chocolate. Your skin is going to love you." "Oh, great!" I laugh. Leila introduces me to the two Austrian women who have accompanied her. One is tall and stands with perfect posture, her hair is gray, and she introduces herself as Miss Anna from the International Rescue Committee. The other is short with fiery red hair, "Everyone just calls me Mrs. M!" she says in Persian. She's our interpreter. "Your Persian is perfect!" I tell her after we've chatted for a bit and I learn she works for the Austrian police and speaks a total of eight languages. "Thanks! I'm married to a Persian man, and I'm Bahá'í also. You can find me at the Bahá'í Center and if you ever get bored, I can keep you busy—we always need help sorting mail and sending out Bahá'í literature." It's a nice offer considering I am quite familiar with just how much time there is to kill in a day when waiting around for visa approvals.

An underground train takes us from the airport to the city center where we catch a lovely little red street car. People here are incredibly respectful of other's personal space—what a change of pace! The tram even moves slowly through the city, so I can catch a good look at all the magnificent architecture. Vienna is so charming. "Am I in a movie?" I ask Leila, gaping at the colorful rows of apartments with trellises climbing up the walls and rose bushes hanging from the window boxes. From our stop, we wind our way uphill through a long corridor. The streets are unbelievably clean. How is it possible? Leila leads us through a small, manicured courtyard to the front door of her four-bedroom flat, puts the key in the lock and turns the knob. We enter a cozy little home and are greeted by the sweetest family. Leila has lived here for six months already with a family of four and has even been given a bedroom of her own. The parents hug me tightly and tell me they are so happy to finally meet me, "We've heard such lovely things about you." They chat with us only briefly knowing that Leila and I "probably have lots to catch up on," so after a quick bite to eat it isn't long before we've flopped ourselves down on her bed and talk the whole night away. I finally hear all the challenging and painful details of her own journey as a refugee.

UN assistance in Turkey had been limited because they had concentrated their efforts to help Iranian refugees in Pakistan instead. For months and months, she waited. After several rejections from the American Embassy in Istanbul, she gave up hope of coming to America. "I started looking for other countries where I might live instead; I considered Bulgaria and some Eastern European countries." Leila had eventually plugged into a Bahá'í community in Turkey and after a year living in Ankara, they were able to help her obtain a visa to Austria. "Such a great day! So much relief." Her joy at boarding the plane to Austria was the same as mine, only hers didn't go so smoothly. "A Turkish Airlines employee in Ankara told me that the airline would need to hold my passport and visa during the flight to Vienna, 'Don't worry,' the woman said, 'all your documents will be returned to you once you land in Vienna.' How stupid I was to believe her but being a refugee and bouncing around for so many months you start feeling like you don't understand a thing about the immigration process and are told to just do whatever anyone tells you to." She sighs. "Mrs. M saved me." "The little red-haired woman? How?"

When Leila's plane landed, she couldn't find the airline agent who took her passport. She tried to get through customs and explain, but the customs agent just smirked and didn't believe a word of her story. Leila was taken straight to the airport detention center and locked up. "I was a mess. An interpreter finally came to explain things to me." The interpreter said the Austrian authorities didn't believe her story because there were too many asylum seekers arriving in Austria without the proper travel documents. What happens is that while they are on the plane, they rip up their passports and flush them down the toilet. "Then," the interpreter said, "they make up a story like yours about what happened to their 'visa'. The plan then is to hold you here until you can be deported back to Iran." Leila's world shattered. They told her she wasn't allowed to contact anyone. There was even a Bahá'í woman supposed to be meeting Leila at baggage claim, but they wouldn't go to try to find her to verify the story. Leila persisted and persisted. "I don't even want to stay in Austria," she said, "I'm just trying to get to America. I have a visa and a passport. If you contact the Bahá'ís of Austria, they can verify this, or even go ask the Austrian Embassy!"

And fortunately for my sister, when the airport security officials phoned the Bahá'í Center it was Mrs. M, the fiery guardian for freedom seeking men and women, who answered the call. She came right to the airport. "I'm going to have the Vienna police verify your story about how you were tricked by that airline agent," she assured her. "This is so common. Turkish agents often identify young women with valid—and valuable—European visas. They steal them and can sell them to smugglers at a high price." Four days later, Leila was released to her host family and Mrs. M brought her to Miss Anna who helped her apply for asylum in the United States. Except that since she no longer had a passport, her process was slowed down while they began the paperwork from scratch.

My only contact with Leila until this point had been through relayed messages from my brothers and parents. She had clearly withheld information from them or they were withholding parts of her story from me, either way, I feel terrible about all that she has endured. "So now what?" I ask her. "Well, the UN has finally approved my asylum request, so now it's just waiting on an interview with the US embassy." I've only just arrived and yet here she is just a few short weeks or months away from completing the last leg of her journey. I can't think about losing her again so soon. I try to shake the idea from my head and focus on the here and now. Leila senses my brooding thoughts, "Don't worry about it," she says. "Tomorrow morning, we're going shopping!"

The day starts at a kiosk in the transit station to get me my own transport pass for the trains and busses. Then we take a ride to the Bahá'í Center to meet with Mrs. M. She registers me with the Austrian police system and gets me a temporary ID. "Make sure you are extra respectful of Austrian laws during your stay here, OK?" "Of course," I tell her, "but like what?" She tells me it's little things. "There are many refuges here right now, people from Eastern Europe, like Czechoslovakia and Yugoslavia, from Turkey and from Russia, and lots of Iranian Jews. I get to work with all of them when they are in trouble since I speak so many languages. I have lots of stories. But the thing is, a lot of refugees don't buy train tickets or pay bus fares. It's on the honor system, which means yes, you could technically board a bus from the back and ride for free, but occasionally, transit police come through to check tickets. If you don't have one, you'll get taken down to the station and fined." She raised just one of her eyebrows at me, "And I don't want to get that phone call from the police." Of course, I understand. Our temporary IDs say we are under the Bahá'ís of Austria's protection—that call wouldn't look good for either Mrs. M who works for the police or for the Bahá'í Faith. She tells me not to do other things—things I wouldn't even ever think of doing—but I appreciate her warnings nonetheless. "Some refugees are breaking the phones, so they can make free calls to their homeland. Others are shoplifting or playing their boom boxes too loudly ("OK, this isn't such a bad crime" she explains, "but it's not polite and can get you a warning"). We should pay our rent and not get evicted, not get drunk or buy drugs or do any crazy things. Mrs. M is basically a parent to teenagers and young adult refugees starting to get wild and experiment now that they aren't under their own parents' watchful eye! "I know I don't really have anything to worry about with you," she says, "if you're anything like your sister."

From there Leila and I make our way to Miss Anna's office where I officially register with the IRC and she gives me information on free English-and German-language classes offered to refugees. "Keep me informed about your whereabouts while I initiate the process for your journey to the US." I nod and tell her I will. She is a woman of very few words, but I find her pleasant. She says she will ask the embassy to combine both Leila and mine's requests for US visas since I am a minor. "I can't promise it will work, but I'll try." That sounds promising, but in a few days, we'll learn from the US authorities that combining our case will not necessarily speed things up for me and will most likely slow things down for Leila. I can't let that happen. Not after all she's been through. I tell Miss Anna not to combine our cases and I mentally prepare for the fact that Leila will probably be leaving in two to three months, and I'll be on my own again.

After all these appointments, we head to the fashion district for some western clothes. Whitewashed jeans and big hoop earrings, off the shoulder tops and lacy crops adorn the mannequins. "I don't think this is . . . my look," I tell Leila, amused at the style, and also a bit horrified. "Look, you don't have to wear anything risqué, but neon colors are definitely *in* and you're definitely getting a jean jacket." For the rest of the day we browse boutiques and try on dozens of outfits and shoes. "I just want you to look good and fit in!" Leila says, "But I also want you to be savvy with money. They do these sales and that's the best time to shop." She explains end-of-season sales, but I need clothes now—for summer—not for next winter. We spend a little extra for a summer wardrobe, and I send out a word of thanks, for Kia and his financial support that made this fun day with my sister possible. "Next on the agenda," Leila says holding up some tweezers later that night, "is to get rid of your unibrow!" In Iran, girls don't pluck their eyebrows until they get married, but it's clearly not the fashion here and I'm only too ready to be done with it. "Go for it!" I tell her. I look like a new person, especially when she fixes my hair in the morning. Inside, I don't feel like the same person, and now the outside is starting to reflect that transformation too.

The next two weeks unfold gently. English classes in the morning and German lessons after that. Our English teacher is really funny. He's an American in his thirties with a thick beard, who likes to talk to us in idioms and slang as if we are already fluent. Like when we're practicing saying really simple things, "Thank you, the cake was delicious. I would like some more." He'll say, "No duh! Who doesn't want more cake?" He tells us if something is really nasty beyond nasty then it's "grody." And if anyone gets flustered, he says, "Take a chill pill. You're doing fine. English grammar is gnarly." But Leila's and my personal favorite is when class is over, and he looks at his watch and says, "Ok gang, it's been rad, but I gotta bounce!"

After classes we usually go visit the Bahá'í Center. There I've met a dozen friends also in transition. We help Mrs. M mail books and publications or set up for special events, and in the afternoons we explore the city or stroll through Vienna's beautiful parks and squares. I cannot get over Vienna's beauty and charm. Everywhere I look there is intricate art and architecture; it's like always being inside a museum while still enjoying the pleasant summer breeze. At Stadtpark, there are statues of famous Austrian composers like Franz Schubert and Johann Strauss; I don't even recognize these names. Instead, I realize that I know absolutely nothing of classical music. I realize I have been deprived of music, and not just any music, classical music, which from the little I have heard since arriving is so unlike any other music! It is so powerful, so moving, so emotional. Words can't even describe what these geniuses composed, and I wasn't allowed to be exposed to that treasure. I feel cheated. But I aim to change that. I can't wait to take it all in now that I have the chance. I don't like thinking about how life was before. I don't talk about it with my new friends and I push the thoughts away when I am reminded. But I like to think about Baba and how much he loved that old Siemens radio and how much pleasure he took in finding a bit of Old Persian folk music for us to listen to. Maybe one day he'll be able to get more stations and I can introduce him to Brahms and we'll listen to classical music together.

Our group especially likes to go to Karntner Strasse where musicians and magicians, puppeteers and mimes, and a whole world of performers line the streets and busk for coins. Sometimes, we even buy ice cream cones, but for the most part we can't afford to do anything except people watch. The first time we walked all the way down Karntner Strasse, Leila showed me that it dead ends at a magnificent church—the first Christian church I've ever seen. I had to go inside. Paintings of saints hang from floor to ceiling and stained-glass windows let in thick, dreamy light. Carved pillars line the rows of pews where people kneel, praying, and statues peek out of every nook and alcove. The pipes of an organ rose high behind the altar and played a melancholic and beautiful song. The place took my breath away. I wanted very much to be respectful, to be quiet and devout, but it was a bustle of activity. Tourists were everywhere, whispering loudly and snapping photos. To the side, people lit candles, sometimes leaving them where they found them others carrying them to tables in front of statues and leaving them there. The soft, wispy light of these candles made me want to offer up a prayer—I am not sure if that is their purpose—but I liked the idea. I lit a candle too and thanked God for the Most Great Peace, for finding light even in a place so different from how I grew up practicing religion. The pictures are different, the prayers, the structure of the building. I wondered what the differences meant to the people who worshipped here, what deeper beauty they knew and felt because they could look into the eyes of their saints and call to mind a hundred different stories testifying to the majesty of God? Every time we come to Karntner Strasse, I decided then and there, I will make a point to come to this church and light a candle. Leila eventually found me and popped my serious little bubble, "Hey," she said, "I'm hungry. Let's bounce!"

Leila wants to show me every place in this magical city. "Vienna just takes your breath away around every corner, doesn't it?" she asks. It's a world away from war-torn Tehran. So charming, clean, and safe. People are respectful and kind. What else can one wish for in life? Two weeks pass by like a happy dream. Leila and I start to realize though that despite how gracious our host family is, the flat is too small for all six of us. We get Kia's permission to start looking for another place to live and with the help of Mrs. M find a nice house with a room to rent just two blocks from the Danube River. The older German couple, who own the home, show us the top floor with the three different rooms available for rent and the shared kitchen and bathroom among them. They only speak German, so we rely on Leila's limited German plus a lot of hand gestures to communicate. We are interested in the largest room—it has two single beds, a small table with chairs, an eleven-inch TV, and a small clock radio whose alarm, they show us, would wake us up to the "Blue Danube Radio" the English-language station. Leila tries to tell them we have the money and that we wish to give it to them right now, so we can move in immediately. Before they are willing to hand over keys, they want to make sure we are aware of all the house rules. We follow them through the house while they point and explain things which we do not exactly understand. We nod our heads and smile and say, "Ja ja" nonetheless. The rules seem to be mostly self-explanatory—keep noise down, lock the front door, keep the common areas clean, we are allowed to receive calls from their downstairs phone but not to make them. It's a deal. Leila and I return to our host family and give them the news. They are sad to see us go because their sweet children have bonded with Leila like an older sister. "Won't you have breakfast with us before you leave tomorrow?" they ask, and we happily agree.

Breakfast turns out to be an astonishment. Whereas I am used to a big breakfast of bread and jam, fruit, and tea, breakfast for Austrians is just one slice of toast and a cup of coffee. And I am a small person compared to their rather large father! Leila tells me they take a mid-morning break to eat cheese and crackers, then have lunch, and then another afternoon snack of cheese, crackers, and perhaps also pâté before finally eating dinner. All I know is that I'm going to need a mid-morning break too or I certainly won't make it to lunch.

On our way to our new apartment we buy a few groceries, bread, jam, eggs, rice, milk, tea and some fruits and veggies. Inside the refrigerator is a note that says "Schwarz," we don't know what this means, so we stock the shelf with our groceries and remove the note. The next morning when we went to make breakfast, we found a new note with the same word on the shelf again and all of our food moved to a different shelf. Leila got out her German dictionary and looked up *schwarz*. It meant "black." We looked at each other, puzzling over the word. "Perhaps they think our groceries are dirty?" "Oh! That could be, let's take everything out and wash it." After scrubbing everything in the sink and wiping it all dry, we replaced our groceries in the fridge. Then we went out for the day and didn't return until evening.

At dinner time, once again we found our food moved to a new shelf and the note was back! We were worried and scared now. "Let's go downstairs and ask what they mean," Leila said. The couple just smiled and nodded and then spoke a lot of German, very fast. Since we still looked confused, they added hand gestures and used even more words and spoke even longer. Leila finally nodded and said, "Danke, danke!" We went upstairs to eat and I asked her, "So what does it mean?" "I still have no idea."

Three days later, our breakfast was interrupted by lots of laughter as people started to move boxes inside and into a room across from ours. Leila and I snuck over to our bedroom window to get a better look at the couple. The woman was tall, and her blonde hair glowed in the morning sun. She and the man went back and forth from their car carrying boxes up the stairs and dropping them in the bedroom. They laughed a lot. We had to hurry off to our English class so we didn't get to meet them. When we returned home, the woman greeted us with a strong handshake and told us her name was Brigitte. "But I prefer to be called Lisa," she said. She's nineteen and doesn't speak much English; the man helping her was her boyfriend, but he lives somewhere else. We aren't sure what to make of her. Austrians are said to be very, very friendly. What did she think of us? Too quiet and reserved? Stuck up?

In the morning, we saw that our groceries were again pushed aside, and the ominous note again taped in the fridge. Lisa was in the kitchen too, making coffee, so we showed her the note hoping she knew what it meant. "Danke!" she said taking the note and throwing it in the garbage. "No!" Leila said, breaking out her dictionary again and trying to tell her about it meaning "black" and how we had washed the groceries, but the note keeps getting put back. Lisa kept saying, "It's OK. It's OK." For some reason, she understood the cryptic note, but we still struggled to grasp its meaning. Finally, Leila and I realized that Lisa's last name is Schwarz! She is Brigitte "Lisa" Schwarz and that shelf is reserved for her! Our food wasn't dirty after all. When it dawned on us, we couldn't stop laughing. Nothing could have helped break the ice between us faster.

Now Lisa, Leila and I do daily language lessons together. She wants to learn more English, we want to learn more German, so we've banded together to share what we know and help each other along. We speak English and fill in the blanks with German words. It's confusing, but we laugh through it and at the end we understand each other. We learn that Lisa comes from a small town where her family earns a living as farmers; she's in Vienna to attend nursing school, and her boyfriend drives up to visit her on the weekends. When he comes, the two of them make a lot of noise and, to our ears, we can't tell if they are arguing or just having a normal conversation. It's difficult to distinguish between sarcasm and joy in the German tongue. But the two of them seem happy. Pretty soon, we become so close that we prepare and eat all our meals together and walk the neighborhoods daily. Sometimes we chase each other up and down the shores of the Danube River. Lisa is so strong. She can easily lift me up in her arms and carry me or give me piggy back rides without breaking a sweat. Our little home feels filled with sunlight. And our friendships are about to expand.

Farah moves in a couple weeks later. She is a Persian Bahá'í in transition like us, but much older, late twenties. She always keeps a cigarette in her hand and likes to touch up her makeup often. Lisa finds Farah's name impossible to pronounce, but it's still easy for the four of us to become fast friends. On the first weekend of every month, many of the local museums and tourist attractions offer free admission, so we start exploring as much as we can together. The museums are incredible, filled with paintings and sculptures beyond imagination. Just like with classical music, it makes me realize how little I know about the art world. I crave to know how it feels to hold a paintbrush and squish clay in my hands. Curious to know if any artistic creativity resides deep inside me too.

We walk the impeccably landscaped Baroque gardens at the Schönbrunn Palace, the former residence of the Habsburg monarchs and also home to the oldest zoo in the world, where I see panda bears and giraffes for the first time. We tour the decadent St. Stephen's Cathedral and climb Vienna's mini-mountain, Kahlenberg, to get 360-degree views of the Danube, the Vienna Woods, and beyond. Sometimes we simply play a game of chess in the park, but we always have dinner together and play cards at night before turning in.

Farah has a hard time sleeping at night. We hear her pacing the floor, sucking on cigarettes, and watching scary movies across the hall. I wouldn't sleep either if I watched scary movies right before bed, but she tells me that's not why she can't sleep. "The attic," she says sticking the butt of her cigarette toward the ceiling. "It's haunted." At nighttime, she hears footsteps above her room. She tells us she's even gone up to the attic and found tombstones. Yeah right, we all think. Clearly, she's joking, just like she does with everything. Farah is always cracking jokes even about her own life, which isn't a very happy story to tell. Back in Iran, she fell in love with a neighbor boy. But he was Muslim and neither of the families supported the marriage and her family forced her to leave the country. She was supposed to join her sisters in Virginia. "Supposed to," she says. "That's what my parents wanted anyway, but that's not what I want." All she wants is to go back to Iran. She wants it so much she refuses to even try to learn English because she will not allow herself to envision a future that doesn't include this man. She cracks a smile. "Ah well, but then again. I've got my cigarettes, makeup, and a pile of horror films, so what more can a girl really ask for, right? And I've got you three crazies. Life is OK." Yet, she keeps talking about the footsteps and voices she hears coming from upstairs. We come to realize that she's actually serious. She takes us up there and she wasn't lying—there are tombstones everywhere! "The tombstones are gateways for ghosts to come back from the dead and they talk to me. Makes it hard to sleep," Farah says. I'm totally spooked but if ghosts are going to talk to someone, I'm glad it's Farah and not me. "The owner of the house must have been a tombstone maker," Leila reasons, "These probably haven't belonged to anyone yet." Then Farah takes us to the basement and out into the yard—tombstones are everywhere. "Maybe the owner was just a tombstone maker, or maybe this house is sitting right on top of a cemetery. Maybe all these dead people I hear are really buried right here," Farah takes a drag on her cigarette and blows it coolly from her nostrils. I shiver. "OK, enough about ghosts," Leila says. "I've got dessert waiting!"

Leila treats us to an amazing dessert she's learned how to make since living in Austria. It's called tiramisu and it is positively heaven whipped in a bowl. "What have you done?" I ask staring wide-eyed after my first taste. "So you like it?" she asks. "It's incredible. I'm going to eat the whole pan." "Not if I eat it first!" Farah says scooping out another big spoonful. Anytime someone has a birthday party, Leila brings her tiramisu, and everyone always gushes over it. She always gives credit to the lady, in whose home she once stayed, that taught her how to make it.

I've certainly been working on my sweet tooth these days. Sweet shops are on every corner and all the pastries are delicate, buttery, delicious. One day I step on the scale and I assume it's broken, but it's not. I've gained twenty pounds. I've always been terribly skinny, but now that I'm not stressed or scared constantly—my appetite seems to have increased and I'm keeping weight on more easily. "You look healthy," Leila tells me. I feel healthy. At a Bahá'í meeting we go to, there's a table full of Viennese pastries and Leila explains what each one is and describes in elaborate detail the talents of the pastry chefs. "Maybe you should be a baker," I say, kind of amazed at how much she knows about pastries. "No, I'd rather just build the machines that make the pastries and then enjoy eating the creations!" she says. "So an engineer then? Not a doctor?" I ask. "Who knows. Wait until I'm in the US and actually in college and then we'll talk." One pastry in particular catches my eye. "Look at that detail!" I exclaim. These pastry chefs really are talented. "How in the world did they get those tiny black dots inside the green jelly? It's magnificent." Leila starts laughing uncontrollably. Tears are actually streaming down her face. "What? What's so funny?" "I'll show you how they do it," she says when she catches her breath, "tomorrow." In the morning, we go to a Turkish market and get some fresh fruit. Leila picks out a fuzzy little oval thing I've never seen before. "You want to know how the pastry chefs do it, watch closely." Leila slices through the fuzzy fruit and little green discs filled with black seeds fall like dominoes. I'm so embarrassed! Leila smiles. "Behold! It's called—kiwi!"

We've met a group of six young Bahá'í men and women through our English course and we often go hiking with them or hang out at the girl's apartment in a small village called Klosterneuburg, about thirty minutes away. We share our trials and triumphs, but hopefully not on the same day—as happened the day Leila learned she had the authorization to finally fly to the US. She was ecstatic, bouncing up and down and clapping her hands. "Dance with me!" she said, spinning me around while she blasted Blue Danube Radio. She shared the good news in our English class and everyone was thrilled, but later that night we got a knock on our front door. Two of our male Bahá'í friends had received word later in the day that they had been rejected, one from the US and one from Canada—they'd been in Austria for two years already. I could smell the whisky on their breath as they stood there smoking in the rain. We invited them in and made tea.

Farah came over and we stayed up late into the night talking. Our friends were devastated, but they were also scared and angry and trying desperately to make light of their situation. "I've got it," one said, "Leila—marry me." "What?" all three of us girls said. "Marry me!" he continued, "It can be a fake marriage, don't worry. I'll release you from your vows when we get to the US. Think about it. It could work." "You're drunk," Farah sneered, "That's a terrible idea." "No really!" he said, "I knew a man who had a fake marriage to a woman who already had a visa ready, and that actually expedited the process for both of them!" He then hung his head. "I know. I'm desperate. Pay no attention to me." I watched Leila from the corner of my eye. She was being so gracious. It's hard to be happy when your friends are so unhappy, and this was supposed to be her day; instead, she looked guilty and embarrassed for her good fortune. Being a refugee, comes with a whole bag of mixed emotions that they never tell you about when you're applying for your visa.

Eventually everyone was yawning, and the conversation had grown sparse and silly. We let the boys sleep in our bed and Leila and I curled up with Farah in her tiny twin bed. It must have been noon before we woke up. Thank goodness the boys didn't remember much from the night before and were apologetic if they had done or said anything embarrassing. We didn't bring up the marriage proposal.

Leila's November departure comes fast. Faster than I'd like to believe. While she prepares for California, a place she'll never have to wear a winter coat again, I buy a pair of boots, a shawl, and gloves to get me through the cold and snowy winters here that I keep hearing about. Leila helps set me up with my own bank account and I ask the Bahá'í girls in Klosterneuburg if I can move in with them since the rent in Vienna will be too much for me on my own. They say yes. The night before Leila leaves, we both pack bags and say tearful goodbyes to Lisa and Farah.

The next day, my sister and I part yet again, and we embark on different journeys to what we can still only hope is a similar end.

21
FRIENDS

I cry the entire train ride to Klosterneuburg. Without Leila, everything feels foreign and the separation insurmountable. I'm just barely treading water alone in the middle of a cold ocean. Is life just playing games with me? Four months of feeling normal, of being with family again, and then it's all taken away. I don't even really know the women I am going to live with that well. My path ahead is lonely. I can't see my way through it.

Soon, decorations go up across the city, which remind me that Christmas and a western New Years are fast approaching. Both will be firsts for me—so perhaps with them will come good "tidings of comfort and joy" for me too.

The train pulls into the station and as I walk to my new home, the adult in me kicks in and I take note of where the grocery store, bank, and post office are all located. This grounds me somewhat. My flat mates are lovely and even though there isn't a bit of room for me they've welcomed me with open arms—and spread an extra mattress on the floor. My bed is beside a queen bed that the oldest woman, Shahin, shares with her two daughters Shiva and Aryana, who are just barely four and six years old, their dolls and toys tumble off their bed and onto the floor around my mattress. On the other side of me is Mahasti's single cot. She is a woman in her twenties, and she fills her little nightstand with makeup, hair supplies, and a mountain of cassette tapes for her boombox. "You like music,

right?" she asks me first thing. "I think so," I say, "I mean, yes I do. It's just
. . . I don't know a lot of music." "Don't worry," she says, "We'll take care
of that." There are also two sisters, nineteen and twenty-four, and a young
woman, Azita, whose sisters are already in Chicago. Our bedroom is just
big enough to scrunch all the beds in side by side. Those who have been
here longer have hung a few photos and posters. I notice there are a dozen
English or German language dictionaries lying all around the room—the
mark of an immigrant. In the corner, there is a big coal stove with a shiny,
brown ceramic chimney, which I'm told does a good job of keeping the
room warm even through particularly long and frigid snowstorms.

"We're pretty organized here. We have to be," Shahin says as she
shows me a chore chart. The main tasks are: taking turns filling up the
plastic water barrel in our makeshift kitchen with water from the hallway
sink; and going down into the cellar for more coal. "It's like a dungeon
down there and you'll come up black and sooty, so wear something you
don't like that much." The coal cellar was used as a bomb shelter during
World War II. The damp chill from the stone walls and earth floor slink
up the steep stairs as we descend with our flashlights and canvas rice bags.
It's my first time venturing down there and images flash through my head
of people hiding, waiting to find out if they will survive another night. My
skin grows cold and damp too, and it's so quiet I think I can almost hear the
sirens at the Mehrabad airport in Tehran again. But no, I can't let my mind
go there. Not now. I shake my head to gather myself and keep moving. My
companions are as anxious as I am to get out of there as fast as we can. We
fill the two sacks and then it takes two women on each bag to haul it up
to our floor. I have never seen coal before; it's amazing that just two pieces
give a whole night of warmth. We let the heat die down in the day to keep
costs low and because we all leave the house to attend English classes for
half the day. We take turns cooking and washing up the food dishes. Our
kitchen consists of two long plastic tables. One with all our cooking supplies and spices, pots pans, bread and oil, and on the other one we have a
hot plate for boiling water and cooking food. There's the water barrel and a

small refrigerator and a couple cabinets filled with mismatched plates and cups. We do have a nice size dining room table in the front room where we can share meals together. The windows in the front room are tall and let in quite a lot of sunlight. There is one toilet with a sink down the hallway and it is shared between two other flats on this level; there's no shower and no running water inside our flat. Twice a week, we'll pay to go to the swimming pool nearby just to use their shower facilities.

Other than a few tense moments, like when I confronted the sisters about smoking inside, we all get along fine. "Let it go, let it go," Shahin is always reminding us. "We're all spread thin. We're all doing our best. It's not worth it to hold grudges." She's become like a mother to us all and is good at helping us resolve conflict. We must rely on each other so much that we cannot help but become like one big family. These are the toughest days of our lives, waiting in limbo. We laugh a lot—especially when we watch old tapes of Persian movies from before the revolution on our tiny TV. Many are Persian comedies. I didn't realize there was such a thing! I don't remember laughter being normal in Iran. We all agree that we were born and raised in the wrong era. We laugh a lot together, but we also cry a lot. The tears come often and unexpectedly, especially when one of us talks to family back home and we get news about a grandparent's failing health, or even the sweet news of a niece or nephew being born and siblings getting married. We're missing important moments and it breaks our hearts. Our emotions are always so heightened that we are ever on the verge of one outpouring or another, be it joyful or mournful. Music helps.

Mahasti's boombox thumps all the time, but none of us really mind because it's just so good to have music again. To take away music should be a crime. It is a basic human right to sing and to dance. But I am only just learning this as I learn to open up my mind, my heart, and my soul, as I learn what the world looks like when there is music and no shame in listening to it. The sisters teach Azita and I how to dance. They teach me Persian dances—dances from home that I've never learned before—graceful moves where it looks like you are floating and your arms paint calligraphy in the sky. Not a day goes by where we don't dance.

Mahasti's boombox isn't the only thing that's loud. Her voice is even louder, her personality the loudest. I start to notice that she really gets on the nerves of the other girls; they are short and sarcastic with each other. But for whatever reason, Mahasti and I get along just fine. Maybe it's because I don't mind her southern accent or that she's always singing. She sings loud and proud like Baba, and because she's from the Persian Gulf she usually sings Bandari songs, which come from that region. I recognize some of them—Baba used to sing them all the time while he worked around the house. One time, Mahasti and I were singing so loud along with the boombox that our neighbors called the cops. Mrs. M was right all those months ago when she warned me about following Austrian laws. When the cops first arrived, I felt a wash of old fear—the fear that we were going to be arrested because music was illegal. I had to talk myself down from the panic. The officers were friendly though and just gave us a warning. We've been more considerate with the noise level since then, but sometimes when things are tough you really just have to blare the boombox and dance it out. It feels good to discover there is still a lot of play in me; even with everything I've been through. Even with all the pressure and responsibility still on my shoulders from living on my own in a foreign country.

I haven't forgotten about Lisa and Farah in all this. Twice a week after English classes in Vienna, I visit them and we still go to Karntner Strasse to watch people, and now, to listen to the Christmas carolers strolling the streets. I feel most at home when I am with them because we talk easily with each other about the deepest parts of our hearts. On one of these visits, Lisa gave us some shocking news. She's decided to become a nun after the new year and continue her nursing studies through the church. I'm not sure exactly what this means or if I will ever get to see her again. She says I can still come visit her at the church convent now and then, but that she cannot leave while she is in training. Farah is deeply upset by the news. I promise to come visit Farah more often, so her days are not so lonely. When Farah and I finally get the chance to visit Lisa after the New Year, we will hardly recognize her when she answers the door. Dressed in traditional robes with her head covered, we decided to play a joke on her and in broken German asked if Brigitte Schwarz was there, explaining that we were her friends. Lisa just laughed and hugged us. She lifted me up and twirled me around just like she always does. We toured the convent, keeping our voices to a whisper. The sterility and silence of the place were such a contrast to the silly and rambunctious Lisa that we have come to love. My heart ached to go run and wrestle with her down by the Danube again.

Christmas came like a dream. My roommates and I took a train to Vienna and when the escalators surfaced from the underground train station, we stepped into a winter wonderland. Big, fluffy snowflakes fell gently and the warm steam of chestnuts roasting in big pans floated up around us. How could we resist? The vendor scooped the chestnuts into a white, paper funnel and sprinkled them with salt. We nibbled the treat and strolled to the church where a choir was singing Christmas songs. Inside everything sparkled. Lights and decorations made everything magical. The songs of the choir echoed through the church with the deep sound of the organ and the glistening handbells. Some songs were so joyful, and others were hauntingly beautiful. We listened for a long, long while then we ended our Christmas experience with mugs of hot chocolate and headed home. I don't think I will ever forget the unbelievable energy of that day, the people dressed in red and green, the vibrancy, the smiles on every person's face. Recently, I saw a movie about Christmas, but it was nowhere near as wonderful as what I had experienced.

Before the new year, I visit Miss Anna at the IRC to check on the status of my request. She too thinks it's strange that we haven't heard anything for five months, especially since she had requested my case be expedited because of my age. She digs around in my file and makes some phone calls. Her news isn't good. "There was a mix-up at the embassy." Apparently, when I told her to drop the request to combine my case with Leila's, they had also dropped the simultaneous request to expedite my interview date.

"Uuugh," I throw my hands over my face and rub my temples. I can't hide my annoyance. All this time! All this time I haven't even been on their radar! "I'm sorry. I'm so sorry," Miss Anna says, "I know this is frustrating. I promise to check your case more frequently and keep you posted." There is nothing to do but keep on waiting.

I call Kia to vent my frustration and he says things can only get better from here. He also tells me that since I'm doing so well in my English classes that I should register to take the TOEFL test to prepare for what's coming. If I take it here, I'll be all ready to start college as soon as I get to the states. My English teacher agrees that I am ready and registers me for February; he gives me some practice tests to work on at home.

What I need is a good old fire ceremony like we have before the Persian New Year. Purge this year of all the frustrations. Give my sickness and regrets to the fire and jump into a warm new year renewed. But there are still many months of a cold, harsh winter ahead after this western New Year.

Just like at Christmas, my roommates and I head into Vienna's city center for the new year holiday. We meet up with our male friends and take another train to Karntner Strasse where we meet Lisa and Farah. The streets are the most crowded I've yet seen. Everyone sings together out in the snow with cups of hot cocoa in their hands. The coffee shops and restaurants are packed and the crowd outside keeps growing larger the closer it gets to midnight. Soon people start dancing—waltzing! —all around us. Lisa grabs my hands, shows me the steps, then leads us away into the crowd. I love dancing. I love spinning in circles under the stars. I love catching the smiles on the faces all around me. There is only joy tonight and I can't help but laugh at the beauty of it all. I dance with all my roommates, with Farah, and with the boys. It's not Nowruz, but it's still pretty spectacular. In the final minute of the final hour of 1988, the crowd starts to count backwards until midnight. At the strike of the tower clock in the square, fireworks light up the night sky. People kiss each other all around me and wish each other a "*Frohes Neues Jahr!*"

Shahin holds her oldest girl's hand and carries her other daughter asleep in her arms. Their cheeks are red from the cold. Always the mother, she tells us that she is leaving, and we should come with her. "The temperature's dropping fast now!" We head to the station, but the subway cars are so crowded we have to split the group up just to fit inside. "We'll meet at the station near home and walk back together, OK?" Shahin says catching all our eyes and making sure we give a verbal agreement. In Vienna, we switch trains for Klosterneuburg, but I can't find anyone in my group. That's OK. The train is so warm and much less crowded now. It's a forty-minute ride and I am so tired. The gentle, clicking movement soon puts me to sleep. When I wake up, there are very few passengers on board. Dread fills me. I leap up and rush to look at the map over the door. I can't make sense of it. Where am I? I must have missed my stop. I try asking people, but they are all drunk and my German is terrible. In a panic, I jump off at the next stop. Mistake! This station is empty. And when the train whooshes away, the only other sound is the howl of dogs in the distance. I should have waited to get off at a busier station. I cross below the tracks and come back up on the other side. The map shows that I've only passed my stop by a few stations. But who knows when another train is coming? It's the middle of the night on a holiday. I was stupid. I wasn't thinking. I am so angry with myself. The silence makes me sick and I start to hyperventilate. No one knows where I am. People are drunk tonight, and crazy things happen when people drink. What if someone comes and kills me here? Oh, dear God, help me. Help me. Help me. Should I run? Do I find someone? What if whoever I find is a bad person? I don't know what to do but pray. *Is there any remover of difficulties, save God?* Where is Baba to comfort me, to tell me everything will be OK and that I am going to be safe? Would he say to me: "You cannot escape your destiny,"? Have I come this far and this close to my destiny just to lose it all simply because I was foolish and fell asleep? The world feels too vast, my parents seem an impossible distance away, and I am not sure I will ever be able to span the distance. I have never felt so alone. It scares me to my core.

It's at least an hour before another train arrives. I jump on, relieved, but can't stop crying. I watch the stations closely this time so I won't miss my stop. When I get off, it's the same thing—empty. I start to run home across icy, snow-packed streets and I stumble and slip the whole way. I must look like just another drunken New Year's Eve reveler. When I burst through the door of the flat, everyone is still up, calmly drinking tea. They see my tears and look confused. "Hi Mahvash. You're here." "What do you mean, I'm here?" "Oh, we just thought you went home with Farah and we wouldn't see you tonight." Not a single person had worried about me. No one had thought to come looking for me. What if something bad really had happened out there—I shudder at the thought. These women have been like family, but even they cannot take on the role of family completely. Family worries about you when you don't show up when you're supposed to. Family goes out looking for you. Family cannot sleep if they don't know you are safe. And my family is a thousand miles away in each direction. I crawl into bed and imagine Baba's fingers running through my hair, his voice singing a low lullaby.

22
ROOTS

My parents sold our house in Tehran. The one with all the fruit trees my dad planted for his children's return. Back in September, the war ended, and it seems people are slowly adjusting to a normal life again. I still don't know what normal really looks like, but I guess my normal would be: be with family, feel safe, go to school. It seems my family is all coming together again but I still don't know when my feet will hit US soil.

Cyrus was granted US citizenship which allowed him to apply for permanent residency for my parents. "Sorry, Mahvash," he told me. "The perk only applies for parents, children, or a spouse . . . not siblings." So still I wait. My parents are already in Turkey. The house was the last of their life savings and gave them enough for plane tickets plus a little extra. Cyrus flew to Turkey to meet them and help them with the paperwork and interviews since they don't speak English. The residency was approved, and their visas came almost immediately. They should be in the US by February. Leila's already in California, in fact, she begins college next month. I keep going about my "normal" routine; no more holidays to look forward to for a while. Just a lot of snow. Then I'm thrown a giant curveball.

Out of the blue, my front tooth began to hurt, but I paid it no mind, thinking it'd go away in a few days. I brush and floss like my life depends on it thanks to Baba's constant preaching. But recently while flossing, I felt a bump up in my gums. I traced my finger around the outside of my gums and the soft tissue above my front teeth. Another bump, this one in my nose. Maybe a pimple? It'll go away.

But it didn't go away. One day, I woke up and half of my face was swollen, my right eye almost shut. The pain kept increasing and turned into headaches. When I broke out in a fever it was clear something was truly wrong. Shahin told me she thought it was a tooth infection or an abscess. "You're going to need antibiotics to get better." I took a train to the city to ask Mrs. M at the Bahá'í Center for help. She took one look at me and my swollen face spoke for itself. "The infection is spreading to your head. You need antibiotics immediately." She told me about a dental clinic that treated refugees and I went straight there. But no one spoke English. And I couldn't figure out how to fill out the German paperwork. I remembered that a Persian Bahá'í family lived nearby, and I went there to ask the daughter to help me. She was attending medical school in Vienna and spoke very good German. The next day, she served as my interpreter and helped with the paperwork. The dentist gave me antibiotics and told me to come back the following week for a root canal.

At night the pain was unbearable. I had a strange idea to put my face against the chimney portion of the coal heater in the room and the heat actually relieved the pain enough for me to relax and eventually go back to bed. But the swelling wasn't going down, in fact it was getting worse, now my right eye was almost completely shut. A week later the infection was so bad the doctor told me she would need to extract the tooth. I begged and begged her to save my tooth. The thought of losing my front tooth devastated me. I sobbed in her dentist chair and asked her please, please, please to save my tooth. She sighed. "OK," she told my interpreter. "I'll try, but I warn you . . . I won't be using any anesthetics." I tried to muster a smile, "Go ahead. That's OK." Anything to save my tooth. The drill started with a buzz and hovered near my mouth. "Ready?" the dentist asked. "Ready," I said. "OK then. Don't move." I could never have anticipated that kind of pain.

I didn't once yell out. I didn't scream or jerk around, but I cried silently in agony, clutching the plastic cushion of the chair, as she drilled away. My tears flooded down my neck and soaked my chest and sweatshirt. Now and again she would stop, pull down her mask and tell the interpreter that she felt really sorry for me. "Does she want me to stop?" No, I told her through my tears. Keep going. Keep going.

"Come back again tomorrow," she said when she had done all she could for the day. I barely made it to tomorrow, the pain was worse, and the swelling hadn't gone down at all. The next day, the dentist again stopped after she couldn't take my tears anymore and spoke to my interpreter. "What?" I asked. "What is she saying?" My interpreter hesitated, then told me: "She says . . . she says a root canal without anesthetics is the worst pain in the world. Worse," she continued, "than childbirth."

If I look on the bright side, this torture means that not only will I get to keep my tooth, but I will be able to handle absolutely anything that comes my way. Ever since I fled Tehran, I've seen over and over and over again just how resilient humans are. Just when we think we have been tested beyond our limits, we learn we are so much stronger than we ever knew. I wish I hadn't had to learn that by sitting in that dentist's chair, but there I was and there I was determined to stay if that's what it took to keep my tooth. How I was going to be able to will myself to take the train and walk there again tomorrow, I didn't know. I just knew that I would because I would choose to.

I went back to the dentist the next day, and the day after that, and every day for one week. Each time she flushed the inside of the tooth and cleaned the root until finally, the pain was relieved, and the swelling started to go down. At my follow-up appointment two weeks later, the swelling had nearly all disappeared. I thanked the dentist profusely. She smiled and said, "You did the hard work. Well done."

It's been nearly a month of living in this painful haze and dealing with all the stress that comes from being sick in a house that doesn't have running water or even a shower. Now that I'm starting to come out of the blur, I realize I had completely forgotten about the rest of my life, reunification, appointments, lessons. Everything. All I could do was just barely manage the pain. I'm not even seventeen. I'm the youngest in my family. This is all so wrong. But what can I do? I'm an involuntary adult forced to take care of every aspect of life by myself. I give myself a day to feel bad for myself and then I'm back on my feet. I figure it's time to pay some visits now that I have energy again.

Miss Anna is first, and she lets me know I'm next on the waitlist. Then I drop by to visit Farah, but no one answers the door, so I head to the convent and visit with Lisa for a bit. Then it's off to the Bahá'í center to check in with Mrs. M. "Oh, Mahvash," she grabs my hands, "I'm afraid I have bad news." I've never seen her eyes so serious before. "Farah attempted suicide." I pull away to steady myself against a chair. "What?" "Farah. She tried to jump out her bedroom window, but the neighbors called for help before she could jump." "Where is she now?" "She's been hospitalized at a mental institution." I head back home but I can't stop thinking about her. How lonely she was and about all the "voices" up in the attic. Part of me feels guilty for leaving her alone in that house, but mostly I feel sad, and just very, very scared for her. I look out the train window the whole ride home, but don't see anything through the fog of tears.

The next day at the mental hospital I have trouble communicating to the receptionist what I want. She says I have to wait for visiting hours to see my friend. My fingers tap everything, my knees, the armchair. I'm not sure I really want to see Farah in her current state. I'm not sure how to handle it, or if I can keep myself together, but I don't get up to leave.

Finally, a nurse leads me to a visiting room where a multitude of other nurses stand around like sentinels. Farah walks in dressed in her hospital clothes. She's missing her signature red lipstick and mascara. I don't think I've ever seen her without makeup. She looks pale. She kisses and hugs me. She's overly calm. When I ask how she's doing, she starts going on and on about someone I don't know. Probably, she's been given a drug to keep her anxiety low or to help with the voices. She tells me about the food here and how it's all disgusting. My smile gets harder and harder to fake. She still doesn't speak any German so she asks me, "Won't you ask someone here when I'm going home?" Instinctively, I know this is not a good question to ask, so I divert the topic and tell her about how I'll come visit again soon. When visiting hours are over, we both cry but I honestly really don't know what I am feeling. This sadness is a well I've never drawn from before. The tears keep coming even as I walk out of the institution. I'm angry and upset. Sad. I bury my head in TOEFL study books and try to distract myself from my poor friend in a mental hospital. The hardships just keep coming.

After that was the toilet. It backed up and overflowed all over the floor and into the hallway. Our German neighbors blamed us for it. "There are too many of you in one unit!" they said. They were so angry with us they wouldn't even call a plumber to get it fixed, and none of us knew enough German to make the call ourselves. Four or five times a day, we bundled up the little kids and trudged through the snow to the train station to use a pay toilet. During the day, it wasn't such a big deal, but at night in the snow and on the ice, it was miserable. We all crossed our fingers that no one got her period. But sure enough, Mahasti's flow started. It doesn't matter if it's the middle of the night, if she needs to go and clean herself up, we all bundle up and are there for her—for each other. I'll never take a toilet for granted again. Being able to take care of the most basic necessities of life go a long, long way at helping you cope with the rest of life.

Visiting Farah is always stressful for me, but I make myself do it anyway. I just can't abandon her in there. Two days a week, after English classes, I head over for visiting hours and try to be as supportive and positive as I can for her. The room is always chaotic though, with patients banging things, breaking dishes, and screaming out at random. If a patient won't behave, then a nurse comes over and quickly gives them an injection. One day, Farah doesn't come in the room. I hope that maybe she has been released. The nurses say no, just transferred to "a more secure unit." I follow a nurse through multiple gated areas. I sneak looks into rooms as we pass and see people tied to beds screaming to get out. Others are so drugged they appear dead. "Farah's been trying to hurt herself again," the nurse explains. That's why she's in here.

I find her on a chair in a corner. She greets me and is chatty, but she's talking about so many things at once and nothing makes sense. She keeps mentioning some person and . . . I'm not really sure they even exist. It's like this every time I see her. She talks about things that don't exist and I get more depressed every time I leave her. She seems to be getting worse. I pay a visit to Mrs. M a couple of days later and she asks me how Farah is doing, then tells me she has good news: the IRC is speeding up Farah's visa process, so she can reunite with her sisters in Virginia. Mental health trumps even my status as a minor. She's at the top of the list now. Good, that's very, very good, I think. She needs to get out of that place before . . . before what? I don't know but the thought scares me.

Farah survived bombs and war and being smuggled. After all she's gone through to get so close to freedom, after all that we—every refugee— has been through and all the strength that we have found, are we still so very fragile? Really, how much can one person take before they break? How much more can Farah take? The war is over now. I cannot believe she has come this far only to fall apart and rot in a country where she cannot speak the language and communicate with anyone in that mental institute. How could she ever hope to get better here? How could she ever hope to survive?

My own interview is, at long last, scheduled for the end of March. Even though I feel excited about getting one step closer to reaching my family, I also find myself resenting the phone calls with my parents. They are preparing to celebrate the Persian New Year and everyone sounds so happy, but I am still so far away and on my own. There will be no Sofreh Haft Seen for me, no Eidee, and no kisses from Maamaan and Baba, no crispy white fish and dill rice. I am so close to being there and yet still so far. It's unfair and though I hate to admit it, I really don't look forward to their calls anymore. The best thing is to not talk to them and just focus on my friends here and now. I learn that Farah's visa has been expedited; she is already on her way to be with her sisters. This makes me happy and brings me peace.

As the snow melts, I find myself enjoying this hilly, little village that's all of a sudden bursting in color and fragrance. My heart ignites when I spot the first bloom of a hyacinth and breathe deeply of the heavenly scent I know and love so well. It takes me back to my childhood, and this time, I don't push the memories away. I let them be. I let the child in me still feel giddy at the unfolding of spring—my favorite season. And I even enjoy celebrating the new year with my roommates. Of course we have a dance party. Of course we play cards and talk long into the night. It is not the new year I imagined and longed for with my family, but I also cannot say that it's not a special new year that I won't always look back fondly on and remember.

After my interview, which went well, came the medical exams. Chest x-rays, blood tests, and a TB skin test. That was the part I was nervous about. Everyone in Iran gets vaccinated for tuberculosis, and so as a result, TB tests often come back positive for us. If it does, the US treats you like you have an active case of TB, which means a months-long treatment. My sister had to do it and it stalled her process. I prayed, I even got Lisa to pray for me, that the results would be negative. And praise God, they were. Now it's just waiting on the go-ahead to schedule a flight. I'm told this can take another couple of months.

It's April by the time I get the news that my flight will depart on May eighteenth. Just like that, I only have a few weeks left in Vienna. Just like that, I've reached the end of this long alone time. In all of my short life, my biggest dream has been to go to America. It's here. It's finally here, just around the corner. I never dreamed, however, that getting there wouldn't be as straightforward as buying a plane ticket. I never dreamed it would take miles cramped in the back of a truck or being betrayed by photographers, or hiding out in dark basements, or being groped by men on busses. Dreams are mysterious and wonderful things. Sometimes they live in the deep, dark soil of our soul, and other times they live in the light of the sun.

But whether a seed or a tree, the dream is good and must be nurtured and believed in. I'm beginning to see the truth in Baba's statement that you can't escape your destiny. Perhaps destiny is not as simple as making a plan and enacting it, as I have long thought, perhaps destiny really does involve surrender. Surrender to the plans of a higher power and the chaos of life. Despite all the setbacks and all the hardships, now that the end is near, I can look back and see that my path has always, only, ever been leading me to this moment in time—to this plane ride back home.

Buying the ticket then has turned out to be the easiest part, and the last part, of the gigantic puzzle that is being a refugee. My emotions come in every flavor. Freedom tastes so sweet, but leaving friends is bitter. Saying goodbye feels like unraveling a sweater. The coziness of the sweater around your body will be no more, but the yarn can still be used to make something new and different. In a way, it isn't really a goodbye at all. Just a farewell to what was, and a hello to what will be. Both are made up of the same stuff, but both cannot exist together. The goodbye must be said. The old must pass on for the new to come.

In my final weeks I reflect on these people who have become like family to me. Together we faced rejection and hopelessness and helplessness, but through it all we had each other's backs and we extended our hands to help when one of us hit rock bottom. We've shared our deepest sadness and our most secret wishes, crying, laughing, singing, dancing. We have been each other's biggest advocates and surest strongholds when we felt weak. We have been refugees giving each other refuge.

It overwhelms me to say goodbye to these kind, generous, and wonderful souls even as I long for and welcome the enormous opportunity that lies ahead of me—the opportunity to put down roots in a rich soil that will accept me for who I am and to watch my life finally blossom and bear the good fruit of my dreams.

PART IV: AFTER

(Reunited after fifteen years. Pictured left to right: Mahvash, Kia, Leila, Cyrus, Maamaan, Baba on a coast in Oregon)

23

DREAMS

"Welcome to the United States." The New York customs agent who spoke those words was like an ayatollah handing me the plastic keys to a heaven here on earth. Though it's been thirty years since that day, I clearly remember how overwhelmed I was in that moment. How excitement and confusion mingled in my body, leaving me speechless. If I had been a child and you walked me into a candy store and told me to have as much as I wanted, of anything I wanted, I wouldn't have believed you and yet I would have loved you desperately for wishing to give me such a gift. Then, as it slowly dawned on me that you were quite serious, my eyes would have lit up, but I would have gone shyly from bin to bin peering judiciously at all the various candies and sweets. Daintily trying just one or two here or there, not to appear greedy, before finally and exuberantly letting down all reservations and running about saying, "Even this? But what about this? But have you seen these . . . I can have these too?" Yes, even those! That's what coming to America as a refugee feels like. America is one big candy store where the treats are being able to become whoever you want to be, to practice your religion freely and without fear, and to speak up and out—the right to your voice; and of course, all the lovely little things that my teenage heart especially held dear back then like dressing the way I wanted, wearing makeup if I wanted, listening to the music I wanted, reading whatever books I wanted, traveling where I wanted, and being respected as a woman.

I had never known such freedoms and I am not kidding when I say they are so very sweet.

And if those two metaphors aren't enough, I have another. The words of that US agent who welcomed me to the United States was like a coach telling you to, "Go get 'em," right before you step into the sports arena, full of confidence and ready to prove yourself to the world. I stepped out of that airport and into the fresh and hot air of San Jose, ready to build my future and the life I'd only dreamed of. It was empowering and daunting, exhilarating and terrifying. I couldn't process it in the moment; I could only feel the monumental shift, like a tectonic plate, that occurred somewhere deep inside me. Welcome to the United States. The words were honey to my soul, they quenched my parched and war-torn spirit and have been a cup that I can drink from all my days. There is nothing exaggerated about these statements. Only if one has known captivity, fear, danger, or imminent death, can they fully appreciate the depth of joy that comes with freedom.

Cyrus was the first to greet me as a newly arrived "resident alien." In New York, I had learned my flight didn't go directly to San Jose but would layover in Dallas. Cyrus was in medical school there at the time, so I found a pay phone and called to let him know I'd be arriving in just a few hours. He dropped everything to come meet me. I tried to call forth an image of him in my mind during the flight. In photos, sometimes he had a mustache and sometimes a beard, sometimes both. His hair was long then short then long again. He never looked the same and I wasn't sure I was going to recognize him. I felt like a thirty-year-old, not an almost seventeen-year-old, after all I'd been through, but be that as it may, as the plane began its descent, it was the six-year-old in me—the child I was when I had last seen Cyrus—that leaped with giddy excitement.

I breathed a sigh of relief when I got off the plane and saw a Middle Eastern man waiting with a big smile at the gate. I smiled back and rushed toward him. "Mahvash!" The sound of my name coming from somewhere behind me—not from the man in front of me who I assumed was my brother—caught me off guard. I froze. I had walked right past Cyrus and nearly thrown myself into the arms of a stranger. Though I was embarrassed, Cyrus hugged me firmly for a long time, and warmly, in the kind of embrace that only a brother can give. We were crying and smiling at the same time. I couldn't get any words out. Where was the tall, skinny seventeen-year-old boy who carried me up and down the stairs when I had the stitches in my foot? Who was this twenty-eight-year-old man with broad shoulders and a full beard? Who, I noted immediately, also happened to be shorter than me! I saw time pass in an instant looking into his face and wondered about his own journey to the United States, just barely older than myself, but without family to greet him. We just held each other for a long time.

When he pulled out his camera to snap some photos of us, something awoke inside me. Memories of him capturing our road trips, his face half hidden behind the big lens. Those long-ago years of innocence and togetherness. We change so much, but still some things never change. His love of photography had endured, and that knowledge brought me an inexpressible happiness. When the time came to board my flight to San Jose, there were again tears in our eyes. Cyrus said he'd see me soon at the graduation, "Didn't you know? Kia is graduating with his master's in Computer Science from Santa Clara University in a few weeks, and I'll be there." Then he hugged me one last time. "You are so beautiful, Mahvash," he said, and I just cried all the harder.

When my feet hit the ground in California, I knew I was in a whole new world and I knew my journey had finally come to an end. Heart racing, I saw Baba, Maamaan, and Leila waving at me from the gate and I took off running. "Hey lady! Slow down!" I stopped in my tracks. It was Kia's voice, I recognized it from our phone calls, but just like with Cyrus, I had walked right past him too! I burst into tears when I turned and saw him for the first time in eleven years. He looked just like Baba. He even sounded just like Baba. Tall, slender, and with lots of gray hair in his curly, black mop! Was he really old enough to have gray hair? Curly chest hair stuck out of his tank top—my brother, the gangly boy who took me swimming every day on the back of his bike was a grown man.

Hugs and kisses abounded, but it wasn't until we got to Kia's house—our own new home—and I was settled in my bedroom that Baba came in and held me tightly and for a long, long time. "Remember," he whispered in my ear, "how I promised you that everything would be fine. I promised that you would come to America to study? Remember?" "I remember, Baba." "And it all worked out, we just had to have faith." I pulled away slightly so I could look into his eyes. Those beautiful and expressive hazel eyes that I'd missed so much. "I believe you now. We can't skip our destiny! I think I understand your faith, our faith, better after everything I've experienced this past year and a half." He smiled and hugged me close to him again.

It was no sparkling, turquoise Chevy, but Kia's Toyota 4-Runner was better equipped for this new kind of excursion he was taking us on—a camping trip—than the Chevy ever could have endured. Of course my father naturally disagreed. Even so, he still gave the 4-Runner some loving pats on the dashboard as it made its way up and over the steep mountain pass of Lake Shasta at the Oregon border. Cyrus had come out for Kia's graduation but then had to get back to medical school. Kia, however, had taken two weeks off from work to take us through national parks and forests all the way up to Seattle. Ironically enough, it was similar to the last family trip we took in 1978 when Cyrus also had to stay behind to get his travel affairs to America in order. As we piled the top of the 4-Runner with Kia's windsurfing equipment, and the back with mats and sleeping bags, pillows, a portable grill, and cooler, the memories from our family road trips in Iran kept coming. "Remember the time we got stuck in the snow?" Kia laughed. This I didn't remember. "Or the time Baba let Cyrus try driving? Never again!" I felt a little lost trying to keep up with the stories, but I was also hungry to hear them. The whole road trip I asked question after question to keep them talking. It was just like old times. Kind of.

It was odd to see Baba in the passenger seat up front and not behind the wheel; he didn't have his California drivers license yet, so navigation

and radio operation fell to him while Kia drove. "Check out 89.9 FM, dad."
"Why?" "Seriously. You'll love it. It's called Reggae." I can't say my dad loved
it, but we were all at least fascinated by it long enough to satisfy Kia's obses-
sion with all things Bob Marley. We drove through the magnificent red-
wood forests. "We're even going to drive *through* a tree just up ahead, it's
so large," Kia said. No way, I remember rolling my eyes at his "joke". But of
course, that's exactly what we did! I couldn't believe it. We went to Yosemite
National Park and camped there. Then we went north and camped at Lake
Shasta. America felt so vast, so wild. None of us, except for Kia and Cyrus,
had ever slept in a tent. It reminded me of sleeping on our rooftop in Iran;
and it was a blast! Nights were spectacular with all the stars out and the
Milky Way visible in the sky. In the mornings, Kia would make his special
omelets and Baba would attempt to make tea over the fire. At night we'd
barbecue chicken and make kabobs. Only one time did we get caught in a
rainstorm; it was on the gorgeous Oregon coast and we all got sopping wet,
but still I wouldn't have changed a thing. The beauty of the mountains, the
woods, and the coast all took my breath away. Nothing felt quite real and I
pinched myself often to remind myself this wasn't all just a dream—it was
my actual life.

Reconnecting as a family after eleven years came in fits and starts.
Sometimes the conversation flowed easily and other times we just basked
in the silence and the nearness of each other. And sometimes the conversations felt insulting and difficult to manage, the reality of being total strang-
ers who just so happened to love each other complicated our attempts at
restoring the years we had lost.

"You and Leila don't know how lucky you are," Kia said adamantly
one night around the campfire. "You had family to meet you at the airport
and to help you pick out your college classes." Lucky? He really had no
idea what we'd been through, but it didn't feel right to try to compare our
past pain and suffering. I wanted to put that time of my life to rest, but I
guess I also wanted to feel understood and not told I was, "lucky," about
the way everything worked out for me. "What are you talking about?" Leila

demanded, "We had a hell of a time and risked our lives coming here." Kia shook his head. "No way, Cyrus and I, we were all alone."

He told us about when they first arrived in New York at sixteen and seventeen years old and how they were robbed during their layover. He shared the hardship of arriving in Nebraska and not knowing a soul, not knowing the system—neither of the US nor of their school. "We had to learn from our mistakes. And we made a lot." The years of the hostage crisis were the worst. Nebraskans made life hard for Iranian students. "Our cars were broken into. Our apartment windows were broken. People got in fist fights with us. We were humiliated, made fun of, and taken advantage of right and left." My heart hurt hearing their stories, and I was saddened at the coming realization of just how big the gap between us really was. It felt impossible to bridge. Could we ever fully reconnect as siblings after having lost all those years? I truly didn't know these men that I loved so dearly and they didn't know me. It gave me a lot to think about as we continued our journey north.

Our final destination was Seattle where we visited the daughter of Baba's old friend, our dear Mr. Danesh from the farm outside of Tehran— what had been my favorite place of refuge from the bombing. Her son, Omid, was my age and I remembered playing with him when we were as young as three or four years old, riding the donkeys, picking fruit, catching frogs—he caught frogs, I just looked on in disgust until he started chasing me with them. When they fled Iran, it was in a rush. One Nowruz, Omid had decided to try an experiment during the Chahar Shanbe Suri, fire celebration. He and his friends put a light bulb into the fire. The glass exploded and a small sliver struck his eye. He lost his vision. They escaped first to Pakistan and then came to the US for treatment to restore his sight. Seeing them again but on brand-new soil was a wonder. How far we had all traveled! Whenever anyone left Iran, it was always with the knowledge that you might never see each other again. Our reunion was very precious indeed and Omid has remained a near and dear friend.

Our family road trip was both fun and sobering. We had the chance to witness unmatched beauty in the wild and to catch up on years of stories and conversation, but we would come to learn down the road that those years apart had created permanent rifts in our family dynamic. When you don't grow up playing and interacting with each other, arguing and making up, just being together all those years as children, it is difficult to bond as a family once you are adults. For refugees, this is a hard reality to face. For so long we hope for the day we will be reunited with our loved ones and everything will go back to normal. This hope is an anchor for our soul during great hardship and struggle.

But the truth is nothing can ever be the same.

We can never fully bridge those gaps. There can still be good, and a lot of it, but re-enacting a family road trip isn't enough to heal and rebuild the bonds that were lost from so many years apart. Even just the couple years that Leila and I spent apart from our parents still created problems. We were used to being independent, making our own choices, being our own people, but here we were under our parent's roof and supervision once again; this turned out to be both comforting and conflicting.

Maamaan tried to enforce so many rules and restrictions and we fought her daily on them. No makeup, no going to parties, curfew at eleven p.m. Why can't you just respect us? We'd yell. You can trust us! We lived on our own and *never* got into trouble. We'd been through so much without her supervision that we just wanted to be treated like adults. You just don't go from being a child to being an adult, and then back to being a child again. But she persisted in treating us like children. Parents will be parents. Now that I am a mother, I can understand how worried she must have been watching Leila and I get picked up in a friend's limo to go celebrate their birthday in San Francisco—a city Maamaan knew nothing about, with friends she hadn't witnessed growing up from the time they were infants. Everything was wildly new and uncomfortable for her, and the thought of her daughters coming this far only to throw it all away on drugs, sex, and rock and roll terrified her. What she didn't realize was that we weren't doing any of those things. Our friends were Bahá'í and we all had such healthy boundaries. After hiding away in Tehran all those years, we just wanted to have fun and feel free. We wanted her to feel the same. But for whatever reason, she could never make the transition that we all did. She continued to carry her past around with her and use it as an excuse. If we tried to get her to learn English, she'd snap, "I can't learn it. I never got past the second grade." When we'd tell her she had learned plenty of incredible things without ever earning a diploma, she'd respond: "Well, it's still no use. Why learn it? I'm going back to Iran." At that point, I'd throw my hands up in frustration. In Iran, I could understand her depression, her excuses, her pain, but now that we were in the US—why not let the past be the past? She, just like all of us, now had opportunities and freedom to change her life. She didn't have to live the same story, and yet she continued to identify with the pain and could not let it go. She did, however, discover the joys of working and being independent in another way. She started babysitting for a Persian family and just loved it. When the child was eventually old enough to go to school, they hired Maamaan to work in their family store stocking shelves and bagging items. And, she got a fresh start on her vegetable and herb gardens in the back of Kia's house.

Baba found work immediately because he wanted to help pay for Leila's and my tuition. He found an ideal job—one at a junkyard where he got to spend his days taking cars apart for resale. He would come home particularly excited when he had come across an old American-made car or a sports car. He was so fond of stick shifts that he even made sure to teach me how to drive one. A few years and a few hernia repairs later though, he gave up the junkyard job to work at a gas station pumping gas and later to bag groceries at a grocery store. Like always, he loved staying busy and productive and just like Maamaan had wasted no time starting her veggie garden, so too did Baba waste no time cultivating a new orchard. This time with avocado and peach and sweet lemon trees alongside the persimmons and pomegranates. Baba had started to teach himself English back when I was in the third grade, and he continued to do so now that he was in the US. I was surprised that he had been able to bring two massive English/Persian and Persian/English dictionaries with him from Iran. He used those books to look up definitions the rest of his life. Strange spellings and pronunciations never ceased to frustrate him though!

Early on living with Kia and Cyrus, I found myself tongue tied. I avoided speaking English around them at all costs because I was so afraid to make a mistake. My reticence worried them, and later they would suggest I join a dorm to improve my English and get more confidence. The truth was, I just felt like I couldn't have an opinion around them because I was so much younger and I didn't know them that well. Despite all this, we were there for each other and willing to muddle through the discomfort of building relationships anew as best we could.

Kia helped me enroll in a "Running Start" program at a local community college for the fall. I was able to skip the rest of high school by passing the college placement exams. That fall I took English, math, and chemistry. Formulas and equations were familiar to me and it felt good to be back in school, but after a semester I told Kia I wanted to try new things too. His eyes twinkled as he opened the course catalog to a section of electives. "I can take *any* of these?" I asked. Like a kid in a candy store. I dove right in. Psychology, sociology, computer programming, even jazz dance! Jazz dance was so different, but so much fun. Let's just say that even though rhythm didn't come naturally to me, at our end-of-semester recital I still found the guts to perform—albeit, from a strategically positioned spot far in the back.

One day while walking to class, I passed the music room. The sounds coming from within were more beautiful than anything I had ever heard, even the symphony in Vienna I went to one time. I had only been able to afford a standing-room-only ticket, but the symphony hall was ornate and unbelievably beautiful, and the heavenly music brought tears to my eyes. The new sort of music emanating from the music room stirred me on an even deeper level. Even just hearing music at random throughout the day could stop me in my tracks. All I had heard for years were Islamic revolutionary songs or the call to prayer. I had no idea how diverse and mesmerizing music could be. What poured from the classroom that day, I learned, was a classical guitar piece composed by a famous Spaniard named Segovia. The performer was a Portuguese professor. "What's the course code for your class?" I asked. He told me, and I signed right up.

Music and dance are pure pleasure. I couldn't imagine how I had ever lived without them. They are so very vital to life. Even when the music is wild—like when Kia would play Pink Floyd on his turntable while he warmed up inside before a run—it is vital and changes you. Electives were invigorating, and they were still aligned with what I needed to fulfill my general education requirements before transferring to San Jose State University. I was on track and working hard—still harder than most, like in my required US history course. While this course was required for gradua-tion, I also knew it would help prepare me for my upcoming citizenship test about this new country I now called home. I, however, didn't realize just how much information would be considered a given. The teacher skipped tons of material because the American students had already learned it in high school. Abraham Lincoln? Who was he? The abolition of slavery? There was a Civil War here? I knew nothing about these things, so I read extra material late into the night to catch up. During class, my teacher would stare at my puzzled face and say, "Right? Right?" nodding her head with a big smile. I'd nod back, jotting down yet another note of something I'd better research later that night.

My counselor at the community college urged me to declare a major before I transferred to the university. Consider what kind of career you want, she told me. I consulted with my brothers. Kia painted a realistic and frustrating picture of the tech industry. "It's a roller-coaster ride and there's a dearth of people contact." But Cyrus encouraged me to pursue medicine, like him. I had always felt like medicine would be in my future, so I began volunteering on Fridays from 5 p.m. to 10 p.m. at a local hospital just to get a feel for the environment. Overworked, unhappy doctors and the lonely and sad, uncomfortable faces of the patients were just not my style. Medicine was out. I tried volunteering at a pharmacy instead. That bored me to tears. Then, my tooth fractured. The one that had been root canaled in Vienna turned dark gray over time and eventually came loose, fractured at the root, and had to be extracted. I cried and cried. All that pain in Austria without anesthesia had been for naught. I was still going to lose my tooth. The dentist wouldn't let me leave, he wanted to extract it that day. I was inconsolable. They called Kia and he calmed me, telling me the tooth could be replaced. But it was still a sad day for me and the loss felt monumental. Yet, that gaping hole in the front of my smile ended up making room for something new and unforeseen to take shape—my future.

It was the summer of 1990 and I was eighteen. Once the gums healed, I was given a bridge to replace the missing tooth. Over multiple visits to the dentist's office my curiosity grew as I watched them work. Dentistry was both an art and a science. It was delicate and precise. One had to understand the finer details about human biology, anatomy and physiology, but also had to have a steady hand, able to create and sculpt. With my growing thirst for art and my love of science, the more time I spent in the dentist office, the more I realized just how much I liked everything about what they did. In the last place I ever anticipated looking and born from one of the darkest and most painful experiences of my life, I'd found my calling. I would major in biology and then go on to dental school.

24
UNITY

A college education is an incredible opportunity for a wealth of reasons, but one of the most meaningful is the chance to be surrounded by people of all faiths and all walks of life. As you all strive toward the same thing—a degree, a career, a new life—you find that your differences are not so great and are in fact, strengths. In school, I had Muslim, Zoroastrian, and Jewish Persian friends. No one cared what I believed, no one got hung up on doctrine. Each of us were deeply committed to our faith, and all of our faiths spoke of inclusion and acceptance. We were finally able to live out the purity of our belief systems in truth and in love, outside of religious extremes and the dictates of corrupt leaders. We ate freely together, respected each other, and just had a ton of fun, playing beach volleyball or camping in Yosemite. This way of living and loving was invigorating. I wondered why we couldn't be this way back in Iran. My father explained to me, his eyes looking far off in the distance, that there was a time when people were like that in Iran, but it was before my time, before my memory.

After college graduation, I was accepted to three dental schools and chose the one in Portland because I'd fallen in love with the Pacific Northwest from camping trips and vacations we'd taken there. Maamaan and Baba would frequently make the twelve hour drive north from San Jose to visit me. "Aren't you tired?" I'd always ask them upon their arrival. "With scenery like that?" Baba would say. "No way!"

One year into the dental program came one of the most exciting days of my life. On May 18th, 1994 I walked myself downtown to the federal courthouse and claimed my US citizenship. It wasn't difficult to let go of Iran because I was deeply convinced I didn't belong there. Iran had made it clear it didn't want me or my faith. With US citizenship, came a true sense of belonging, one I had waited and wished for many years That day, I became a member of the most powerful country in the world. I was granted the same rights and the same treatment as any other citizen, and that was itself a powerful feeling. Now, I could vote and participate in the affairs of my community. The court took my alien resident card when I entered the courthouse. No wonder everyone called it a "green card." Alien just sounds so derogatory and unwelcoming. Today, they are called permanent resident cards and this small change goes a long way to helping new refugees maintain their dignity and humanity. Then, I took a test on US history, the constitution and the judicial system, and answered a few questions orally before the naturalization ceremony where I took an oath of allegiance to the United States of America. Then, someone asked me if I wanted to change my name. That caught me off guard. The idea was humorous to me, I'd never considered such a thing. I declined, but to my surprise nearly everyone else in the room was picking American first names and some even changed their last names. I'd skipped my morning dental school classes to participate in this momentous ceremony, and when I returned to campus that afternoon a few of my classmates asked, "So, do you feel any different?" I told them everything was different. Everything.

The first thing I did with my certificate of naturalization was to apply for a US passport, the freedom to travel the world. I wanted to see the whole world. With so many places to visit, I had to start early to get to them all. But before my big plans to live in New York and travel could be realized, I needed to get through dental school and pass my board exams. My father continued to tell me, "You work hard now, it pays off for the rest of your life. You can always travel later, but for now stay focused on school work." Of course, he was right.

Dental school was no walk in the park. As an undergraduate, I had felt pretty smart and did well, but once I was in a professional school where only the best of the best were culled and invited to study—I was no longer top of my class. I still needed to carry a dictionary with me most of the time and review my notes and textbooks two or three times for the information to sink in. Every day I was reminded that English was not my first language.

Commencement day rang out clear and bright in early June of 1997 during Portland's famous Rose Festival. Scottish bagpipe music played in the background and sent happy chills up my spine as I recited the Hippocratic Oath. I was a month shy of my twenty-fifth birthday, and the youngest member of our graduating class. While waiting in the hallway for our hooding ceremony, my Baba found me in the crowd and came up to me, pulling my face close to his with his big, thick hands. "Remember," he whispered with excitement, "remember how I promised you will be a doctor one day? Today is that day!" He kissed me on both cheeks, looked deeply into my eyes, and gave me his widest and proudest smile.

After graduation, while I waited on the results of my dental board exams to confirm that I could indeed practice dentistry, I grabbed my passport, a backpack, and headed off on a European tour where I visited several major cities and hopped from youth hostel to youth hostel. During the trip, I learned that I had passed the exams. I then decided I'd try living in Seattle before, perhaps, moving back to California or maybe even to New York. This time when I got back to the US and handed my American passport to the customs agent, I was greeted differently. Instead of saying, "Welcome to America!" he said, "Welcome home!" This was my home and I was counting on it.

Sea-Mar Community Health Center was in South Seattle, across from Boeing Field. It was my first job out of dental school and I am forever grateful to the fabulous dentists and specialists who mentored me while I worked there. The clinic primarily served the low-income population, and particularly Hispanic immigrants and farm workers. To be successful, I quickly realized I'd need to learn Spanish, so I could speak directly to my patients and not through an interpreter. I enrolled in night classes. My patients were a delight, so pleasant and hardworking. I woke up every day thankful to give my time and talent toward serving them. There are so many patients I will never forget, but two are forever etched in my memory because of the ways they expanded my heart and opened my eyes.

The first memory is of the time I walked into the treatment room and found a man in orange overalls and handcuffs sitting in my chair, with police officers at the treatment door. I hightailed it out of there and back to the clinic manager's office. "What kind of criminal am I treating?" I asked, honestly too frightened to find out. To my surprise, the patient was not a common criminal. He was a Hispanic man being held in detention while awaiting deportation to his home country. My heart instantly broke for him and I found a flood of empathy and understanding that outweighed the fright. Had I not been in a similar situation a few years back? I understood the immigrant man's pain, his fear. I understood it intimately. I looked my manager in the eyes and told her, "I want to treat all the immigrant detainees who come to the clinic from here on out."

The other patient I will never forget was a man who made me tremble with anger and fear while I worked on him. He was an Iraqi. And he was chatty. I tried desperately to avoid all conversation and just do my job, while I silently attacked him, blaming him for all my suffering through the years of war and bombing. All the anger, terror, and negativity about the war I'd ever felt gushed through me and I directed it at him. I hated him for all the nights I couldn't breathe or even swallow because of the fear that gripped me. I hated him for every single Iraqi jet that ever dropped a bomb. I hated him for robbing me of my childhood. I hated him.

But this man was undaunted by my silence, and the more I listened to his story, the more my feelings turned to embarrassment and then to empathy. During the Iran-Iraq war, my patient had escaped to Kuwait to avoid reporting for military duty for a war he didn't believe in. Iraqi guards came to his home looking for him and when they discovered he'd fled the country, they shot his sister inside the home, in front of his mother. Tears streamed down my face as he recounted trauma after trauma of what he and others endured. For the first time, I realized that we were all victims of the war. The innocent people of both countries had no choice. We were all injured, all traumatized, all sacrificed by regional and international politicians whose decisions defended only their own interests. I could not stop apologizing to the man in my dental chair.

Our conversation enlightened me in more ways than one. It also brought to light the deeply-rooted anger and resentment I still carried. In all my years in the US, I had never spoken about the war or my life in Iran to anyone. I'd tucked them away into boxes and shoved them into the darkest corner of my mind. Now I could see that they weren't really gone and they still weighed me down. For ten years, I thought if I just focused on my education and my gratitude for what I had been given after coming to America, then I wouldn't have to examine my past, I wouldn't have to revisit those dark times. But there I was face to face with the person I had presumed to be the enemy, and he was not—at all—my enemy. It would still be some time before I would go to therapy and work through the stories, confront my trust issues, and learn to understand my PTSD, but what I was able to grasp immediately was just how deep the scars of war go, how they are not so easily erased. I considered the Palestinian and Israeli conflict, and how near-impossible it may be to resolve. Later in 1999, after I'd met and married the love of my life, we visited Israel for one month to visit the Bahá'í gardens in Haifa. We also traveled the country and witnessed the oppression of the Muslims in the West Bank and the anxiety of the Jews in the shores of Red city in Ellott. Both sides have wounds that go back generations. Loved ones have been lost on both sides and can never be replaced. Perhaps the only way to achieve peace and unity in the world is to bring the innocent people of today together, to mingle and to forgive each other.

25
HOME

There are only a few events that drastically change one's life, turning the world upside down and inside out. Revolution and war, for me, certainly fall into that category. So does falling in love. I met Dave during my first year working at the Sea-Mar Community Health Center. I had gone to his office seeking a referral to an endocrinologist. "I'm new to Seattle," I had explained. "Oh?" he raised his eyebrows and turned a little pink in the cheeks. "I have this thyroid problem that I need to just finally get some answers to." "Well, I know someone who can help." He gave me the name and I turned to go, but he stopped me. "Oh, but by the way, I can also give you a tour of the city . . . since you are new in town." "That would be nice," I said. A few days later he came to my office to follow up about "that tour we discussed" and we ended up on a lunch date. Followed by a few more "city tour"/lunch dates.

Our clinic was located by the industrial Duwamish River near Boeing Field and we liked to stroll along the polluted river banks after lunch taking in Boeing's junk yard of burned and warped airplane wings, torn up fuselages, and other bits of abandoned aircraft. We were so madly in love we thought everything was beautiful. The first time he invited me to his apartment in Capitol Hill he surprised me with a candlelit dinner. Flowers on the table, the smell of steak and potatoes coming from the kitchen— he'd thought of everything. He introduced me to Blue, his sister's dog. He was dog sitting for her while she was out of town. The poor thing was fifteen years old and couldn't walk anymore, but his sister refused to put him down. She would carry the eighty-pound mutt up and down the stairs. I admired how gentle and attentive Dave was with the old "man". With Blue at our side, and the candles gently flickering, Dave served up the feast. We were about to take our first bite when old Blue let loose a gush of diarrhea. Dave jumped up in a frenzy, mortified and apologizing profusely as he cleaned up the mess. The smell remained unbearable. We ran out and went out for dinner.

It didn't matter what we were doing we could find a way to enjoy ourselves. We went to concerts and learned to tango, stayed up late at coffee shops drinking hazelnut lattes and eating German chocolate cake. The taste of hazelnut always takes me back to a pleasurable, childhood memory. I told Dave about the emerald hills of the Gilan Province in Iran known for their hazelnut groves. How we took a family trip there with Ms. Molook, the woman who pierced my ears. I had never seen a place so green and lush—until I came to the Pacific Northwest! Dave listened to all my stories intently and lovingly. He wanted to know everything about me and I wanted to share those memories with him, all the while holding back some parts of me. There was this secret part of me I had been hiding. The thought of opening those doors petrified me. I suppressed the past, yet the past would sometimes show its ugly head, percolate out in my dreams. Dave never pushed me to share those pieces of my life but assured me I could trust him, and he was here to listen whenever I was ready. He was always there for me, like the time he held me until I stopped shaking when I heard the roar of the US Navy Blue Angels jets flying overhead in military formation, jets booming to the applause of the Seattle Seafair crowd.

My PTSD never stopped us though, and it wasn't long before we began to share our love of travel together. It started with hiking and backpacking and evolved into camping, setting off for the volcanic Mt. Rainier, experiencing the wild coast of the Olympic Peninsula, visiting the Skagit Valley when the salmon were running, and hundreds of eagles came back to nest in the trees and feast in the streams. In Costa Rica he taught me to snorkel, unlocking a world I did not know existed. On our first Christmas together, I was like a child getting the biggest Christmas present that Santa could ever possibly bring down the chimney! Dave surprised me with my first bicycle ever. As a child, I rode a tricycle but that was before the revolution. After the revolution, all girls were forbidden to ride bikes. This giant adult size bicycle thrilled my heart! Dave had gone as far as trying to wrap it for me, which I thought was so cute, and he got to teach me how to ride my bike too. Our joy truly knew no bounds.

Almost a year after Dave and I started dating, Leila called me up. "Ooo! Get ready!" she gushed with excitement at the other end of the line. "For what?" "There is a ring coming your way!" "Leila, what are you talking about?" "Dave is going to propose. He just called and asked me what your ring size is!" She never could keep a secret. My parents on the other hand, could.

After they had come for a visit, Dave insisted on driving them to the airport. Apparently, he made a detour along the way at a coffee shop and somehow, with their limited understanding of English, he made them understand that he was asking for their blessing to marry me. My parents loved and adored Dave. They enthusiastically approved the marriage proposal and kept the secret to themselves. If Dave were planning to propose, I ended up forgetting all about Leila's words because it did not happen, not for weeks, not for months. When the day finally came, it was a complete surprise.

Dave had planned a beautiful dinner for us at a fancy restaurant, but when the day came, I was so exhausted from work I just wanted to stay home. He would not take no for an answer and came up with some excuse why we couldn't cancel our reservation. He dropped me off in front of the restaurant and went to park the car. I decided to go in and let the host know we needed a table for two. The host sat me at a small table in a corner. When Dave came in, he said, "Oh, no no. This is wrong. We had a reservation." The host apologized and said that I had not given him Dave's name for the reservation. He moved us to a table by the water set with candles and flowers. "Wow, Dave!" I said, "How nice." Our menus were huge, probably two feet tall. I was studying mine closely when out of the corner of my eye, I saw Dave kneeling on the floor. "Dave, what are you doing? Tying your shoe? I am debating between the Alaskan King Salmon or a New York Steak. What are you getting?" Dave pulled my hand away from the menu. He was on his knee smiling at me so big that I could see his gold tooth in the back of his mouth, his ears pulled back, his eyes watery. It hit me. Oh my god. He is proposing.

What an idiot I am! Of all the things I could have said, I ask if he was tying his shoe? Here he is trembling, his voice quivering, and that's a ring box in his hand! I was overcome with emotion staring deeply into his eyes. The world around us disappeared. He was talking to me, but I can't remember anything he said except when he got to the end: "So what do you say?" he asked. I looked around and the whole restaurant was staring at us. I smiled, a smile probably as big as his. "Yes," I said, "Yes, yes, yes." We laughed and hugged and kissed. Then he asked me to hurry up and order because we had tickets to a musical. The man had made all these incredible plans for the entire evening, and all I had wanted was to stay home after a hard week of work!

Our wedding was intimate, surrounded by family and friends, and hundreds of blooming flowers at the Seattle Rose Garden. Before my father walked me down the aisle, he repeated the same sentiment he had told me so many times before. Holding my face in his big hands, he said, "Remember how we cannot escape our destiny? Remember those dark days? Look at how far you have come. Look at where life is taking you with Mr. David. He is a good man, one of a kind. His heart is so pure." Baba always called Dave, Mr. David. Some say a girl tends to marry a man like her father, and for me that is very true.

About a year into our marriage, we had an incredible opportunity to travel overseas together for three months for both a European vacation and to offer our services as volunteers for a month on the island of St. Lucia in the Caribbean. Sea-Mar clinic had offered Dave a three-month sabbatical. The trip turned out to be a turning point in my career. While Dave worked in the emergency room at the hospital, I worked in a dental clinic with a Cuban dentist and two assistants. The first two days were the most difficult. I came back to our room crying, feeling helpless. There were not enough anesthetics and other basic dental materials, and what they did have was expired. Anesthetics were only allowed for root canals and extractions. There was no x-ray machine. How was I supposed to diagnose my patients' problems without x-rays? By the third day, I pulled myself together. These people needed me. I was determined to find a way to give them excellent care and help them. I remembered the dentist in Vienna who did so much to help my tooth many years ago. Even though I did not receive anesthetics, I appreciated her skill and attentive work. Now it was my turn to perform root canal after root canal without x-rays. Now I have decided to take a deep breath and trust my knowledge of dental anatomy along with relying on my tactile senses to find the curvature of the roots. With a gloved finger, I closed my eyes and traced the roots, gently working my way through any blockage or curvature in the roots, feeling how deep they went. Often, I had to remove teeth never knowing how long or curvy the roots were or how close they were to the sinuses or nerves.

The knowledge I gained in that month was immense. It humbled me and also excited me to have learned what was possible and how resourceful one can be under pressure. For dental posts, I straightened paper clips, sterilized them and pushed the metal down into the roots to keep teeth and fillings together. No matter what it took, I was committed to do the best I could for the people of St. Lucia. Their lives were not easy. Even though the international community was providing medicine, equipment, and other aid, the corrupt government was diverting the majority of it and it was being sold privately for profit on the black market. Most of the men were unemployed. Women ran the households by themselves. If they became pregnant, they were abandoned by their husbands or boyfriends. I hoped that for my small part, I had helped to ease some of their physical pain. The conditions they lived under made me appreciate what I had and to also make a commitment to do my part to fight such adversity.

Dave and I knew volunteering was a core part of who we were and who we would continue to be. If there could be opportunities to go above and beyond to care for others, we would not say no. It is a precious gift to be able to share our resources and talents with those who cannot or do not have access to health services. This is what being a part of a community means and for us "community" extends globally. We are neighbors, near and far, and as such have a responsibility to care for each other. As we help and heal others, we are helped and healed in many different ways. When we returned home from the Caribbean, we learned that I was pregnant.

Dave and I had basically planned our life together even before we were married. Now with a little one on the way, we talked more extensively about the concept of home. It is a conversation we have continued to have over the years. Where is home exactly and what is home? What defines a home for us? While the conversation may be different for each person, I imagine there are many similarities. For Dave and I, home is where we feel safe and welcomed. It is where we can be together in love and at peace. Home is where we can build community and raise our family. Our home is where we put down roots knowing we belong and that we can create memories to be cherished for a lifetime.

Together, Dave and I had already created so many memories and our sense of home was about to feel truly complete as we prepared to welcome our son, Zachary, into our lives. Following him three years later came Parisa. Six years later, we asked the two of them: "What do you think about us having another baby?" To which they replied, "Can we get a puppy instead?" So we got a spaniel and then let them know we were also having a baby—a new sister, Sheyda.

With my parents here in Seattle, we would pack into our Honda minivan, complete with kayak on the roof and bikes on the back, camping up and down the coast, out on the San Juan islands, up to the Canadian Rockies and out to Glacier National Park. Baba would say with a smile,

"Remember the Chevy? Well Honda is a good car too! Very roomy." One time we took my parents on a vacation to Kauai. We were in my most favorite place, Hanalei Bay. With the beautiful beach in front of us, tall, lush mountains on the other side, the waterfalls behind us and a rainbow over the ocean, I turned to Baba and asked, "Are you enjoying your life?" I was remembering those dark days. His response has always stayed with me: "Is this what heaven is like? Can it get any better than this?" Indeed, is there anything more perfect and heavenly than creating beautiful memories with your loved ones while living in peace and safety?

Dave and I feel fortunate to have called Seattle home for over twenty years and to be raising our precious family here, in a place so welcoming, accepting and supportive of all people. I have called America home for thirty years and throughout those years I have enjoyed a peaceful coexistence with my fellow American citizens. America offered me a second chance at life. Not just any life or any kind of existence, but the chance to build the life that I dreamed of and the chance to provide rich experiences for my children, raising them to be conscientious, caring and respectful citizens of this world.

Slowly, sometimes imperceptibly, sometimes forcibly, the times have changed. The climate in America has become more divisive since the 9/11 attack and a wave of fear and suspicion has spread over this great land bringing with it more prejudice and discrimination, less understanding and acceptance. No bigger risk have I ever taken than to leave my homeland but the sense of belonging and the opportunities afforded me as a US citizen, have been worth it a hundred times over. Not everyone is so fortunate. Refugees are continually denied access to basic human rights and needs, displaced and homeless for too many years, if not for their entire lives. I do count myself blessed.

26

COURAGE

"Did you hear what happened?" Dave asked over the phone.

"No. What?"

"Turn on the TV."

How many other Americans had a similar experience on 9/11? How many remember turning on the television only to fall to their knees as they watched planes crash into the Twin Towers? Everyone remembers where they were and what they were doing at the moment of the 9/11 attack. Everyone has their story.

I was at home, in my pajamas, with my son, Zack, who was barely a month old. Dave called from his clinic, "Turn on the TV."

The live broadcast chilled me to the bone. As I watched the smoke rising from the towers followed by the two crumbling to the ground, that old suppressed feeling of terror filled my chest and I could not breathe. This is not happening in my world again. Not *again*. I grabbed my baby and ran for the basement of our Wallingford bungalow for shelter. I talked nonstop to my child, sang to him, remembering my father's comforting voice in the dark, dark nights of Tehran as we waited for the bombs to drop. Any minute now, I thought. Any minute now and I'll hear sirens and fighter jets. I waited for hours, expecting that at any moment, the house would shudder from the blast of the bombs.

Finally, I got a hold of myself. I mustered enough courage to turn on the TV and what I saw was horrifying and familiar. Unsuspecting, innocent people going about their day then being attacked. This was a paralyzing, devastating and nightmarish experience. After that day, I found the reaction of my fellow citizens shocking and puzzling. Anger! Fear! Then I came to understand how completely foreign of an experience this attack on American soil was for the majority of people. Not since Pearl Harbor had there been an attack on US soil. Americans knew nothing about the pain and heartbreak of a war unless they had lost a loved one on an overseas battle. Most Americans are untouched by war for the simple (and wonderful) truth that they have not grown up on war-torn soil. Thank goodness that this is the reality for most Americans. Yet it remains crucial that we recognize the gap of understanding this sense of safety and invincibility creates in regard to how we approach global affairs—how hard it is to really imagine and understand the day-to-day reality of people living in war zones. We cannot remain ignorant because our influence as a nation is widespread, reaching far across our borders and into other lands. War may not be our daily reality, but it is the reality for millions of humans across the world today. I saw this attack and the subsequent reactions to it pointing to the greater problem of lack of understanding on both sides of the issues that face the world, not just one nation or one group. The misguided approaches to resolve them, perhaps from a lack of willingness, even if unintentional, to see the world from the other's point of view, and the lack of genuine acceptance of others as equals with the same rights and desires to live in peace and harmony. One side wishing, nay demanding, that the other converts to accept its beliefs and views of the world, while the other does not acknowledge and respect the sovereignty of the other and undermines their independence.

After the 9/11 attack, I was often asked how I felt about it. I struggled to explain my feelings without hurting theirs, so I usually remained silent. But I can be silent no longer. War destroys the lives of innocent people. It is from personal experience that I can say with confidence that war achieves no good, does not bring freedom, and does not foster good will. Trauma does not end when the war does. Perhaps before we elect and appoint leaders with the decision-making powers to inflict a lifetime of suffering on people, and all for causes that mean nothing—money, oil, power, etc.—we should insist that these leaders have served in a war and seen firsthand the devastating effects of decisions like these. When we lead from a place of fear, we continue a never-ending cycle of suffering. When we inflict suffering on others, we scar them, and their suffering often breeds hostility which gets passed down to children and future generations. This never-ending cycle of fear-mongering, prejudice, and egotistical supremacy, only leads to more conflict and war, wasting precious and limited resources.

Five months after 9/11, Dave, Zack, and I boarded a flight to Florida to visit family. We had a layover in Chicago and when we lined up again at the gate to board the connecting flight a young airport security guard stopped me. "ID please." I handed him my American passport. He studied it and asked me to step out of the line. Dave started to follow, but the guard put up a hand and asked him to stay in line and board the plane. I passed Zack to Dave and followed the security guard to a small room. The questions were perfunctory. What's your background? Have you been back to Iran since you left? Are you in contact with people in Iran? Then things took a sinister turn. A wide grin spread across his face when he pulled a baby bottle from my backpack. "What is this?" he asked. "Expressed breast milk," I explained. "I save it for plane rides. You know, to help my baby's ears to pop during takeoff and landing. "So, what is in the bottle?" he asked again. "I told you, breast milk." "You'll have to drink it to prove it is not anthrax." I asked him if he was crazy. "Drink my own breast milk?" "If you want to board that plane, you will drink it." I honestly asked him if he was out of his mind. "You saw my baby! You saw my husband carry him onto the plane. Surely there is another way to determine what is in the bottle?" He handed me the bottle, "Not enough time to send it out for testing. Drink it." "Let's just get rid of it then. Run it down the drain," I told him. He refused. I was beside myself. "Let me go get my baby then and feed him the bottle." "Sorry, you can't leave this room until you're cleared. Your lack of cooperation is holding up this flight for everyone else." My lack of cooperation? The heat from my cheeks spread down my neck. His demand was ludicrous. He threatened to put me in jail if I did not follow his orders. "You have no choice but to accept. Drink the milk, if that is what you claim it is." Finally, he actually gave in and said he'd bring the baby to me. He locked me in the room and returned in ten minutes with Zack who was just as furious and red faced as I was. It took quite some time to calm him down long enough to take his bottle.

The struggle with the airport security guard was unwarranted. Was it created by the incompetence of an officer enforcing rules he didn't fully understand? Was it an abuse of power? Was it the racial profiling that defined the experiences of Middle Easterners and other non-whites in America after 9/11? The profiling continued.

Our family has long enjoyed vacationing in Vancouver, BC. It is just a short drive north from Seattle and we can enjoy magnificent, natural beauty. We used to go to Whistler in the winter to ski, but after 9/11 the "random" checks at the border were happening far too frequently to be mere chance. My American passport, which indicates my birthplace to be Iran, seemed the likeliest culprit. Many times while traveling, we were stopped at the border while the car was searched. Sometimes it took hours and eventually we stopped making the short 140-mile drive north as often as we had in the past. A couple years ago we decided to apply for Nexus cards to be able to cross into Canada in the Nexus lanes. Nexus is designated to expedite border crossing for pre-screened, "trusted and frequent" travelers. We submitted the applications for our entire family, paid the fees, and scheduled the required interviews. My interview was much longer than my husband's or our children's. When our cards arrived, we packed up the car for a ski trip up north. When we returned to the US border from Canada, we were pulled over and had to be interviewed. The US officials insisted—unconvincingly—that we were randomly selected for additional screening.

In the aftermath of 9/11, America drew a tight bubble around herself. I witnessed, and my children encountered, acts of racism and crimes against certain populations, races, and religions more than ever before. There was a racism exacerbated by fear and exclusivity of anyone deemed "other" and who were perceived as a threat. For example, Sikhs were killed for wearing turbans based on the assumption that they were Arabs.

Those who "are not like us" were seen with suspicion and assumed to be terrorists. Foreign policy has increasingly come to reflect the same sentiment in shaping how those outside of the US are perceived and treated. It has helped to justify embarking on wars and engaging in conflicts across the globe. Wars based on false pretenses that have accomplished nothing but destruction, loss of lives and resources, all of which destroy the infrastructure of the "host" country. All in the name of stumping out terrorism and bringing the gift of democracy to them.

In the recent years, white supremacy has been implicitly promoted, and racism and violence encouraged. All are a flagrant violation of our constitution and the values this country was built upon. We are not practicing a culture of worldliness. We are not sensitive to the injustices happening on our very shores and certainly not to those abroad. We are not utilizing our great power and position in the world to coordinate and lead efforts to improve the lives of others. We are not demonstrating maturity or wisdom. Because of fear, we've limited specific immigrant groups from entering the US based on blatantly false premises. For centuries, the diversity of immigrants has helped to create a rich American culture, a vibrant society which has made us leaders in technology as well as a beacon of democracy and freedom.

Discrimination and racism are complex task, I know. But there are patterns to racism that are so predictable we cannot sit back and only respond to them in the moment, as they happen. We cannot simply stand on the sidelines and allow these patterns to grow like a cancer in our society. We must put in place solutions that not only identify the root causes of these problems but also give us the tools to combat them.

It may start at the dinner table. A passive comment, our body language in how we react to the news on TV, our reaction to our neighbors, our relatives, or our friends' comments—these all teach our children how to think and behave. We transfer our values to them and if we are not conscious about it, we may inadvertently be helping to raise an unaccepting and intolerant future generation. All of these attitudes and skills are also taught, fostered, and practiced at schools and at our workplace.

If we, the adults, can learn to accept that our religious beliefs, our skin color, our gender, and where we were born doesn't determine our inherent dignity and worth as humans, then we can take down our walls—indeed, there will be no reason to build them in the first place—and we can live together in harmony with and in acceptance of one another. We can achieve success beyond our imaginations. While the current state of our country brings with it a fair share of ugly, frightening, and discouraging truths, I am thankful that the discomfort is also pushing us to have conversations that we otherwise wouldn't be having. We have a great opportunity to think deeply about our values as individuals, as families, and as communities and to reassess and realign our thoughts, words, and actions. The conversations can be uncomfortable, but it is my hope that we find the courage to face our discomforts and fears and to embrace the people who are our neighbors and the people with the drive and desire to become our neighbors.

'Abdu'l-Bahá, the eldest son of the Baha'u'llah, says in Bahá'í writings that prejudices of all kinds—whether religious, racial, nationalist, or political—are destructive to the divine foundation of humanity. All the warfare and bloodshed in human history has been the outcome of prejudice. This earth is one home and native land and God created humankind, of all races, with equal endowment and the right to live upon it.

Knowing this, may we then be courageous in our acceptance and bold in our love for all who ask for freedom and safety, never turning our backs on those whose rights are being abused.

"The children of Adam are the members of one another, since in their creation they are of one essence. When the conditions of the time bring a member to pain, the other members will suffer from discomfort. You, who are indifferent to the misery of others, it is not fitting that they should call you a human being."

Saadi Shirazi, 13th Century Persian poet

EPILOGUE

I wrote most of this book while sitting by Baba's bedside late at night. My presence helped settle his anxiety from the dementia that was slowly creeping through his brain and fogging the details of his past. Despite his suffering, Baba never lost his positive demeanor. It would shine through his beautiful hazel eyes even until the end of his life while he would tell me, "I have had a full life, a beautiful life. God granted my wishes for all my children to get higher education." I lost my beloved father before I finished the book, but through my grief and loss I was given a window of opportunity to reflect on both his life and mine in ways I could not have anticipated. Much of that reflection has been on how people come to make the difficult choices that they do.

My own difficult decision to be smuggled in the back of a dark and dusty pick-up truck across the Iranian border is not one I would wish on any child or adult. Because of this, however, I intimately understand how people come to make the agonizing choices they do to emigrate. When faced with difficult decisions in impossible situations, it often isn't really a question of choice. It isn't a question of: How could you choose that? How could you risk that? It is more a question of dignity, of our inherent worth as an individual or group. The United Nation's Universal Declaration of Human Rights says that "recognition of the inherent dignity and of the equal and inalienable rights of all members of the human family is the foundation of freedom, justice and peace in the world."

I spent eight years of my childhood at the mercy of sirens and bombs during a war that took hundreds of thousands of lives, on both sides.

Despite the terror, the persecution, and my family's diminished status, I never learned to give up on my dignity. Perhaps it was something innate in me. Perhaps it was the way my parents raised me. But perhaps too it was because of the brave and difficult decision Mr. Goodarzi made to stand in the gap for my family the night our Muslim neighbors were coming with torches to burn our house down. Mr. Goodarzi made the dangerous choice to stand up for my family's inherent worth and dignity when we had been stripped of our voice and right to do so for ourselves. In doing so, Mr. Goodarzi's actions saved our lives and showed me that by preserving someone else's dignity, we actually preserve our own.

Now consider: I could have drunk my breast milk that day in the airport. My parents could have told me to just marry a nice Bahá'í boy and live a quiet, unassuming life in Iran. Mr. Goodarzi could have joined the mob with torches that terrifying night. But in each of those instances, dignity was at stake—the inherent worth and value of an individual. And dignity is not easily relinquished. We fight to preserve it in ourselves, and we fight to preserve it for others because—how can we truly honor and uphold our own dignity if we deny it to others? Sadly, the dignity of a refugee or immigrant is always at question, even thirty-one years later.

Right before I sent this book to publication, I had to let go of an employee who was not the right fit for my office. This person become verbally aggressive with me and later sent a stream of texts to my past and present employees and myself saying: "Muslims are all the same. You can't trust them as far as you can toss them." Then they followed it up saying, "Persians are Muslim. They believe in Islam. They are the nasty people who blew up the World Trade Center." This incident shook me deeply, and I am not even Muslim. But as we know, those words clearly indicate an Islamophobia that breeds further ignorance, hate, ugliness, and racism.

On first reflection, this experience left me shattered, angry, and confused. Have we learned nothing from history? It's truly frightening. On further reflection, I feel only sadness and compassion. Such hate can indeed grow from ignorance, but underneath ignorance usually lies pain.

The office manager, I learned later, had lost their spouse in a drunk driving accident that was the fault of an undocumented Pakistani man. The drunk driver wasn't prosecuted. In light of the pain the office manager carries, I see they are also innocent—innocent in that they loved their spouse and lost them in such a tragic and unexpected way. Their grief has had nowhere to go because they didn't have the chance to say goodbye. As often happens with deep pain, it boils up and out scalding other innocent people around you. This person didn't treat me as a human deserving of dignity, but I am left wondering: perhaps they have been unable to heal their own wounds, so they inflict prejudice on anyone who appears to be like the people who were the original cause of their pain. This understanding makes the anger in me dissipate, but of course, it does not make right their actions and words.

This episode makes me think even harder about what happens to all the asylum seekers today who are going to have to wait for an unforeseeable amount of time to be evaluated. Will the action or nonaction of US citizens contribute to the further division, exclusion, and oppression of others? Or can we soothe the lives broken by fear and pain with the possibilities of hope, freedom, safety, and opportunity? Can we look for ways to transcend our fears, the core beliefs that fuel our hesitation, and accept one another? Can we heal our own hearts so there is no need to heap abuses on anyone else's? And how do we, those with passports and privilege, choose to stand in this difficult moment in time? How do we live with ourselves knowing what we know? How else are we supposed to preserve the dignity of our nation if we do not uphold human rights and the dignity of those who would seek refuge from us? Difficult questions and difficult choices indeed, but for me, I find there is only ever one right answer when dignity is at stake. Only one right way. We do not turn our backs on those whose rights are being abused.

And so, the choice—although it might appear on the outside to be rash, risky, or crazy—is actually quite simple.

ACKNOWLEDGMENTS

Just like my immigration to America, the writing of this book has also been a long and winding journey full of destiny. I could not have done it without the love and support of my family, friends, and community, who embraced and encouraged me every step of the way.

To my dear father, Aziz, for his wisdom, love, and commitment to educating his children. His sacrifices and his positive outlook on life has made me the person I am today.

To my husband, Dave, the love of my life and my true partner, who stands by me, believes in me and empowers me every day. Thank you for keeping me centered when my PTSD kicks in and turns my world upside down.

To my wonderful children, Zachary, Parisa and Sheyda—you are my reasons for living. Your kindness and big hearts, your unconditional love, your deep understanding and respect of my past is immense. I love you very much and thank you for bringing smiles to my face every day. I feel very lucky to be your mother. I am very proud of all of you and what beautiful world citizens you are becoming.

To my nieces Aava and Saba for their love, interest, and support of this book. Thanks for filling our small family with your energy and excitement.

To my dear friends: Beth Ebel, Jane Park, and Monika Kashyup, for their friendship, love, and support in my life and especially during the creation of this book

Special thanks and recognition to United Nations for providing me support and safety when I most needed it by accepting my asylum request.

They granted me the gift of a second chance at life—a beautiful and wonderful life beyond anything I could have possibly imagined.

Special thanks to my editor, Asha Myers, who first came to me as a dental patient. Through small talks (while she was partially numb in my dental chair), we created an immediate connection. Her genuine interest, enthusiasm, and passion has made this book blossom. I am thankful for your continuous support through this unknown journey.

To our family friend and my first editor, Kathy Sheehan, who helped guide me in the early stages of the book with all the faults of writing in English as a second language.

My sincere gratitude to National Spiritual Assembly of the Bahá'í of the United States review committee for their guidance and commitment to fact check the Bahá'í content of this book and for their spiritual love and support.

My deep appreciation for Michael and Sara Nicolaï, who generously provided the book's cover photo from their travels to Iran. The picture has special meaning to me because it was taken in Yazd, the city my parents were from. You can find more of their beautiful photography at exploreforevermore.com

PHOTOGRAPHS

(Sitting with her siblings on top of the Chevy. Mahvash is on the left.)

(In Yazd, in front of the cracked mud walls. Mahvash is on the right.)

(Mahvash on a family road trip with Chevy in the background.)

(Visiting Persepolis in Shiraz. Mahvash is in her mother's arms.)

(The last family photo before Mahvash's brothers left for the US.)

(Photo of Mahvash's 1ˢᵗ grade Bahá'í class. She has the white pin in her
hair to the left of the teacher.)

(Seventh grade classroom. Mahvash is third from left.)

(In the school yard with her history teacher. Mahvash is second from the left.)

(Mahvash with her parents in their backyard before she is smuggled out of the country.)

(Final bus trip from Lahore to Islamabad. Mahvash is seated in the center in the front.)

(Mahvash in Vienna.)

(Kitchen in Klosterneuburg, Austria showing the water barrel that was filled daily for washing dishes.)

(The Harvey Family. Pictured left to right: Zack, Mahvash, Sheyda, Parisa, Dave)

RESOURCES AND FURTHER READING

THE BAHÁ'Í FAITH

You can learn more about the Bahá'í faith by visiting: https://www.bahai.org

PRINCIPLES OF THE BAHÁ'Í FAITH

- The oneness of mankind.

- Universal peace upheld by a world government.

- Independent investigation of truth.

- The common foundation of all religions.

- The essential harmony of science and religion.

- Equality of rights of men and women.

- Elimination of prejudice of all kinds.

- Universal compulsory education.

- A spiritual solution to the economic problem.

- A universal auxiliary language.

BAHÁ'Í WORLD NEWS:

The Bahá'í World News Service:

The Bahá'í World News Service makes available thoughtful essays and articles on contemporary issues and developments at:

https://news.bahai.org/

A particularly important development for Bahá'ís in Iran was captured in this article from The Bahá'í World Publication in November of 2018, "UN resolution calls for end to Iran's rights violations against Baha'is", which can be found at:

https://news.bahai.org/story/1295/

The US Bahá'í Office of Public Affairs

The US Bahá'í Office of Public Affairs offers many human rights related documents and resources concerning the crimes against Bahá'ís of Iran:

http://publicaffairs.bahai.us/what-we-do/human-rights/
related-documents-and-resources/

HISTORY OF IRAN:

Iran: A Modern History

"This history of modern Iran is not a survey in the conventional sense but an ambitious exploration of the story of a nation. It offers a revealing look at how events, people, and institutions are shaped by currents that so metimes reach back hundreds of years. The book covers the complex history of the diverse societies and economies of Iran against the background of dynastic changes, revolutions, civil wars, foreign occupation, and the rise of the Islamic Republic.

Abbas Amanat combines chronological and thematic approaches, exploring events with lasting implications for modern Iran and the world. Drawing on diverse historical scholarship and emphasizing the twentieth century, he addresses debates about Iran's culture and politics. Political history is the driving narrative force, given impetus by Amanat's decades of research and study. He layers the book with discussions of literature, music, and the arts; ideology and religion; economy and society; and cultural identity and heritage."

—Yale University Press, book summary of *Iran: A Modern History*

Abbas Amanat is William Graham Sumner Professor of History at Yale University and director of the Yale Program in Iranian Studies at the MacMillan Center for International and Area Studies. He lives in North Haven, CT.

PERSIAN LITERATURE:

Shahnameh: The Persian Book of Kings by Abolqasem Ferdowsi

"Originally composed for the Samanid princes of Khorasan in the tenth century, the Shahnameh is among the greatest works of world literature. This prodigious narrative tells the story of pre-Islamic Persia, from the mythical creation of the world and the dawn of Persian civilization through the seventh-century Arab conquest. The stories of the Shahnameh are deeply embedded in Persian culture and beyond, as attested by their appearance in such works as The Kite Runner and the love poems of Rumi and Hafez."

—Penguin Random House book summary of the *Shahnameh*

Divan of Saadi: His Mystical Love-Poetry translated by Paul Smith

"Sadi of Shiraz (1210-1291), a contemporary of Rumi who influenced him, was another Perfect Master Poet who expressed himself in the ruba'i form as well as hundreds of ghazals in his beautiful Divan that often also contained images from dervish dancing. Sadi was a great traveller who spent forty years on the road throughout the Middle-East, North Africa and India and many of the incidents he experienced he wrote down in his two most famous works when he finally returned to his beloved birth-place... The Rose Garden (Gulistan) and The Orchard (Bustan). Sadi's mystical love poetry, his ghazals, although almost unknown in the West, are loved by his fellow-countrymen almost as much as those of Hafiz whom he greatly influenced."

—New Humanity Books book summary of the *Divan of Sadi*

HUMAN RIGHTS ORGANIZATIONS:

Mona Foundation:

Mona Foundation supports grassroots initiatives that provide education to all children, increase opportunities for women and girls, and encourage service to the community. The initiatives that we support includes schools that serve economically disad-vantaged communities globally. The schools focus on academic excellence, fine arts and character development to train capable, ethical, and altruistic leaders who contribute to the betterment of their families, communities, and ultimately their nation.

https://www.monafoundation.org/

Tahirih Justice Center:

Tahirih Justice Center stands alone as the only national, multi-city organization providing a broad range of direct legal and social services, policy advocacy, and training and education to protect immigrant women and girls fleeing violence.

https://www.tahirih.org/

Northwest Immigrant Rights Project

Northwest Immigrant Rights Project promotes justice by defending and advancing the rights of immigrants through direct legal services, systemic advocacy, and community education. They work to keep families together, protect people from violence, and stand up to injustice.

https://www.nwirp.org/

ABOUT THE AUTHOR

Dr. Mahvash Khajavi-Harvey is a dentist in private practice in Seattle where she lives with her husband and their three children. A firm believer in the power of community—both far and wide—she has volunteered dentistry services overseas in third-world communities and also provides free dental care in Seattle at local homeless clinics every year. Dr. Harvey is an outspoken advocate of human rights issues and supports numerous nonprofits including: the Mona Foundation, the Tahirih Justice Center Foundation, and the Northwest Immigrant Rights Project. For several years, she served on the board of "Journey with an Afghan School," a non-profit, non-governmental organization (NGO), which was founded post 9/11 to build schools for girls in Afghanistan.